LAUGHING IN THE FACE OF CHAOS

A POLITICALLY INCORRECT SHAMANIC GUIDE FOR MODERN LIFE

RUDÁ IANDÊ

THE VESSEL

CONTENTS

Cataloging-In-Publication (CIP)
(eDOC BRASIL)

Iandê, Rudá.
I11l Laughing in the face of chaos: a politically incorrect shamanic guide for modern life / Rudá Iandê. – Belém, Brazil: The Vessel, 2025.
360 p. : 6" x 9"

ISBN 978-65-5278-251-9

1. Shamanism. 2. Self-acceptance. 2. Spiritual healing. I. Title.
DDC 299.8144

Prepared by Maurício Amormino Júnior – CRB6/2422

PREFACE

I'm a restless explorer of myself. My journey began thirty-five years ago. I've tried many religions, philosophies, and esoteric schools. I embraced the New Age Movement with great excitement. I studied dozens of different therapies, healing techniques, and methods of self-development. With every discovery, I was sure I'd found my path, only to become disillusioned later. I couldn't fit in with any of the paths offered to me. What I did not realize at the time is that to find my true path, one day I would need to unlearn everything I thought I knew about spirituality.

For decades I found myself utterly exhausted—not just from disappointment, but from the labyrinthine world I had entered. I walked among shamans, warlocks, and witches, seeking truth but encountering shadows. Time and again, I was disillusioned, learning the hard way that not all that shines is gold. Even the most profound knowledge and the highest spiritual gifts can become weapons in the hands of those who crave power and control. I faced not only the brilliance of the divine but the treachery of the human heart, wrapped in veils of mysticism.

This journey forged my being. It broke me open, shattered my illusions, and stripped me of every false certainty I once clung to. But in the depths of that darkness, when I had nothing left to hold onto, I was not rescued by a human hand. My salvation came from a being older than time itself—a whispering vine, a teacher rooted in the very fabric of the earth.

Ayahuasca, the mother spirit of the jungle, took me in when I had lost my way. Not as a god, not as a doctrine, but as a presence—both ruthless and profoundly nurturing. If a plant could garden a human, then *Ayahuasca* was my gardener. She dug into the hardened soil of my soul, breaking apart the knots of pain and ignorance that had taken root there. She watered me with visions, pruned away my arrogance, and forced me to confront the hidden decay within. She showed me who I was, long before I was ready to see it.

Like any true master, she did not coddle me. She shook me awake when I was drifting toward the abyss. She tore through the veils of my self-deception and set before me a path where I had only seen endless night. With brutal honesty and boundless love, she stripped me bare—until all that remained was the raw, unfiltered essence of my being.

And so, I dedicate this book to *Ayahuasca*, the vine that whispers through the veins of the jungle, carrying the wisdom of the earth, the cosmos, and all that lies beyond. She is the serpent and the vine, the mother and the storm. With her, I saw the infinite labyrinth of existence, the vast interplay of light and shadow, the silent intelligence humming beneath all things.

She opened my eyes to behold the Great Mystery—the force that does not speak in words, but in the breath of the wind, the rhythm of the rivers, the pulse of the earth beneath bare feet—the same force that shaped me and the same force that has drawn you to these pages. This Mystery moves through her, through me, through you. It is the whisper of the unseen, the breath of something vast and unfathomable that flows through all living things.

It is the force that fills our lungs with breath and lifts us from the depths of despair, urging us to rise like wildflowers blooming through the cracks of ruin. It is the thread that weaves all things into one vast, unknowable tapestry—the pulse of life itself, whispering through creation in the silent language of the unseen.

And it is always waiting. Not in the distant reaches of the cosmos, nor in the promises of gods and men, but here—in the untamed depths of our own being, calling us home. This book is a culmination of the emotions, memories, and wisdom I've gathered over the last thirty—five years, including self-discovery, frustration, anxiety, and wonder. However, what you're about to find here, dear reader, is not my personal experiences, nor my worldview. My truth belongs only to me. There's something much more enjoyable for you to explore: your own truth.

All I can offer is a guide that will help you break through the mythological constructions that keep you away from your true self. Once you break these mirrors and meet your true being, you'll find a universe that belongs only to you.

Both humans and gods fear your true self. An awakened human is a natural anarchist fated to destroy the age-old constructions that keep us as pawns in the ruthless game of life.

Your true self has been painted as the devil. Your real power has been labeled as weakness. You've been taught to fight your own self, so you are kept distracted, divided, and weakened while the true evil prevails and feasts on your ignorance.

I hope, in the course of this book, that you can embrace your "inner beast" and turn this aspect of your being into an ally. There's no better friend you can find in this life!

Enough spiritual philosophies and religions talk about goodness while teaching us how to better torture ourselves in the pursuit of purity and perfection. I have indeed learned to contemplate the beauty of my own imperfections amid the chaos of life. Under the guidance of an ancient witch, I've learned to open my path to such chaos with the power of my laughter. I invite you to embrace this journey with this same spirit: by relaxing and having fun along the way.

As Alan Watts once said: "Man suffers only because he takes seriously what the gods made for fun."

Chapter One

The Fabricated Truths We Hold Dear

A young seeker—hungry for truth—set out across the globe in search of answers. That seeker was me, driven by a longing to wander beyond the frontiers of my own culture, to learn from the variations and echoes I would meet along the way. I craved a wider lens on life and, in the end, a clearer view of myself.

In the back of my mind, I also hoped to find an antidote for my deepest insecurities. I believed that somewhere out there, I would uncover the ultimate truth that would help me make sense of life and fill me with unshakable confidence, inner peace, and strength. This truth, I thought, would be a safe harbor of clarity and purpose, guiding me through the chaos of existence. The journey was a quest to uncover the wisdom hidden in diverse traditions, to find common threads that unite humanity, and to discover how these insights could illuminate my own path.

From the ancient temples of Mexico to the sacred mountains of Peru, I sought out gurus, shamans, and wise elders, eagerly absorbing their teachings and practices. And for a fleeting moment, I believed I had found it—the key to unlocking the mysteries of the universe. I felt a surge of self-assuredness, a certainty that I had finally grasped the fundamental nature of reality.

But as I clung to this newfound "truth," I realized that it had become a prison of its own making. The weight of certainty became a burden, blocking my ability to see beyond my own perspective. In that moment I understood that life is a kaleidoscope of countless perspectives, each offering a unique glimpse into the vast ocean of the Cosmos. The truth I had been seeking was not a fixed destination but an ever-evolving dialogue between my consciousness and the universe itself.

My journey was not one of acquiring truth but of losing certainty. Every conviction I once held eventually unraveled, forcing me to question who I really was. Perhaps you have felt this too—the disorienting moment when the foundation you stood on crumbles beneath you. Instead of resisting, I invite you to step into the unknown, where transformation begins.

What if we could learn to embrace the discomfort of not knowing? Rather then seeing the cracks in our convictions as weaknesses to be feared, why not facing them as opportunities for growth and expansion?

This journey is not a search for absolute truth, but rather a letting go of attachments to our knowledge and perspectives. It's a leap into the diverse and multifaceted nature of life, to embrace the mystery that lies at the heart of our existence. Life is wild, chaotic, and beautifully unpredictable. By releasing our need for certainty, we open ourselves to the fullness of the present moment, experiencing life as it unfolds in all its richness and complexity. This gives us the opportunity to step beyond the limits of our preconceived realities and engage with the unknown—not as something to be solved, but as a living experience to be felt with curiosity and wonder.

Are you prepared to question the core of your beliefs and assumptions? To peel back the layers of your reality and uncover what lies beneath?

Our journey begins with a force as ancient as humanity itself, one that has guided our dreams and shaped civilizations. This force—both a source of limitless potential and a web of limitation—shapes how we see ourselves and the world. It has built empires and bound them, connected us across generations, and yet kept us tethered to illusions.

In this chapter, we'll examine the invisible threads that influence how you see yourself, relate to others, and make choices. As we navigate this terrain, long-held assumptions may begin to dissolve, revealing deeper truths hidden beneath the stories you've inherited. What emerges is not just a new understanding, but the freedom to redefine your own path.

In the pages that follow, you'll learn to recognize the spells that your imagination has cast over you and break free from self-imposed confines, stepping into a boundless realm of possibility—where the reality you inhabit is not just discovered, but created.

Storytelling: Superpower and Prison

IN the dawn of human history, our ancestors faced a world that was as beautiful as it was unforgiving. They were not the strongest, the fastest, or the most physically imposing creatures in their environment. They stood naked against the elements, their skin battered by the sun, their bodies shivering in the cold. They watched as predators lurked in the shadows, ready to pounce at any moment. They foraged for food, never knowing where their next meal would come from, always at the mercy of the land and the changing seasons.

But amidst the chaos and the constant struggle for survival, something extraordinary happened. Our ancestors, who had once lived much like apes, in small family groups of twenty to fifty individuals, began to develop remarkable new ways to thrive. This moment in human evolution was nothing short of magical. Early humans started to harness the power of their minds, crafting tools, and creating art that spoke to their burgeoning creativity. They formed complex social structures, weaving together the fabric of early societies. They developed sophisticated methods of communication, sharing knowledge and stories that would be passed down through generations. This period marked the dawn of human ingenuity, a pivotal moment when our species began to transcend mere survival and step onto the path of cultural and intellectual evolution. It was a time of wonder and innovation, laying the foundation for the incredible advancements that would follow. Humans began to unlock the full potential of their minds and spirits.

Unlike chimpanzees, who were often torn apart by instinctive competition and aggression, our early human ancestors learned to cooperate and communicate in ways that no other species had before. From their imagination, they created stories and myths that could unite them and give their lives meaning and purpose.

Around the flickering light of the campfire, they wove tales of great hunts, of brave heroes, and of the spirits that inhabited the world around them. They painted on cave walls, etching their stories into stone, leaving a legacy that would endure for millennia.

And with each story told, something miraculous occurred. Our ancestors began to work together in ways that transcended their individual limitations. They formed tribes and clans, pooling their resources and their knowledge to overcome the challenges that had once seemed impossible.

They learned to hunt together, to share food and shelter, and to protect one another from the dangers that lurked in the shadows. They forged intricate social bonds, fostering cooperation and empathy within their communities. They created language, art, and culture from their shared stories and collective imagination. Through rituals and traditions, they celebrated births, mourned deaths, and marked the passage of time. They explored the mysteries of existence, pondering their place in the cosmos and seeking meaning through spirituality and mythology. They formed deep connections with each other, laying the foundations of human civilization.

This was the birth of human civilization, and it was made possible not by brute strength or physical prowess, but by the power of the human mind and the human spirit. Our ancestors had discovered a new kind of magic, a force that could transform the world and shape the course of history. This magic was the ability to weave experiences, dreams, and wisdom into narratives. These stories became the lifeblood of their culture, transcending time and space, connecting generations, and uniting communities. Through the enchanting power of these tales, they could heal, inspire, and illuminate the path forward, leaving an indelible mark on the foundations of human civilization.

As time passed and human societies grew larger and became more complex, this magic only grew stronger. The stories and myths that had once united small tribes and clans evolved into the great epics and religions that would define entire cultures and civilizations.

From the Mesopotamian city-states to the Roman Empire, from the Maya to the Ming Dynasty, human beings used their imagination and their storytelling prowess to create new worlds, technologies, and ways of living that would have been unimaginable to their ancestors.

But this power came with a price. As human societies grew more complex and hierarchical, the stories that once united us began to sow division. Myths and legends that had inspired cooperation and shared purpose transformed into ideologies and dogmas, pitting human against human, tribe against tribe, and nation against nation. What was once a source of unity became a tool for control, wielded by those seeking to manipulate others. Like all great powers, storytelling carries a shadow we must confront.

Imagine for a moment that the stories we tell collectively and personally are like rivers, carving the landscape of our existence. These rivers of meaning guide civilizations, unite tribes, and shape individual lives. But as they flow, they also erode, carrying away the raw essence of what they touch. A tree becomes "wood," a person becomes a "name," and the vast mystery of existence is reduced to symbols and labels.

At the personal level, these rivers of narrative can nourish or confine. For years, I lived within a story shaped by childhood trauma—a story that whispered I was never enough. Achievements, no matter how grand, felt hollow, as if measured against an impossible standard. This story, subtle yet powerful, kept me from fully inhabiting my own life. It was only when I paused, examined, and rewrote this narrative that I began to see my true worth. By stepping out of the river's current, I could finally experience life in its fullness, untethered by the chains of limiting beliefs.

We all live immersed in stories, from the myths that shape our cultures to the silent narratives running in the background of our minds. These tales can inspire and connect us, but they can also blind us to the profound reality beyond their reach. Beneath our constructed realities lies something vast and untamed, waiting to be felt rather than named—a pure experience that defies the boundaries of language and invites us into the mystery of existence.

The Sensory Matrix and the Conceptual Veil

IMAGINE standing in a forest at sunrise, the light filtering through the canopy, the scent of earth and leaves surrounding you. Now consider this: a bee in that same forest sees patterns on flowers invisible to your eyes, guiding it to nectar. A bat flying above navigates through echolocation, painting a sonic map of its surroundings. A wolf catches scents carried miles by the wind, experiencing an intricate world of smells we can't fathom. Each of these creatures inhabits the same forest, yet their realities are profoundly different, shaped by the sensory tools their evolution provided.

For humans, reality begins with the raw input of our senses—sight, sound, touch, taste, and smell. These inputs interact with the unfathomable matrix of existence: a boundless realm of energy, matter, and possibility. Our senses act as translators, distilling this infinite complexity into something our brains can interpret. What we call "reality" is, in truth, a biological hologram—an imagined construct based on what our bodies are capable of perceiving.

This shared sensory hologram connects us as a species. The colors we see, the sounds we hear, the textures we feel—these are the building blocks of our collective experience. Yet even within this shared framework, there are infinite variations. A person with synesthesia might see sounds as colors, while someone with colorblindness perceives hues in a way most of us cannot. Our individual realities are as unique as our fingerprints, shaped by the specific interplay of biology and experience.

But humans possess something extraordinary that sets us apart: the ability to transcend the boundaries of our immediate sensory experience. Through language, imagination, and abstraction, we construct an additional layer of reality—a conceptual veil draped over the sensory matrix. This veil enables us to assign meaning to the world, to organize chaos into patterns, and to create narratives that guide our understanding of life.

At the core of this process lies language itself. Through words, we name and categorize the world, transforming raw experience into something we can grasp and communicate. A tree becomes a "tree," not just an intricate organism but a concept—a symbol in our mental landscape. This act of naming is both a gift and a limitation. While it allows us to share ideas and collaborate, it also simplifies and reduces the world's complexity, filtering out the nuances of its infinite essence.

Consider the tree again. To a biologist, it's a living system of cells and chemical processes. To an artist, it might be a muse, its twisting branches an invitation to create. To a logger, it's timber, and to a child, it might simply be a place to climb and dream. The tree itself, however, transcends all these interpretations. It exists beyond the labels we impose, rooted in a reality we can never fully capture with words.

This dual nature of our conceptual veil is both liberating and constraining. It allows us to build civilizations, write symphonies, and send spacecraft to distant planets. Yet it can also entangle us in a web of constructed meanings that disconnect us from the raw, unfiltered experience of existence. We mistake the map for the territory, the name for the essence, and the story for the truth.

The same dynamic applies to our understanding of ourselves. From the moment we are born, we are named, categorized, and labeled. These labels become the foundation of the stories we tell about who we are—stories shaped by culture, family, and personal experience. Over time, these narratives accumulate, forming a conceptual overlay that colors how we see ourselves and the world. And just as with the tree, these stories can never fully encompass the vast, dynamic reality of our being.

When we internalize these external narratives, we risk confining ourselves to a narrow and static identity. We might mistake a label or a role—parent, professional, student—for the entirety of who we are. Yet beneath these constructs lies something far more profound: the living, breathing mystery of our existence, an essence that defies categorization.

Our capacity to create and inhabit conceptual worlds is both our greatest gift and our greatest challenge. It enables us to dream and innovate, to build connections and meaning. But it also tempts us to cling to these constructs as if they were absolute, blinding us to the deeper, uncharted reality that lies beyond them.

What lies in the space between the sensory matrix and the conceptual veil? Could it be where our truest essence resides—unfiltered, untamed, and boundless? To inhabit this space is not merely an intellectual exercise but a journey of awareness and detachment. It requires us to see through the stories and labels we impose, to let go of the constructs that confine us, and to embrace the raw immediacy of existence as it unfolds in each moment.

This is the delicate balance: to honor the creative power of our minds without becoming enslaved by it, to use the conceptual veil as a tool rather than mistake it for truth. It's in this space, between perception and imagination, that we glimpse the mystery of life in its fullness. Here, we are no longer defined by the narratives we tell or the roles we play, but by the living, breathing reality of being.

To live in this space is to reconnect with the vast, untamed reality that no story or concept can capture. It's to reclaim the freedom to see the world as it truly is—not as we name or categorize it, but as a dynamic, infinite unfolding. And in this act of seeing, we can reimagine ourselves and our lives, not as static identities but as fluid, ever-evolving expressions of the universe itself.

Chapter Two

Deciphering the Programs That Run Your Mind

In the next pages we will dive deep into the heart of the stories that structure human reality. We'll weave a thread to guide us through this maze of stories, allowing us to pierce through their hypnotic veil and discover the tools to author our own narrative, on our own terms.

From the heart of the Amazon rainforest to the streets of Uruguay, from ancient myths and legends to the emerging narratives of our time, this chapter takes us on a whirlwind journey through the stories that shape our world. Along the way, we'll meet remarkable individuals who have broken free from the chains of cultural conditioning to forge their own paths toward meaning and purpose. Together, we'll explore profound questions about reality, identity, and the essence of the human experience.

Through it all, we will discover the power of stories to transform our lives and our world, to help us make sense of the chaos and the complexity that surrounds us. We will learn to see the world through new eyes, to find magic and meaning in even the most mundane of objects and experiences.

As you delve into these pages, you'll embark on a journey of liberation, discovering the tools to break free from the shackles of conditioning and reclaim your place as the author of your own story. Together, we'll explore how to navigate our human experience with grace, wisdom, and resilience, learning to live each day with authenticity, purpose, and joy.

Unraveling the Knots of Family Programming

FROM the moment we enter this world, we are enveloped in a web of stories spun by those closest to us—our families and immediate environment. These narratives form the foundation of our understanding of ourselves and the world around us, shaping our identities long before we have the capacity to question or resist. For many of us, this begins with our parents, who serve as the master storytellers, crafting tales of who we are and who we should become. For those raised in alternative care settings—whether by adoptive families, foster parents, or supportive communities—the master storytellers are no less influential. These caregivers, mentors, and communities shape the foundational narratives just as profoundly, offering stories that guide and influence the development of identity and perception. Together, these narratives intertwine to create the fabric of our initial experiences, like an invisible veil that frames how we see ourselves and the world.

Consider the expectations and dreams your parents may have held for you since your conception. Perhaps they imagined you as a successful professional, a loving partner, or someone embodying their ideals of achievement and happiness. These projections often extend far beyond careers or roles, touching on personality traits and even life choices. Shaped by their own experiences, hopes, and societal pressures, these visions, while well-meaning, can quickly become restrictive—pre-written scripts that leave little space for your authentic desires to take root.

Through my work, I've witnessed how deeply these inherited stories can impact an individual's life. Time and again, I've guided people back to their true selves, helping them chip away at layers of external expectation and conditioning. Often, these stories create such profound mental and emotional blocks that individuals struggle to access their inner voice, let alone honor it. In the pursuit of fulfilling inherited dreams, people can become disconnected not only from their deepest desires but also from their essence.

These familial narratives are not inherently harmful. They provide a structure, a survival toolkit of beliefs and values to navigate the world. But true personal growth requires us to deconstruct this inherited framework. To honor the gift of life, we must break through these limitations, allowing our innermost essence to flourish.

As we mature, we often realize that the stories we inherited no longer align with the narratives we wish to write for ourselves. This realization is both liberating and terrifying—it demands that we challenge the foundation of our identities. The process of individuation is not a rejection of love or support but a necessary step in our evolution. It requires us to discern which inherited beliefs serve our true selves and which must be transformed or discarded.

This journey is rarely easy. Confronting deeply ingrained patterns and fears can be painful, particularly when weighed down by the responsibility for others' emotions. We may fear that asserting our individuality betrays those we love. Yet true love is not contingent upon fulfilling someone else's expectations. It thrives when we honor our authenticity and live in alignment with our inner truths. By doing so, we not only liberate ourselves but also inspire others to embrace their own.

The tension between our true self and the expectations imposed upon us is an inevitable part of the human experience. Many of us shield our parents from disappointment, using this as an excuse to avoid claiming our individuality. But let's face the truth: being human means inevitably disappointing and hurting others, and the sooner you accept this reality, the easier it becomes to navigate life's challenges.

From the day you were born, you've been a source of both joy and pain for your parents. Your very existence transformed your mother's body in ways she could never fully recover from, and your arrival marked the end of their carefree days as a couple. Your incessant crying, constant demands for attention, and endless needs placed immense stress on their lives. For years, your upbringing consumed their time, energy, and financial resources.

While there was undoubtedly love in the mix, don't fool yourself into thinking you were the perfect embodiment of their dreams. Unless your parents are masochists or have attained a state of enlightenment, you have always fallen short of their expectations on some level.

This is not a personal failing, but rather a universal truth that applies to all of us. To cope with the inevitable disappointment and frustration that comes with raising a child, your parents likely convinced themselves that you were the center of their universe, and you may have grown up believing this narrative. The price of feeling so special is the burden of responsibility that comes with it—the deeply ingrained belief that it is your duty to please your parents, to make them proud and happy, even at the cost of your own happiness and fulfillment.

Many of your parents' expectations were programmed so long ago that they may already feel like an intrinsic part of you, intertwined with your sense of identity. This deep-seated programming can obscure your true desires, making it difficult to distinguish between what you genuinely want and what has been imposed upon you.

The path of self-discovery requires experimentation and courage. It's an exploration of uncharted territories, where we disentangle the threads of external expectations to uncover our innermost desires. Life is vast, offering infinite possibilities beyond the confines of inherited programming. Embracing this journey is not selfish; it's essential.

Recognizing that our primary duty is to ourselves—not others—is essential to living authentically. You have both the right and responsibility to explore and try until you know yourself deeply, because this journey is the essence of honoring the unique combination of potential, creativity, and purpose that only you can bring into the world. Since you cannot escape making your own choices, it is crucial to take full responsibility for who you are and who you aspire to become.

This path may lead to moments where you disappoint your parents or others, but they must learn to live with it. Their happiness is their responsibility, not yours. Your choices, your life, and honoring your truth are your responsibility. By embracing your genuine self, you honor the seed of life that was given to you, allowing your innermost essence to blossom.

Often, the journey toward self-actualization is mistaken for selfishness. Yet, true self-discovery is not about disregarding others but about living authentically. While selfishness prioritizes personal gain at others' expense, self-discovery fosters a deeper understanding of oneself—allowing for more meaningful connections. Prioritizing this journey is not an act of selfishness but a commitment to truth. By embracing who you are—bringing your love, struggles, and desires fully into the world—you contribute uniquely to the rich mosaic of life.

Redefining Honor: A New Approach to Respecting Our Parents

IN the Western world, where Judeo-Christian values have long held sway, the notion of honoring one's parents is deeply ingrained. But what does it truly mean to honor our mothers and fathers? Is it to blindly obey their every wish, to sacrifice our own identity on the altar of their approval? Or is there a deeper, more nuanced way to pay respect to those who gave us life?

As a shaman, I believe that true honor lies in embracing our role as evolutionary beings. Like a tree growing from a seed, we are not meant to be static replicas of our progenitors but dynamic expressions of the life force that flows through us. Our duty is not to preserve the past unchanged, but to transform it—to take the raw materials of our genetic and cultural inheritance and alchemize them into something new and vital.

In this sense, honoring our parents means having the courage to question the stories they have told us, to challenge the limiting beliefs and concepts that shaped our early years. It requires recognizing that their expectations, however well-meaning, are projections of their own dreams and desires. Honoring them, then, is not about blind adherence, but about charting our own unique course, embracing the freedom and responsibility to live authentically.

This is no easy task. Breaking free from the gravitational pull of our family's narratives demands tremendous will and self-awareness. It calls for confronting the fear of disappointing those we love, the guilt of "betraying" our ancestral legacy, and the existential vertigo that comes with stepping into the unknown. Yet, as we learn to assert our own voice and trust the wisdom of our inner being, we uncover a deeper truth: our parents, like us, are imperfect creatures, grappling with their own unresolved wounds and unmet needs. Their dreams for us were never entirely about us, but reflections of their unconscious desires and fears.

With this realization comes a profound sense of liberation. No longer bound by the weight of our family's expectations, we are free to embark on a journey of self-discovery, to uncover the essence that lies beneath the layers of conditioning and programming. We can begin to craft our own stories, to shape our reality in accordance with our deepest truths and most cherished values.

Ultimately, honoring our parents means honoring the life force that flows through us all—that ineffable spark of creativity and potential seeking expression in ever-new and wondrous ways. We are not static endpoints of a lineage but dynamic participants in an ongoing process of evolution and transformation. Our DNA is not a fixed blueprint to follow rigidly but a living code, inviting interpretation, expansion, and personal expression. By embracing our role as co-creators of our genetic and cultural legacy, we pay homage to the countless generations before us while taking responsibility for shaping the future.

Honoring our parents, then, is not about rigidly adhering to their expectations or beliefs. It is about having the courage to question, explore, and innovate, becoming active agents of evolution and contributing our verse to the grand poem of life. Let us approach our familial inheritance with both gratitude and reverence, embracing our sacred duty to challenge, grow, and transcend. In doing so, we pay the highest possible tribute to those who gave us life and step into our power as co-creators of the reality we wish to inhabit.

The Inherited Lens: Recognizing the Filters of Cultural Conditioning

IT was a warm October morning in the heart of the Amazonian jungle. The air was thick with humidity, and the sounds of exotic birds and insects filled the atmosphere. I found myself standing amidst a sea of semi-naked bodies, more than three hundred native men and women, their skin glistening with sweat and mud. The energy was palpable, a mix of excitement, reverence, and pure, unadulterated joy.

Just moments before, we had been engrossed in the bee's game, a sacred ritual that held deep significance for the *Yawanawa* tribe. A bunch of bananas, symbolizing the hive, was fiercely guarded by the women who played the role of the bees. The mud on the ground represented the honey, a precious commodity that the men, as the thieves, were determined to steal. The game was a flurry of activity, with the women chasing down the men and throwing them into the mud, their laughter echoing through the jungle.

As the game progressed, the roles reversed, and soon everyone, men and women alike, was covered head to toe in the earth's rich, brown embrace. The tribe then gathered in a large circle, their voices rising in unison as they began to sing and dance, their feet stomping the ground in a rhythmic beat that seemed to pulse with the very heartbeat of the jungle.

I found myself swept up in the moment, my own body moving in sync with the tribe as we made our way down the hill toward the river. The singing grew louder, more passionate, as we approached the water's edge, and I could feel the ecstatic energy and joy of the *Yawanawa* people washing over me like a cleansing wave.

This was the final day of the *Yawanawa's* annual celebration, a week-long event that honored their ancient traditions and way of life. The *Yawanawa* are an indigenous tribe that has called the Amazon rainforest home for countless generations. Their history is one of resilience and adaptation in the face of immense challenges.

A few decades ago, Christian missionaries made contact with the *Yawanawa*, introducing not only their religion but also the scourges of alcohol and the societal ills that often accompany such cultural invasions. The impact on the tribe was devastating, leading to widespread alcoholism, depression, and even suicide.

But the *Yawanawa* are a strong and proud people, and they refused to let their culture be erased. Around twenty years ago, a group of young tribal leaders made the courageous decision to expel the missionaries and begin the process of reclaiming their heritage. They started a movement to revive their ancient traditions, to remind their people of the beauty and value of their way of life.

The annual celebration I witnessed was a testament to the success of that movement. For a full week, the entire tribe came together, welcoming visitors from around the globe to share in their rituals and festivities. The games they played were not mere entertainment, but powerful tools for strengthening social bonds, resolving conflicts, and marking important milestones in the life of the community.

At night, under a canopy of stars and around the flickering light of the bonfire, the *pagés*, or shamans, would lead us in *Ayahuasca* ceremonies, guiding us on a journey into the realm of spirits. We danced and sang, celebrating the wisdom of the jungle, the power of the earth, and the eternal cycle of life and death.

The bee's game, with its playful mixing of mud and laughter, held a special significance. It was the *Yawanawa's* way of inviting the Mother Earth herself to join in the celebration, to share in their joy and gratitude. By offering the party to her, they were reaffirming their deep connection to the land and all its creatures.

As I looked around at the faces of the *Yawanawa* people, I saw a resilience and wisdom that humbled me. They had faced unimaginable challenges, but they had emerged stronger, more committed than ever to preserving their way of life. They understood that the key to their survival lay not in assimilating to the ways of the outside world, but in staying true to their own culture, their own sacred traditions.

In a world that often seems bent on conformity and consumption, the *Yawanawa* stand as a shining example of the power of cultural identity and the importance of living in harmony with the earth. They have become skilled diplomats, learning to navigate the complexities of the modern world while never losing sight of who they are and where they come from.

As I left the celebration, my skin still caked with mud and my heart full of wonder, I couldn't help but reflect on the profound diversity of human cultures and the myriad ways in which societies around the world shape the beliefs, values, and behaviors of their members. There's beauty in the diversity, and there is no single "right" way to live, no single path to fulfillment and meaning.

In a world filled with countless cultures, religions, and ideologies, each with its own unique history and traditions, it can be easy to fall into the trap of believing that our own way of life is somehow superior or more valid than others. But the truth is that every society, from the most technologically advanced to the most isolated indigenous tribe, is a product of its own particular set of circumstances and influences.

As we move through our own lives, it's essential to remember that the roles, expectations, and beliefs that we are taught to accept as "normal" or "natural" are, in fact, the result of complex processes of social conditioning. From the moment we are born, we are immersed in a web of cultural narratives and practices that shape our understanding of ourselves and our place in the world.

But just as the *Yawanawa* were able to recognize the limitations of the belief systems imposed upon them by outside forces, so too can we learn to question and challenge the assumptions and expectations that govern our own lives. By exposing ourselves to the rich kaleidoscope of human diversity, by learning from the wisdom and experiences of cultures different from our own, we can begin to expand our own sense of what is possible and to chart our own unique course through life.

In the vast array of cultures and societies that make up the human universe, each one has its own unique set of beliefs, values, and ideas about what constitutes a "perfect" way of life. For many of us, our own society's vision of utopia is so deeply ingrained that we may not even realize the extent to which it shapes our worldview and expectations.

Take, for example, the Christian conception of Paradise – a realm of eternal love, goodness, and equality, where the faithful are protected and blessed by a benevolent God. This vision has shaped the aspirations and moral frameworks of countless individuals throughout history, offering a powerful incentive to adhere to a particular set of religious and social norms.

In stark contrast, the ancient Vikings held a very different view of the ideal afterlife. For these fierce warriors, Valhalla represented the ultimate reward – a place where they could feast, drink, and fight alongside the gods, enjoying the company of the most beautiful women (the Valkyries) for all eternity. This vision of paradise, shaped by the Vikings' highly patriarchal and militaristic society, reflects a set of values and priorities that is radically different from those of the Christian worldview.

But these are just two examples among countless others. In the highlands of Papua New Guinea, the Huli people have traditionally believed in a complex spirit world, where ancestors and nature spirits play a critical role in shaping human destiny. For the Huli, the ideal life is one lived in harmony with these spirits, adhering to a strict set of social and ritual obligations that maintain the balance between human and non-human realms.

Meanwhile, in the bustling cities of Japan, the concept of "*wa*" – social harmony and the subordination of individual desires for the greater good – has long been a central pillar of their culture. For many Japanese, an ideal society is one in which everyone knows their place and works diligently to fulfill their prescribed roles, creating a sense of order and stability that benefits the collective whole.

In contrast, the modern capitalist societies often prioritize individual achievement, competition, and the pursuit of personal wealth and success above all. In this worldview, the ideal society is one in which everyone is free to pursue their own self-interest, with the belief that the invisible hand of the market will ultimately lead to the greatest good for all.

However, the relentless focus on individualism and competition has led to a range of social and environmental problems, from growing inequality and social fragmentation to the exploitation of natural resources and the destruction of traditional communities. The pursuit of individual gain often comes at the expense of the collective good, and that the concentration of wealth and power in the hands of a few can lead to the erosion of democratic values and institutions.

Moreover, the pressures of modern capitalist society can take a heavy toll on individuals, leading to high levels of stress, anxiety, and social isolation. The constant need to compete and succeed, to keep up with the latest trends and technologies, can leave people feeling disconnected from themselves and from others, with little time or space for the cultivation of deeper values and relationships.

In this context, the example of the San people of the Kalahari Desert offers a powerful counterpoint. For the San, the ideal existence is one in which everyone has equal access to the resources and knowledge needed to thrive, and in which the bonds of community and reciprocity are the foundation of social life. Their way of life prioritizes connection, sharing, and a deep respect for the natural world, values that are often lost or marginalized in the rush to achieve individual success and material wealth.

However, it's important to recognize that no culture or society holds the ultimate truth or the perfect way of life. Even in traditional societies like the San, there can be problems and challenges, such as conflicts over resources, gender inequalities, or the struggle to maintain cultural identity in the face of external pressures and changes.

Similarly, while the Japanese emphasis on social harmony and the collective good has many admirable qualities, it can also lead to conformity, suppression of individual expression, and a lack of creativity and innovation. The pressure to fit into prescribed roles and to prioritize the group over the individual can be stifling and may lead to feelings of alienation and disconnection.

Across history, societies have struggled to balance individuality and collective well-being. In early human communities, survival depended on cooperation, where personal desires took a backseat to group needs. Over time, civilizations introduced systems that either reinforced collective identity, such as the Confucian emphasis on social duty, or promoted individual ambition, as seen in Western capitalism. Each model shaped not only societal structures but also how people defined success, purpose, and belonging.

No system is flawless. Cultures that emphasize community often risk suppressing personal freedom, while those that celebrate individualism can breed isolation and inequality. Throughout history, humanity has continuously adjusted this balance, reshaping traditions, values, and expectations to navigate the evolving tension between self-expression and social responsibility.

As we explore these different cultural perspectives and ways of being, it's essential to approach them with an open and critical mind. We must be willing to question our own assumptions and biases, to learn from the wisdom and experiences of others, but also to think for ourselves and to chart our own course in life.

The key to finding fulfillment and meaning in any society is to strike a balance between the needs of the individual and the needs of the community. It's to find a way to honor our own unique gifts and passions while also contributing to something larger than ourselves. And it's to recognize that there is no one-size-fits-all answer, no perfect blueprint for the ideal life or society.

Instead, each of us must do the hard work of questioning the social standards and expectations that mold our perspectives, of looking deeply within ourselves to discover our own values and priorities, and of creating a life that is genuine and true to who we are. It's a journey that requires courage, compassion, and a willingness to step outside our comfort zones and to embrace the unknown.

But in the end, it's a journey that can lead us to a deeper sense of purpose and connection, to a life that is rich in meaning and fulfillment, and to a world that is more just, equitable, and sustainable for all. By learning from the diversity of human cultures and experiences, and by staying true to our own inner compass, we can begin to weave a new story of what it means to be human – one that celebrates our differences even as it recognizes our common humanity, and that seeks to create a world in which all people can thrive and reach their full potential.

As we continue this journey, let's keep this lesson in mind, and let's approach each new culture and way of life with an open mind and a willingness to be transformed by each encounter. For it's only by stepping outside the bounds of our own cultural programming that we can truly begin to appreciate the full richness and complexity of the human experience.

In Aldous Huxley's "Brave New World," the pursuit of societal perfection takes a chilling turn. The citizens of this dystopian future are not only genetically engineered and socially conditioned but also kept in a state of artificial contentment through the widespread use of a drug called soma. This government-provided substance offers an instant escape from any residual unhappiness or dissatisfaction, ensuring that everyone remains blissfully compliant with their assigned roles. As one character explains, "And if ever, by some unlucky chance, anything unpleasant should somehow happen, why, there's always soma to give you a holiday from the facts."

Moreover, the society in Huxley's novel has reduced human intimacy and sexuality to a mere distraction, a superficial pleasure that keeps people docile and emotionally detached. Promiscuity is encouraged, while genuine emotional connections are viewed as a threat to the stability of the social order. In a world where "everyone belongs to everyone else," the very concept of individual love and commitment becomes subversive.

While the specifics of Huxley's vision may seem far-fetched, the underlying themes of social control and the suppression of individuality are all too relevant to our modern world. Just as soma and sexual promiscuity are used to pacify the citizens of Huxley's dystopia, our own society often relies on consumerism, entertainment, and instant gratification to keep us content and compliant.

We are bombarded with advertisements that promise happiness through the acquisition of material goods, urged to define ourselves by our possessions and appearances. Social media and online entertainment provide a constant stream of distraction, keeping us engaged in superficial interactions and preventing us from grappling with deeper existential questions. In the pursuit of economic growth and efficiency, our unique talents and passions are often sacrificed in favor of conformity and productivity.

While these modern-day "soma" may not come in the form of a pill, they serve a similar function: to numb us to the inherent imperfections and challenges of life, to keep us focused on short-term pleasures rather than long-term fulfillment. And just as in Huxley's world, this pursuit of a false sense of happiness and stability comes at a great cost to our individuality, our creativity, and our authenticity.

Despite the inherent flaws in the pursuit of societal perfection, we often find ourselves embroiled in fierce ideological battles, fighting tooth and nail to impose our vision of the ideal world upon others. We engage in passionate debates over political systems, economic theories, and moral frameworks, as if the very fate of humanity hinged on the universal adoption of our preferred ideology. We pour our time, energy, and resources into defending and promoting our beliefs, sometimes at great cost to our relationships, our peace of mind, and even our own well-being.

But what if we were to take a step back and reevaluate our approach? Instead of striving for an unattainable utopia, we can begin to accept and even embrace the idea that society, like the humankind itself, is inherently imperfect.

This isn't to suggest that we should abandon our efforts to create a better world, but rather that we should approach the task with a greater sense of humility, compassion, and openness to diverse perspectives.

When we look at the fundamental role of society, we see that its primary purpose is not to ensure our individual happiness, but rather to provide the conditions necessary for our survival and collective growth. The structures and institutions that we create – from governments and economies to schools and families – serve to organize our efforts, pool our resources, and transmit our accumulated knowledge and skills from one generation to the next. Without this collaborative framework, our species may never have made it past the early stages of our evolutionary journey.

However, as essential as society is to our continued existence, it often demands a certain sacrifice of our individuality. To maintain order and stability, social systems require us to conform to certain norms, roles, and expectations. They ask us to temper our wild impulses, to channel our energies in socially acceptable ways, and to prioritize the needs of the group over our own desires. While this trade-off has allowed us to build complex civilizations and achieve incredible feats of cooperation, it can also leave us feeling stifled, disconnected, and yearning for something more.

It's also important to understand that a society is not a monolithic entity, governed by a single ideology or set of beliefs. Rather, it's a complex set of competing forces, each with its own agenda, biases, and desired outcomes. Political parties, religious groups, corporations, media outlets, and countless other institutions and organizations are constantly vying for our attention, our loyalty, and our resources. They seek to shape our opinions, our behaviors, and our understanding of the world in ways that serve their interests.

In this context, we are often reduced to little more than pawns in a larger game, our individual agency and autonomy consumed by the machinations of those in power. We are bombarded with messages and narratives that seek to polarize us, to pit us against one another, and to keep us locked in a state of perpetual conflict and division.

Consider, for example, the way in which political discourse has become increasingly polarized in recent years. The rise of echo chambers and filter bubbles, fueled by social media algorithms and partisan news outlets, has created a landscape in which people are exposed only to information and opinions that confirm their existing beliefs. This has led to a hardening of ideological boundaries, a decrease in empathy and understanding across political divides, and an erosion of the structures of civil society.

The impact of this polarization can be seen in the way it has torn apart friendships and even families. Heated debates over politics, once confined to the realm of the abstract, have now become deeply personal, with individuals defining their very identities by their partisan affiliations.

In such a climate, it can be tempting to view those who disagree with us as enemies to be vanquished, rather than fellow human beings with their own unique perspectives and experiences. We may feel a sense of righteousness in our beliefs, a certainty that we are on the right side of history, and that those who oppose us are misguided or even malevolent.

Amidst the noise of division, we often forget that beneath every ideology lies a human being shaped by unique experiences and fears. To break free from this cycle, we must cultivate curiosity, empathy, and a willingness to learn. By viewing those who differ from us as teachers rather than adversaries, we can expand our understanding of the world and develop a more nuanced and compassionate view of the human condition. For no single ideology or belief system has a monopoly on truth, and the path to a more just and harmonious society lies in our ability to bridge divides, to find common ground, and to work together toward shared goals.

This openness to learning from others not only fosters personal growth but also equips us to navigate the broader forces that shape our societies. In a world where powerful institutions often seek to impose conformity, reclaiming our individuality becomes an act of resistance and renewal.

As human beings, we are both individual and social creatures, and this duality can create an ongoing tension within us. On the one hand, we need to find our place and purpose within the larger group, while on the other, our individuality yearns for expression and fulfillment.

But individuality without connection is just another illusion—a selfish rebellion that changes nothing. Real power lies in the ability to break free from our ideological bubbles and build bridges where others see walls. It's not about polite coexistence; it's about fierce collaboration. It's about acknowledging that every voice—no matter how inconvenient or uncomfortable—has a role to play in shaping the world we share.

Our society is not some static ideal carved in stone but a living, breathing organism that changes with every choice we make. By embracing curiosity, rejecting blind conformity, and leaning into the discomfort of true cooperation, we stop being mere spectators and become the architects of something better.

In the end, the path forward lies not in clinging to the false comfort of uniformity but in embracing the untamed diversity of human thought and experience. By standing in our truth while daring to hear others, we stitch together a world where individuality and community thrive—not despite each other but because of each other.

The Myths of Modernity: Media's Storytelling Sorcery

AT the heart of every culture lies a rich mosaic of myths and stories, woven together over generations to create a shared understanding of the world and our place within it. These myths are far more than entertaining tales; they are the threads that bind societies, shaping values, beliefs, and behaviors in ways so profound they often go unnoticed.

Picture this: you're sitting around a flickering fire in a small village centuries ago. The night is dark, the only light coming from the dancing flames and the stars above. An elder, his face etched with wisdom, begins to speak. His voice is low and melodic, and as he weaves his tale, the world around you fades away. You're transported into the story—heroes, monsters, love, loss, and the mysteries of the cosmos come alive before you.

With every word, metaphor, and symbol, the elder is planting seeds—seeds of your culture's myths, its understanding of the universe, and your place within it. These aren't just stories. They are blueprints for how you see the world, guides for your actions, and the foundation of your identity.

For millennia, myths were passed down through oral traditions. Each generation added its own layers, embedding these narratives into ceremonies, art, music, and rituals. These stories taught morality, social norms, and the mysteries of human existence. But as their power became apparent, so did their potential for manipulation.

Religious institutions began codifying myths into strict doctrines. Sacred texts, divine revelations, and ritualized practices were used to solidify authority, reinforcing existing power structures and maintaining social order. What began as shared wisdom became tools of control. Similarly, political leaders learned to wield myths to build national identity, foster patriotism, and justify their rule. Grand narratives of origin, destiny, and heroic leaders mobilized entire populations while entrenching the authority of those in power.

In this way, myths became instruments of social control, used to shape the thoughts and actions of individuals in ways that served the interests of the ruling elite. And as these institutionalized myths spread and took root, they became increasingly difficult to challenge or question, their power and influence growing with each passing generation.

But with the advent of the printing press, a seismic shift occurred in the way stories were told and disseminated. Suddenly, myths could be written down, mass-produced, and spread far beyond the confines of a single village or community. The printing press, invented by Johannes Gutenberg in the 15th century, marked the beginning of a new era in human communication and the birth of what we now know as the media.

As time passed, the media evolved, finding ever more sophisticated ways to tell stories and shape public opinion. From newspapers and magazines to radio and television, from the internet to social media, the channels through which we receive information and entertainment have proliferated at an astonishing rate.

Today, we are bombarded with stories from every direction, each one vying for our attention and seeking to influence our thoughts and behaviors. The myths of our modern age are no longer confined to the fireside tales of our ancestors; they are created in the boardrooms of corporations, the studios of Hollywood, and the newsrooms of media conglomerates.

These modern myths are carefully crafted, their messages honed through the use of sophisticated marketing techniques and psychological research. They play on our emotions, our desires, and our fears, tapping into the deepest recesses of our collective unconscious.

In the past, if an organization wanted to inspire people to take action or make a donation, they would have to rely on the power of the spoken word. A priest, for example, would spend hours at the pulpit, passionately preaching about the importance of being a peaceful, generous servant of God. He would paint vivid pictures with his words, appealing to the congregation's sense of morality and urging them to give generously to the church.

In the age of the media, agencies, companies, and institutions have much more powerful instruments at their disposal. An environmental organization like Greenpeace, for example, can use powerful imagery and storytelling to inspire action and encourage donations not only in a single location, but worldwide. A harrowing video of a whale being hunted, its blood staining the blue waters of the ocean, or a photograph of a once-lush forest reduced to ashes and stumps—these visual narratives evoke a visceral response, stirring our emotions and compelling us to act.

Unfortunately, the same techniques that can be used promote worthy causes are also be employed to manipulate us into buying products we don't need or subscribing to ideologies that may not serve our best interests. The advertising industry has become a master of the art of mythmaking, creating elaborate narratives around the products they sell.

A smartphone isn't just a communication device—it's a symbol of status and innovation. Fashion trends are no longer about aesthetics; they're declarations of identity and values. These myths are so pervasive, so seamlessly integrated into our daily lives, that we often accept them, allowing them to shape our desires, our self-image, and our understanding of success and happiness.

The power of these media-driven myths cannot be overstated. They shape public opinion, influence political discourse, and define the very boundaries of what we consider to be possible or acceptable.

In a world where the media holds such sway over our collective consciousness, it's more important than ever to develop a critical awareness of the stories we are being told and the myths we are being sold. We must learn to question the narratives that surround us, to look beyond the surface appeal of the images and slogans, and to examine the underlying assumptions and agendas at play.

This is not an easy task, for the myths of our culture are deeply ingrained, cemented in the bedrock of our identity and our understanding of the world. But by becoming more conscious of the stories that shape us, by learning to deconstruct and analyze the messages we receive, we can begin to sift through the noise and discover something deeper—our own voice, clear and steady, amidst the multitude of competing narratives in our minds.

In the following sections, we will delve deeper into some of the most pervasive and influential myths of our modern age, examining how they shape our beliefs, our behaviors, and our sense of ourselves. From the cult of consumerism to the illusion of perfectionism, from the polarization of politics to the distortion of reality, we will explore the ways in which these myths both reflect and shape the world we live in.

The Righteous, the Wicked, and the Ambiguous: Tales from the Moral Badlands

DURING the Cold War, the world was divided into two opposing camps: the capitalist West, led by the United States, and the communist East, dominated by the Soviet Union. Both sides engaged in extensive propaganda campaigns to convince their respective populations of the righteousness of their cause and the evil of their enemies.

In the West, media, government, and educational institutions all painted the communist world as a dark, oppressive, and dangerous place. The Soviet Union was portrayed as a ruthless, totalitarian regime that sought to crush individual freedom and impose its will on the world through force and subversion. Communists were depicted as godless, immoral, and bent on destroying the American way of life.

This narrative was reinforced through popular culture, with movies, books, and television shows often featuring Soviet agents as villains, scheming to undermine democracy and enslave the free world. Children were taught to fear and despise communists, with duck-and-cover drills in schools and public service announcements warning of the ever-present threat of nuclear annihilation.

On the other side of the Iron Curtain, the communist propaganda machine was equally hard at work. The United States and its allies were portrayed as decadent, imperialist powers, intent on exploiting the working class and oppressing the peoples of the world. Capitalists were depicted as greedy, heartless monsters, willing to sacrifice the lives and well-being of millions in the pursuit of profit.

Communist citizens were told that they were the true heroes of history, fighting a noble battle against the forces of evil and injustice. They were promised a utopian future, where the workers would control the means of production, and all would equally share in the fruits of their labor. Any hardships or sacrifices endured in the present were justified by the glorious struggle for the greater good.

These competing narratives left the world divided, not just by political and economic systems, but by fundamentally different views of reality. Each side saw the other as the embodiment of evil, an existential threat to be vanquished at all costs. This led to a state of constant tension and conflict, with proxy wars, arms races, and the ever-present specter of nuclear Armageddon.

While the Cold War may have ended, the myth of good and evil remains deeply embedded in the way societies perceive and engage with the world. The ideological battle between the United States and the Soviet Union may have faded into history, but the underlying narrative structure—us versus them, the righteous against the wicked—continues to shape global and domestic affairs.

In its simplest form, this myth offers a sense of clarity and purpose, casting complex issues as moral struggles. Nations, movements, and even individual leaders use it to rally support, foster loyalty, and simplify the messy realities of human conflict. The binary of good and evil is a potent tool: it inspires action, justifies sacrifice, and absolves self-reflection. If you are the hero fighting darkness, then any means become permissible in service of the cause. Instead of seeking understanding, you can just cling to the comforting illusion that your motives are pure and theirs are not.

The danger, of course, lies in its reductive nature. By framing conflicts as battles of good against evil, the narrative obscures nuance, erases context, and silences dissent. It fosters polarization, painting those with differing perspectives as adversaries to be defeated rather than partners in dialogue. Complex realities—rooted in history, economics, and cultural dynamics—are flattened into black-and-white caricatures.

The myth of good and evil is a powerful tool for manipulation precisely because it taps into our deepest emotions and our most primal instincts. When we are convinced that we are on the side of good, fighting against the forces of evil, we are willing to do almost anything to win. We are more likely to accept authoritarianism, to tolerate violence and oppression, and to sacrifice our own freedoms and values in the name of the greater good.

But who decides what's good and what's evil, and with which criteria and intentions? This question lies at the heart of the manipulation, for those in power often wield these labels as weapons to further their own agendas.

Moreover, by framing complex social and political issues in simple terms of good and evil, the dominant elites can avoid addressing the underlying causes of conflict and injustice. They can deflect blame and responsibility onto the designated enemy, rather than confronting how their own policies and actions may be contributing to the problem.

But the pernicious force of the myth extends its reach far beyond the grand theatres of geopolitics and ideological conflict. Indeed, it infiltrates our personal relationships, professional interactions, and community dynamics. It has the power to transform even the most trivial of disagreements into a cosmic battle between the forces of righteousness and depravity.

Consider, for example, a dispute between neighbors over the placement of a fence or the boundaries of a property line. What might begin as a minor difference of opinion or a misunderstanding can quickly escalate into a full-blown moral crusade, with each party convinced of the utter wickedness of the other. The complex realities of property law, zoning regulations, and the inevitable ambiguities of human communication are reduced to a simplistic narrative of hero versus villain, good versus evil.

In this storytelling framework, there is no room for nuance, no space for compromise or mutual understanding. The neighbor who encroaches on one's land is not seen as a fallible human being, perhaps acting out of ignorance or a different interpretation of the situation. Instead, they are cast as a malevolent force, a representation of all that is wrong with the world, an enemy to be vanquished at all costs.

This dynamic repeats in countless areas of daily life, where ordinary disagreements are elevated into full-blown moral dramas. The myth of good and evil turns what could be opportunities for collaboration and understanding into battlegrounds of division, eroding trust and progress in the process.

The consequences of this myth are profound and far-reaching. By reducing the complexities of human interaction to a binary of good and evil, we create a world of stark divisions and irreconcilable differences. We lose the ability to see humanity in those with whom we disagree, to recognize the common fears, hopes, and aspirations that unite us all. We become locked in cycles of recrimination and retribution, unable to find the common ground necessary for progress or reconciliation.

If we are to transcend the limitations of this myth and build a more just, compassionate, and harmonious world, we must learn to resist the temptation of moral absolutism. We must strive to cultivate a nuanced and empathetic understanding of the human condition, recognizing that even those with whom we disagree are complex beings, shaped by their own unique experiences, beliefs, and circumstances.

However, this is easier said than done. After all, the myth of good and evil is deeply ingrained in our psyches, and the desire to see ourselves as righteous and our opponents as wicked can be incredibly seductive. It's all too easy to fall into the trap of moral self-righteousness, to convince ourselves that we are the heroes of our own story and that anyone who stands in our way must be a villain.

In a world ruled by strict moral codes, where our anger boils repressed under the surface, it's convenient to have a villain around. By casting our enemies as the embodiment of evil, we give ourselves permission to unleash the worst aspects of our nature, all in the name of justice and morality. We can indulge our darkest impulses, our most destructive tendencies, and still maintain the illusion of righteousness. We can set our inner beast free without losing our sanctity.

This is the seductive trap of the good-evil dichotomy, the way it allows us to justify our own harmful actions and attitudes by projecting all that is bad onto some external "other." But in doing so, we lose touch with our own humanity. We become prisoners of our own self-righteousness, unable to see the complexity and nuance of the world around us.

If the myth of good and evil distorts the complexities of life into a binary narrative, to move beyond it we must confront the uncomfortable truths about our own roles in sustaining these divisions. This requires us to take an honest look at the ways we have been complicit in perpetuating the very conflicts we claim to oppose—whether through our silence, our biases, or our unquestioning acceptance of simplistic narratives.

By enriching our principles with humility and self-awareness, we create space for transformation—within ourselves and in the broader world. This is the starting point for weaving a new narrative, one that embraces complexity, honors diversity, and recognizes the shared humanity in all of us.

To rise above the stark divide between good and evil, we must set blame aside and begin the harder work of introspection and reconciliation. Only by confronting our inner shadows can we mend society's fractures and build a world where understanding replaces enmity, nuance outshines absolutes, and collaboration becomes the bedrock of progress.

The Eden Complex

THE rhythmic beat of the drums pulsed through the air, mingling with the ancient songs that seemed to emanate from the very heart of the earth. I found myself in the midst of a sacred ritual, a celebration of the Orishas, the gods of the Yoruba tradition. The ceremony was being held in honor of my friend, Thiago, who had just emerged from the Roncó, a sacred initiation room where he had spent the past ten days in deep meditation, dieting, and undergoing profound rituals of initiation to consecrate his life to his father Orisha, Ogun.

As Thiago stepped into the ceremonial lounge, his eyes glazed over in a trance-like state, the energy in the room shifted. The drums intensified, and the songs grew louder, more urgent. Thiago's body began to move, not of its own accord, but as a vessel for the spirit of Ogun himself. He danced with a sword in hand, his movements both powerful and graceful, a physical embodiment of the god of progress and technology.

The Orishas tradition had its roots in Africa, brought to Brazil by slaves who carried their spiritual beliefs and practices with them across the Atlantic. In a cruel twist of fate, many of these slaves were political and religious leaders, sent to Brazil as part of a deliberate plan to strip the African continent of its leadership. Yet, in the fertile soil of Brazil, the Orishas tradition found a new home, a place where it could grow and flourish.

Each Orisha represents a different aspect of the natural world and of human experience. Ogun, the god of progress, is known for his simplicity, humility, and loyalty. He's the one who forged the metals, bringing the first tools to the world, paving the way for technological advancement. But Ogun is also a fierce and furious god, the one who brought the war and spilled blood to feed the thirst of the earth.

As I watched Thiago dance, embodying the spirit of Ogun, I was struck by the stark contrast between the Orishas tradition and the dominant religious narratives of our time, particularly those of the Judeo-Christian faith. While the Orishas tradition acknowledge the complex interplay of light and shadow within the human soul, the Judeo-Christian religions often present a more simplistic and polarizing view of morality, one that has had profound consequences for the way we understand ourselves and our place in the world.

At the heart of this worldview lies the myth of basic goodness, the idea that we are all fundamentally pure and innocent, and that any deviation from this state is a result of sin or corruption. This myth has been used for centuries to manipulate and control the masses, to instill a deep sense of guilt and inadequacy in the hearts of believers.

The idea of the seven deadly sins—pride, envy, gluttony, greed, lust, sloth, and wrath—is a prime example of this manipulation. By labeling natural human emotions and impulses as inherently sinful, the Church has effectively pathologized the very essence of what it means to be human, creating a system in which the mere experience of these feelings, even if not acted upon, is seen as a stain upon the soul.

The concept of sin itself is deeply problematic, as it implies a fundamental flaw or defect in the human condition, a state of perpetual unworthiness that can only be redeemed through the grace of God. This idea has been used throughout history to justify all manner of abuses and atrocities, from the subjugation of indigenous peoples to the oppression of women and minorities.

By convincing us that we're inherently sinful, that we're forever falling short of some impossible standard of goodness, the Judeo-Christian tradition strips us of our inherent dignity and self-worth. It makes us feel like eternal sinners, forever in pursuit of a redemption that always seems just out of reach.

The Orishas tradition, in contrast, offers a more grounded and compassionate alternative to these limiting and oppressive narratives. By acknowledging the full complexity of the human experience, by honoring both the light and the shadow within us, it frees us from the tyranny of impossible ideals and the endless pursuit of external validation.

It reminds us that we are not inherently sinful or flawed, but rather complex, multifaceted beings, capable of great beauty and great destruction. It invites us to take responsibility for our actions and choices, to confront our shadows with honesty and compassion, and to strive for greater wisdom and understanding.

To glimpse our nature, start with a newborn—, the most untouched state of a human being. From the first breath, their needs take center stage. They cry, demand, and consume without hesitation—milk, yes, but also attention, energy, and entire nights of sleep. As they grow, the tactics evolve: tantrums morph into shrewd negotiations, and budding charm becomes a precision tool for getting what they want. By peak mischief age, parents are coasting on caffeine, reflexes, and a faint memory of hope.

Our nature is not completely evil, and our babies are not just little tyrants, but let's face it, the capacity for selfishness and havoc is as much a part of the human experience as pooping and drooling. We carry this potential for cruelty with us throughout our lives, like a beloved childhood toy we just can't seem to part with. From the petty schoolyard squabbles over who gets to play with the shiny new truck to the grand-scale atrocities that make history textbooks read like a Stephen King novel, we humans have a real knack for being absolute bastards to each other.

Even in our most loving relationships, there is always an element of shadow, a potential for hurt and betrayal. Sometimes we must fight a war against our own instincts to avoid controlling, manipulating, or even attacking those we love most.

These impulses are not aberrations or deviations from our true nature, but rather an integral part of who we are as human beings. To deny or suppress them is to engage in a form of self-deception, a refusal to confront the full complexity of our own being.

The solution, then, is not to strive for some impossible ideal of goodness, but rather to accept and integrate the full range of our human experience. We must learn to acknowledge our own capacity for destruction and cruelty, not as a source of shame or guilt, but as a reminder of our own inherent fragility and imperfection.

Finding the courage to embrace the fullness of our own being, we can learn to dance with both the light and the shadow, and to trust in the inherent wisdom and resilience of our human spirit. When we accept that we are not inherently good, we can develop a different relationship with our spirituality. We can evolve, not motivated by guilt or the desperate pursuit of redemption, but by true consciousness and love.

No longer weighed down by the burden of original sin or the belief in our own fundamental corruption, we can begin to see ourselves in a new light. We can recognize the incredible progress we have made as individuals and as a species, the countless ways in which we have overcome our destructive impulses and strived to create a more just and compassionate world.

That's something to be celebrated, something to be deeply respected and honored. When we look at ourselves and each other through this lens, we begin to see the true beauty and potential of the human spirit. We begin to understand that our struggles and imperfections are not sources of shame, but rather opportunities for growth and transformation.

We can approach our own being with self-respect and appreciation. We can choose to see ourselves not as miserable sinners groveling for forgiveness, but rather as brave and resilient beings, doing our best to navigate the complex landscape of the human experience. This is actually a much more realistic and fair perspective that honors the hard work and dedication it takes to be a good person in a world that often makes this difficult.

In doing so, we cultivate a deeper, more authentic relationship with the divine—one rooted not in fear or guilt, but in love, trust, and a profound reverence for the sacred nature of all life. Our evolutionary path is not about striving for an unattainable ideal of perfection, but about embracing the depth of our essence and allowing it to guide our actions in creating a meaningful impact on the world.

The Road to Hell is Paved with Perfect Intentions

THE myth of perfection, a close relative of the myth of inherent goodness, is one of the most insidious and pervasive delusions of our modern age. Its roots trace back to the idea of a perfect God who created humans in his image, a concept that has fueled centuries of theological and philosophical debate. However, let's set aside the metaphysical implications for a moment and consider what the pursuit of perfection looks like in practice.

What would it mean to achieve your ideal of perfection, to reach a state of flawless, unchanging excellence? Is such a thing even possible, given the dynamic and ever-evolving nature of life? The answer, of course, is a resounding no. Perfection is an illusion. In a universe that is constantly in flux, where change is the only constant, the very notion of perfection is a contradiction in terms.

If we were all perfect, having reached the pinnacle of our potential with nowhere left to go, what would the point of existence be? Life would become a stagnant, monotonous affair, stripped of growth, challenge, and the thrill of discovery. We might as well call it a day, for there would be no new frontiers to explore, no struggles to shape us, and no aspirations to ignite our spirit.

The myth of perfection not only robs us of the joys of growth and discovery, but also stifles our creativity and holds us back from reaching our full potential. When we become obsessed with achieving some imagined ideal of perfection, we paralyze ourselves with fear and self-doubt. Every action becomes a potential misstep, every choice an opportunity for failure.

We see this play out in countless ways, from the writer who agonizes over every word, convinced that a single misplaced comma will ruin their masterpiece, to the artist who spends years tinkering with a painting, never quite satisfied with the result. In the relentless pursuit of perfection, we become our own worst enemies, sabotaging our efforts and draining the joy from the creative process.

Perhaps the most insidious aspect of the myth of perfection lies in its entanglement with our sense of self-worth and value. In a culture that equates success with flawlessness, it's easy to internalize the message that our worth is only as good as our last perfect performance. We become terrified of making mistakes, of revealing our human fallibility, lest we be judged and found wanting.

This fear manifests in all sorts of counterproductive ways, from chronic procrastination to self-sabotage. We might shy away from new challenges, convincing ourselves that it's safer not to try than to risk falling short of our impossible standards. Or we may work to the point of burnout, convinced that if we just push ourselves a little harder, we'll finally achieve that elusive state of perfection.

But the game of perfection is a losing game. It's a standard that no one, no matter how talented or driven, can ever truly meet. And in the relentless pursuit of this impossible ideal, we risk losing sight of the imperfect but ultimately beautiful reality of our lives.

In recent years, Silicon Valley, the tech world's beating heart, has adopted a game-changing philosophy: the MVP, or minimum viable product. The idea is simple yet revolutionary—launch creations as soon as they're functional, even if they come with a few bugs or rough edges, rather than waiting for perfection. And guess what? It's working. By putting their products out there early and iterating based on user feedback, these companies are able to innovate and improve at lightning speed. They're not shackled by the fear of imperfection; they're fueled by the opportunity to learn, adapt, and grow.

This approach has given rise to groundbreaking technologies: smartphones that place the world at our fingertips, social media platforms that bridge continents, and artificial intelligence capable of diagnosing diseases and predicting natural disasters. None of these innovations would exist if their creators had been paralyzed by the myth of perfection.

So, what can we take away from the Silicon Valley mindset? First, we need to embrace the power of iteration, focusing on small, incremental steps toward our goals rather than fixating on an unattainable ideal from the outset. Feedback should be welcomed, not feared, as a tool to refine and improve our creations over time. Alongside this, cultivating humility is essential. Mistakes and imperfections aren't shameful flaws to be hidden but valuable opportunities for growth and learning. Every misstep brings us one step closer to mastery.

Perhaps most importantly, we must learn to enjoy the process—warts and all. Striving for excellence is commendable, but it shouldn't come at the expense of our sanity or joy. Approaching creative pursuits with a sense of play and experimentation, rather than rigid determination to meet arbitrary standards of perfection, allows us to find fulfillment in the journey itself.

In the end, the myth of perfection is exactly that—a myth, a seductive illusion that lures us away from the messy, imperfect beauty of reality. When we learn to embrace the chaos and imperfection of the creative process, we unlock a world of endless possibilities. And if we truly are made in the image of a divine, all-powerful being, perhaps that God is just as messy, unpredictable, and beautifully imperfect as we are.

So why not give ourselves a break? Why not embrace our own chaotic, imperfect humanity with humor, curiosity, and a willingness to grow? Life isn't about achieving some unattainable ideal; it's about finding joy in the journey, not just the destination. When we let go of the need to be perfect, we free ourselves to live fully—embracing the mess, complexity, and richness of a life that's delightfully real.

Eternal Sunshine's Fallacy

YOU wake up one morning, groggy and disoriented, the remnants of last night's dreams still clinging to you like a fog. Stumbling into the kitchen, you hope a hot cup of coffee will bring you back to life.

As you sip your coffee, your phone pulls you into a digital reality where every face smiles, every moment sparkles, and every life seems effortlessly perfect. It's a jarring contrast to your groggy reality.

A sinking feeling starts to creep in, a nagging suspicion that maybe there's something wrong with you. If everyone else seems to have figured out the secret to happiness and fulfillment, why do you still struggle to get out of bed in the morning? Why do you always feel like you're playing catch-up, never quite measuring up to some impossible standard of success and joy?

This feeling is all too familiar—the gnawing sense that everyone else is at some grand happiness party, while you're stuck outside, staring through the window. And it's no wonder, given how relentlessly our society pushes the idea that happiness is the ultimate goal of human existence.

From an early age, we're bombarded with messages proclaiming that happiness is life's true purpose. We're told to "cheer up" when we feel down, to "look on the bright side" when challenges arise, and to "fake it till we make it" when our emotions don't cooperate. Meanwhile, we're inundated with products, services, and experiences, each one promising to unlock the elusive secret to lasting joy and fulfillment.

The myth of perpetual happiness is one of the most insidious and pervasive narratives fueling our consumer culture, keeping us on an endless treadmill of desire and acquisition. "Not happy? Maybe you need some new clothes," it whispers. "Perhaps a shiny new car will do the trick," it suggests. "Work harder, buy a beach house, and then you'll finally be content," it promises. Even more subtly, it whispers, "Your unhappiness comes from not having a family yet. Have kids, and your life will be filled with joy."

But here lies the deception: happiness cannot be sought in external milestones alone, least of all in bringing children into the world as a remedy for your own discontent. True fulfillment begins within. Only when we cultivate inner happiness can we create a nurturing environment for others, including the next generation. To reverse this dynamic is not just unfair—it's unsustainable.

The truth is, no one is happy all the time, no matter what their meticulously curated social media profiles might suggest. Life is an unpredictable journey, filled with highs and lows, moments of great joy and deep sorrow. Expecting ourselves to maintain a constant state of happiness is like trying to stay dry while running through a thunderstorm—it's not just unrealistic; it misses the point of the journey entirely. The richness of life lies in its unpredictability, in the way we learn and grow through both triumph and adversity.

Social media amplifies the pressure to appear happy, creating a distorted mirror where struggle and imperfection are erased. The documentary The Social Dilemma, directed by Jeff Orlowski, offers a sobering look at how these platforms shape our perceptions and, in turn, our mental well-being. Through interviews with former tech insiders, the film exposes the deliberate design choices behind social media—features aimed at fostering addiction and maximizing user engagement. While these strategies succeed in keeping us scrolling, they also contribute to rising rates of depression, anxiety, and

The documentary carefully traces the alarming rise in mental health issues, revealing how the relentless quest for online validation and the pressure to present an idealized version of one's life can have profound psychological consequences. Social media, as a microcosm of the larger media landscape, sells a fantasy of endless happiness and perfection—a standard that is not only unattainable but also deeply harmful.

The constant exposure to curated snapshots of other people's lives—stripped of the challenges, struggles, and imperfections that are inherent to the human experience—sets an impossible benchmark for happiness and success. This digital illusion of perpetual bliss distorts our self-perception and undermines our mental well-being. As we chase a happiness that always seems just out of reach, dangled before us on our screens, we risk falling into a vicious cycle of comparison and despair. We begin to see ourselves as fundamentally broken or defective, as if we're missing some essential ingredient in the happiness recipe that everyone else seems to have managed to find.

The human experience is far too complex and multifaceted to be reduced to a simple binary of happiness and unhappiness. Life is a rich tapestry, woven with moments of joy and sorrow, triumph and struggle, clarity and confusion. Trying to flatten this nuanced landscape into a one-dimensional pursuit of happiness is to rob ourselves of the full depth and meaning of what it means to be alive.

And yet, this is precisely what society often pressures us to do. We're led to believe that if we're not perpetually happy, there's something inherently wrong with us—some flaw that needs fixing. We're made to feel like failures if we can't maintain an unwavering state of positivity and enthusiasm, regardless of the challenges and uncertainties life inevitably brings.

What if we could learn to embrace the full spectrum of human emotions, recognizing each one as a vital and meaningful part of our lives? Instead of relentlessly chasing an unattainable ideal of constant happiness, what if we sought purpose and growth in our struggles, viewing moments of discomfort and pain as opportunities for growth?

Buddhism offers profound insights into the nature of human suffering and happiness. It teaches that the root of suffering is desire, including the desire for perpetual happiness. True peace, it teaches, comes not from grasping after fleeting pleasures but from cultivating a deep understanding of the nature of reality, which includes accepting impermanence and the inevitability of suffering.

Chögyam Trungpa, the renowned Tibetan Buddhist teacher, offers a thought-provoking perspective on the nature of existence. He famously said, "The bad news is you're falling through the air, nothing to hang on to, no parachute. The good news is there's no ground." This seemingly paradoxical statement encapsulates the Buddhist view of life as a constant state of change and uncertainty, with no solid ground of permanent happiness to land on. Trungpa's paradoxical wisdom invites us to embrace life's uncertainties instead of clinging to the illusion of permanence. By letting go of our obsession with unchanging bliss, we open ourselves to the richness of life's fleeting, unpredictable beauty.

From this perspective, the myth of eternal happiness is not just an unattainable goal; it becomes a source of suffering in itself. Clinging to the belief that we should always be in a state of uninterrupted joy sets us up for inevitable disappointment, blinding us to the richness and depth that the full spectrum of human experience has to offer. A more grounded and harmonious approach invites us to accept life as it is, in all its imperfect beauty, recognizing that true fulfillment comes from embracing the totality of our emotional landscape.

By letting go of the pursuit of happiness as the ultimate goal, we can start to cultivate a more balanced and realistic approach to life. We can learn to welcome and value the full range of human emotions, understanding that each one has its place and purpose.

This shift in perspective doesn't mean that we should stop seeking joy and contentment in our lives. Rather, it suggests that we recognize happiness as just one aspect of the multifaceted human experience, rather than the single defining factor. It means learning to find meaning and fulfillment in life's ups and downs, in our challenges and struggles as much as in our triumphs and successes.

It means cultivating resilience and adaptability, trusting in our innate ability to navigate life's storms. It calls us to embrace the present moment fully—without resistance to what is or attachment to what could be—rather than perpetually chasing an idealized future that may never come.

And perhaps most importantly, it means extending compassion and kindness to ourselves, even in moments when happiness feels out of reach. It means recognizing that our inherent worth and value as human beings is not dependent on our ability to maintain a constant state of positivity, but rather flows from the very essence of who we are, from the unique light that each of us brings to the world.

In a culture that often equates success and fulfillment with material possessions and external validation, this shift in perspective can be profoundly transformative. By acknowledging that life encompasses a rich spectrum of experiences beyond the narrow confines of happiness, we open ourselves to a deeper sense of beauty and meaning. We discover joy in life's simple moments, wisdom through our struggles, and resilience in the face of adversity.

This approach doesn't diminish the importance of happiness or suggest that we shouldn't strive for joy and contentment. Rather, it invites us to place happiness within a broader context, to see it as one of the many colors that make up the vibrant prism of human experience.

When we open our hearts and minds to embrace the full spectrum of emotions and experiences life has to offer, we unlock a profound sense of freedom and authenticity. No longer constrained by the impossible standard of perpetual happiness, we begin to find meaning and purpose in the entirety of our journey. This openness allows us to be more fully present in each moment, more deeply connected to ourselves and others, and more attuned to the inherent beauty and mystery of existence.

In this way, the path to genuine fulfillment shifts from a relentless pursuit of elusive happiness to a courageous and compassionate acceptance of life in its entirety. It becomes a journey of self-discovery and growth, inviting us to find peace and contentment by engaging with life's challenges as integral parts of our experience, rather than just obstacles to overcome.

It's time to set aside the myth of eternal sunshine—the illusion that happiness is a prize waiting to be claimed. Instead, let's embrace the rich and varied terrain of life, trusting in our resilience and capacity to grow with each twist and turn. In doing so, we may just discover a deeper sense of joy and fulfillment than we ever thought possible—a joy that is not dependent on external circumstances, but rather springs from the very core of our being.

Life is a precious gift, a grand adventure woven with moments of breathtaking beauty and profound challenge. When we learn to welcome the full spectrum of this journey and seek meaning in all its shades and textures, we open ourselves to a world of limitless possibilities. In that openness, we may finally grasp what it truly means to be alive—not in perpetual happiness, but in wholehearted engagement with life's endless possibilities.

Rethinking the Finish Line

AN elderly man, his face lined with the weight of years and experience, his hair a shock of white, walks barefoot through the streets of Montevideo. He is dressed simply, in a worn shirt and trousers, his feet callused and tough from a lifetime of walking the earth. He greets the people he passes with a warm smile and a kind word, his eyes twinkling with the sort of wisdom that can only be earned through a life of struggle and service.

This man is no ordinary citizen, no common passerby on the streets of the Uruguayan capital. He is, in fact, the former President of Uruguay, Jose Mujica, a man who has become a global icon for his unwavering commitment to social justice, equality, and human rights.

As Mujica walks, he is approached by a group of children playing football in the street. He stops to chat with them, listening intently to their stories and their dreams for the future. He encourages them to study hard and to never give up on their hopes for a better life, his words carrying the weight of a man who has seen the very best and the very worst of what humanity has to offer.

Later, he climbs into his old, beat-up Volkswagen Beetle, the same car he has driven for decades. The car is a reflection of his values, his belief in living simply and humbly, without the trappings of wealth or power. As he drives through the streets of Montevideo, he's greeted by honks and waves from the people he passes, proof of the deep affection and respect he has earned from his fellow citizens.

Mujica's leadership style was unlike any other. As President, he eschewed the lavish lifestyles and entourages of his predecessors, choosing instead to live in a small, modest farmhouse on the outskirts of the city. He donated ninety percent of his salary to charity, living on just eight hundred dollars a month, a sum that would be considered a pittance by the standards of most world leaders.

For Mujica, this was not a sacrifice, but a conscious choice, a way of living in solidarity with the people he served. He understood that true leadership was not about accumulating power or wealth for oneself, but about using one's position to uplift and empower others.

Under Mujica's guidance, Uruguay underwent a remarkable transformation. He legalized marijuana, same-sex marriage, and abortion, progressive policies that put the small South American nation at the forefront of social change. He welcomed Syrian refugees with open arms, offering them a safe haven in a world that had turned its back on their suffering.

Mujica also invested heavily in education and renewable energy, understanding that the key to a sustainable future lay in empowering the next generation and protecting the planet we all share. He fought tirelessly against corruption and inequality, working to build a more just, more compassionate, and more inclusive society.

Through it all, he remained humble and grounded, a leader who led by example and who never forgot his roots. He spoke often of his time in prison, of the years he spent in solitary confinement, tortured and beaten by the oppressive regime he fought against. But rather than being broken by these experiences, Mujica emerged stronger, more committed than ever to the cause of justice and human dignity.

In stark contrast to Mujica's example of success stands the mythological figure of the modern-day achiever- a figure held up as the pinnacle of accomplishment in today's society. Celebrities, billionaire CEOs, and influencers embody a version of success measured by wealth, power, and public adoration.

It's a vision that's hard to resist. After all, who hasn't, at some point, been captivated by the allure of the rich and famous? The sprawling mansions, private jets, and adoring fans—it's a fantasy that has been carefully packaged and sold to us as the ultimate fulfillment of the human experience.

Yet, the myth of success that pervades our culture is not only unattainable for most—it's inherently contradictory. Just think about the "perfect" successful person we're meant to aspire to: they're supposed to be wealthy, famous, stunningly attractive, effortlessly cool, highly intelligent, in peak physical condition, and endlessly charismatic—all at once.

When you really think about it, this vision of success is not just unattainable—it's a logical impossibility. No one can embody all these traits simultaneously, as they often require sacrificing one aspect of life for another. The person who dedicates all their time and energy to achieving wealth and fame, for instance, may end up neglecting their physical health or personal relationships in the process.

Similarly, the person who focuses on maintaining the perfect physique or the most enviable social life may have to put their career aspirations or intellectual pursuits on the back burner. The idea that anyone can have it all, excelling in every area while maintaining a happy, balanced life—is a myth, one that inevitably leads to disappointment and a profound sense of failure.

In reality, the pursuit of this mythical ideal of success feels more like a prison than a path to fulfillment. It demands that we constantly curate and maintain an image of perfection, concealing any trace of weakness, vulnerability, or simple humanity. We become consumed by the fear of letting our guard down, terrified of revealing that we're not the flawless, unassailable paragons of success we're expected to be.

The irony is that even for the rare few who manage to achieve something resembling this idealized vision, the reality is often far less glamorous than it appears from the outside. Behind the glossy magazine covers and meticulously curated social media profiles, there is often a deep sense of emptiness, loneliness, and profound dissatisfaction.

The relentless pressure to maintain an image, stay relevant, and remain at the top can be utterly exhausting, emotionally and physically. It's like spinning endlessly on a hamster wheel of endless striving and self-promotion, chasing an illusion with no clear destination or deeper sense of purpose.

Ultimately, the myth of success we've been sold is not only unattainable but also a trap. It locks us in a cycle of anxiety, self-doubt, and constant comparison to an impossible standard. This relentless pursuit blinds us to our own uniqueness, preventing us from embracing our limitations as essential and natural parts of the human experience.

And perhaps most tragically, it cuts us off from the very things that bring true meaning and fulfillment to our lives—the depth of our relationships, the pursuit of our genuine passions, the simple joys of living in the moment and appreciating the world around us.

From a young age, we are bombarded with messages that tell us we are not enough as we are, that we must constantly strive to be better, faster, smarter, more attractive, more successful.

We internalize these messages, and they become voices in our heads, a constant nagging reminder of our shortcomings and failings. No matter how much we achieve, how many milestones we reach, there is always the sense that it's not enough, that we're still falling short of some standard.

This is the real trap of the success myth—not just that it sets an unattainable bar, but that it fundamentally undermines our sense of self-worth and value. It teaches us to measure our worth by external metrics, by superficial opinions and validations of others, rather than by the quality of our character and the depth of our relationships.

And in doing so, it robs us of the very thing that true success is meant to bring—fulfillment, meaning, and connection. We become so focused on chasing the next achievement, the next level of recognition, that we lose sight of the things that truly matter—the joys and challenges of the journey itself, the people we love, the beauty and wonder of the world around us.

This is where Mujica's example offers such a powerful counterpoint. In living simply and humbly, in dedicating his life to the service of others, he showed us that true success is not about what we accumulate for ourselves, but what we give back to the world. It's about living in alignment with our deepest values and convictions, and using our talents and resources to make a positive difference in the lives of others.

In my own life, I've had the privilege of meeting and interacting with people from all walks of life, including billionaires and celebrities. And while I've certainly met some remarkable individuals among the rich and famous, I can say with conviction that the most successful people I've known were not necessarily those with the most wealth or the highest profile.

Instead, the people who have left the most profound impression on me—the ones who seem to embody the essence of a well-lived life—are those who have faced adversity head-on and emerged stronger, wiser, and more compassionate. These are the individuals who navigate life's complexities with grace and resilience, staying true to themselves while making meaningful contributions to the world around them.

These individuals may not grace magazine covers or capture the attention of millions, but they possess an inner success far more valuable than any external measure of achievement. They have cultivated a profound understanding of their values, passions, and purpose and demonstrate the courage to live in alignment with those convictions—even when it means defying societal expectations.

In many ways, these unsung heroes embody the same spirit of authenticity and service that we see in the life of Jose Mujica. They understand that true success is not about accumulating wealth, power, or fame for their own sake, but about using one's gifts and resources to make a positive impact on the world, however small or large that may be.

And the great lesson we can take from these examples is that this kind of success is within reach for all of us, regardless of our circumstances or background. It doesn't require some superhuman level of talent, intelligence, or luck—it simply requires a willingness to look within ourselves, to get clarity on what really matters to us, and to live each day with intention, integrity, and a commitment to making a positive difference.

Success must be defined on our own terms—honoring our unique gifts, passions, and values. It begins with cultivating self-awareness and self-respect, which serve as the foundation for a life of purpose and meaning.

It requires a kind of courage and attention that can be challenging to cultivate, especially in a world that often values conformity and superficial measures of success over true authenticity and purpose. But it's a path that is deeply rewarding, not just for ourselves but for all those whose lives we touch.

Chapter Three

THE QUEST FOR YOUR TRUE SELF

We live immersed in an ocean of stories, from the collective narratives that shape our societies to the personal tales that define our sense of self. These stories are powerful, weaving meaning and connection into our lives, yet they also confine us. Paradoxically, while we are the authors of these narratives, we are also shaped by them, often losing sight of where the story ends and our genuine being begins. This realization invites profound questioning: Who are we beneath the stories? What belongs to us, and what have we merely absorbed? To uncover the answers, we must step beyond the boundaries of these narratives and reconnect with the essence of who we truly are.

This process requires a delicate balance of awareness and playfulness—a willingness to detach from the stories we tell and inhabit them with the lightness of a child at play. Detachment does not mean rejection; rather, it is a conscious recognition that our stories are tools, not our masters. By holding them lightly, we create space for spontaneity, curiosity, and self-expression to arise naturally. This playful approach allows us to cut through the layers of narrative, peeling back the scripts we follow to reveal the vibrant core of our being. In this state of openness and presence, we rediscover the freedom to live authentically, guided not by the weight of inherited stories but by the creative rhythm of our true self.

The beauty and power of spontaneity lie in its ability to liberate us from the confines of our mental constructs and preconceived notions. In the pursuit of our purpose, we often fall into the trap of believing that the path must be clearly defined, meticulously planned, and strictly adhered to. We create elaborate roadmaps in our minds, convinced that if we just follow the right steps, we will arrive at our desired destination.

But life rarely unfolds according to our carefully laid plans. The universe has a way of presenting us with unexpected detours, surprising opportunities, and challenges that we could never have anticipated. And it is in these spontaneous moments of uncertainty that we often achieve our greatest growth and transformation.

When we cling too tightly to our concepts and strategies, we risk missing out on the richness and depth of the journey itself. We become so focused on reaching some distant goal that we fail to appreciate the beauty and significance of the present moment.

This is where the detachment from our conceptual mind becomes so essential. By learning to not engage with the constant chatter of our thoughts, we create space for a different kind of awareness to emerge—one that is rooted in the immediacy of our sensory experience and the inherent wisdom of our being.

In this state of presence, we begin to notice the countless miracles that are unfolding within and around us at every moment. We become attuned to the intricate dance of our bodily functions, the delicate balance of our ecosystem, and the profound interconnectedness of all life.

We realize that the true essence of our being is not confined to the narrow boundaries of our mental constructs. And in this realization, we find a sense of freedom and expansiveness that goes beyond anything our conceptual mind could ever imagine.

Think of a moment in your life when you were overcome with deep anguish—a time when a problem loomed so large it seemed insurmountable. Perhaps it was a heart-wrenching breakup, a career crisis, or the sudden loss of something you held dear. In such moments, the mind often becomes a storm of relentless thoughts, searching frantically for answers, replaying every possible scenario, and desperately trying to find a way out. Yet, the harder you try to untangle the mess, the more ensnared you feel, as if every attempt to escape only tightens the grip of the problem. It's like sinking in quicksand: the more you struggle, the deeper you sink.

Now imagine taking a step back, even in the midst of anguish. What happens if, instead of grasping for an immediate solution, you simply observe? By shifting perspective, curiosity replaces panic, and new possibilities emerge.

It is in this space of awareness that we reconnect with life's rhythm, stepping out of resistance and into collaboration with the unfolding moment. No longer bound by the need to control or predict, we begin to see life as a dynamic dance, one where challenges and opportunities flow together to shape our journey. In this state of presence, we become co-creators with life itself, responding authentically to whatever arises. This responsiveness is our true power—not in imposing rigid plans, but in meeting each moment with an open heart and a clear mind, trusting in our capacity to adapt, evolve, and grow through each experience.

When we step into this space of presence, curiosity becomes our guide, leading us beyond the confines of fear and rigidity. Curiosity invites us to approach life as a grand, unfolding mystery, where every moment is an opportunity to learn, grow, and discover. It encourages us to trade judgment for wonder, to see challenges not as roadblocks but as invitations to ask deeper questions and explore new possibilities. By quieting the chatter of our minds and tuning into the subtleties of our experience, we begin to notice the extraordinary within the ordinary—the gentle rhythm of our breath, the intricate dance of light and shadow, the quiet wisdom contained in the simplest moments.

Practicing curiosity in our daily lives means embracing the unknown with openness and a sense of adventure. It means asking questions without demanding immediate answers, challenging assumptions that no longer serve us, and remaining receptive to perspectives that stretch our understanding. This mindset transforms how we engage with the world. Instead of rushing past life's moments, we pause to observe them, allowing ourselves to be captivated by their depth and richness. The quiet beauty of a sunrise, the laughter of a stranger, or the texture of a passing breeze becomes more than fleeting occurrences—they become reminders of life's infinite complexity and wonder, grounding us in the present and inviting us to engage more deeply with the world around us.

Curiosity doesn't just invite us to observe life with wonder—it also calls us to take risks, step outside our comfort zones, and embrace the unfamiliar. It challenges us to venture into new experiences and perspectives, to surround ourselves with people and environments that support our growth, even if they push us to evolve in ways that feel uncomfortable at first. This path requires courage and a willingness to stumble, but it also asks for self-compassion. When we inevitably fall short of our ideals or struggle with the unknown, curiosity reminds us to approach ourselves with kindness, to see these moments not as failures but as steps in our ongoing journey of self-discovery.

Start small. Each day, carve out a few minutes to sit quietly and connect with your breath. Notice the sensations in your body, the thoughts that arise, and the emotions that stir—without judgment or the need to fix or change anything. Simply allow yourself to be fully present, even if only for a moment. As you move through your day, look for opportunities to bring this sense of presence and openness into your interactions and activities. When mental chatter pulls you away, gently guide yourself back to the reality of the present moment. And when challenges or setbacks arise, let curiosity be your anchor. Instead of resisting discomfort, explore it—ask what it can teach you, what new paths it might reveal. Every moment, no matter how difficult, is an invitation to begin again, to embrace life's uncertainties with a spirit of exploration and growth.

In this dance of curiosity, detachment, and spontaneity, we may find ourselves no longer captivated by the stories we once clung to, but enchanted by life. The rhythm of existence unfolds before us, not as something to be conquered, but as a living mystery to be embraced. With each step, we let go of the need to control and instead surrender to the flow, trusting in the quiet intelligence that guides us. It is here, in this state of presence and wonder, that we encounter the profound beauty of simply being. From this place of enchantment, we act—not with the fierce urgency of striving, but with the natural ease of one aligned with the heartbeat of life. And in this flow, we may discover that our true self is not something to be found through effort or achievement, but something that emerges effortlessly when we are fully present, open, and alive to the miracle of existence.

Peeling the Layers of Desire

IF our journey calls for detachment, then it also demands that we turn our attention to the natural force that makes us cling so fiercely to our mental and material constructions: desire. This primal energy is what compels us to grasp, to hold, to build meaning from the shifting sands of life. It is the force that fuels our attachments, shaping the narratives we tell ourselves and the structures we create to feel secure. Yet, far from being a flaw, desire is a vital part of our humanity—a raw, untamed energy that, when understood, becomes a doorway to deeper awareness and transformation. To truly embrace detachment, we must explore this force not as an enemy to be subdued, but as a sacred current to be navigated.

The Buddhist teachings offer a profound insight into the nature of desire, recognizing it as a fundamental source of suffering in the human experience. They suggest that our constant craving for more, our insatiable hunger for pleasure and satisfaction, is ultimately a futile endeavor, doomed to perpetual frustration in a world defined by impermanence and change.

Yet, upon closer examination, there is a curious paradox at the heart of the Buddhist path. The very desire to be free from desire, the yearning to transcend the cycle of attachment and suffering, is itself a form of desire. It's a longing, however noble and elevated, that propels the seeker forward on their spiritual journey.

In this sense, the Buddhist approach to desire is not one of total annihilation, but rather of skillful transformation. It's a process of sublimation, of redirecting the raw energy of our wanting into the pursuit of a higher goal—the realization of enlightenment, the attainment of nirvana.

This is a subtle but crucial distinction. The Buddhist path does not seek to eradicate desire completely, for to do so would be to extinguish the very spark of life itself. Rather, it aims to purify and refine our desires, to align them with our deepest aspirations for freedom, wisdom, and compassion.

Our desires are not our enemy, but our greatest ally. They are the fuel that drives us forward, the spark that ignites our creativity and our passion. And nowhere is this more evident than in the dreams and goals that we set for ourselves, the visions of the future that beckon us onward.

But here's the challenge: not all dreams are created equal. In the vast universe of ideas and aspirations, it's all too easy to get caught up in pursuing the dreams of others, to chase after the shiny objects and glittering prizes that society holds up as the ultimate measures of success and happiness.

Perhaps it's the dream of a bigger house, a faster car, a more prestigious job title. Or maybe it's the dream of fitting in, of being accepted and admired by our peers, of conforming to the narrow standards of beauty, intelligence, and charm that our culture valorizes. These are the dreams that are sold to us from every angle, the dreams that we are told will bring us joy, fulfillment, and meaning.

But are they really our dreams? When you strip away the expectations and the conditioning, the voices of your parents, your teachers, your friends, and the media, what is left? What are the dreams that spring from the depths of your own being, the visions that set your soul on fire?

These are the dreams truly worth pursuing, the ones aligned with your authentic nature and deepest values. Dreams that emerge from the quiet stillness of your heart, not the cacophony of the world around you.

But accessing these dreams, even beginning to hear their whispers amidst the noise, requires a profound journey of self-discovery. It demands peeling back the layers of our social conditioning, the masks and personas that we have adopted to navigate the complexities of human interactions.

From the moment we emerged into the world, helpless and dependent, we began the process of learning how to survive in a social environment.

We quickly discovered that certain behaviors and attitudes were rewarded with affection, attention, and approval, while others were met with punishment, rejection, and shame.

Over time, we crafted an entire repertoire of strategies and techniques to get our needs met, to secure our place in the social hierarchy. We learned to mold ourselves to the expectations of others, suppressing and hiding those parts of us deemed unacceptable or undesirable.

And so, piece by piece, we constructed a social self, a persona to present to the world. This mask became a filter, concealing vital parts of our true being while projecting only a curated facade. Over time, much of our true self was retained behind this mask, unseen and unexpressed.

As we grew and evolved, something strange began to happen. The persona that we had created, the character that we were playing, started to take on a life of its own. It began to develop its own dreams and desires, its own ideas about what constituted a well-lived life.

These are not our genuine dreams, but rather aspirations and ambitions that have been programmed into us by the forces of culture and conditioning. Aspirations of being recognized, respected, admired, and loved—not for who we truly are, but for how well we can perform the role assigned to us.

Like a method actor lost in a role, we began to identify with the character, believing that the mask we wear is our true face. We ended up trapped on the wrong side of the equation.

And yet, our true nature, the wild and untamed essence of our being, never forgets its own dreams. It has always been there, whispering in the depths of our consciousness, urging us to remember who we truly are.

To reclaim our authentic self, to break through the shell of our social conditioning, is a process of distillation, of separating the pure gold of our being from the dross of our persona. It's a journey of self-knowledge, of stripping away the layers of false identity to reveal the radiant core of our existence.

And as we begin to ground ourselves in the primal source of our own creative power, we start to realize that we already possess everything we need. We hold within us the power to nurture our being and to grant ourselves the recognition, acceptance, respect, and love we have long sought from others.

We discover that our true nature is a wellspring of infinite possibilities, a universe of magic and potential that is not dependent on external validation or approval. From this place of deep self-connection, we can begin to dream our own dreams, to set goals and intentions aligned with our soul's deepest yearnings.

But this is not a path of isolation or self-absorption. Our persona is not our enemy—it is a tool, a vehicle to navigate the complex web of human relationships. The key is not to reject or suppress this aspect of us, but to bring it into harmonious alignment with our being.

As you learn to navigate the terrain of your desires with discernment, you may find that your dreams begin to shift and evolve. You may discover that the goals that once seemed so important, the external markers of success and status, lose their luster in the light of your growing self-knowledge.

In their place, new dreams begin to emerge—dreams of meaning and purpose, of contribution and service, of living in alignment with the deepest truths of your being. These dreams that have the power to transform not only your own life, but the lives of all those you touch.

For decades, I believed I was playing an important role in the web of life. As a shaman, I held the conviction that my sacred mission was to raise awareness, to awaken people to their true nature and unlock their potential to create a more balanced and sustainable world. My ultimate purpose, as I saw it, was to protect the environment and ensure the survival of our species.

When the pandemic first struck, I saw it as a difficult but necessary lesson for us all. As the world grounded to a halt, I witnessed the planet and its ecosystems taking a much-needed breath. The air became clearer, the waters cleaner, and the animals reclaimed spaces that had long been dominated by human activity. I hoped that we would learn from this experience, that we would emerge from the crisis with a newfound appreciation for the delicate balance of life and a commitment to change our ways.

Yet, as time passed, my hopes began to fade. Despite the clear warnings from scientists and the unmistakable signs of environmental distress, society seemed to rush headlong back into its old patterns of greed, consumption, and destruction. The latest reports from the Intergovernmental Panel on Climate Change (IPCC) were unequivocal: we had already crossed the threshold of irreversible climate change, and the window of opportunity to avert catastrophe was rapidly closing.

As I watched the relentless march of the capitalist machine, the fabrication of new wars by global powers, and the insatiable consumer hunger of the masses, a painful realization dawned on me. The battle I had been fighting, the grand dream of saving the world's biodiversity that had driven me for so long, was already lost. The very purpose that had defined my existence seemed to crumble before my eyes, leaving me adrift in a sea of despair and uncertainty.

For a couple of years, I wandered aimlessly, my sense of direction and meaning lost in the wreckage of my shattered dream. I felt like a failure, like all my efforts had been in vain. The weight of the world's suffering bore down on me, and I couldn't see a way forward.

And then, amidst the darkness, a small, quiet voice began to emerge from within. It whispered to me of a different kind of purpose, one that was rooted not in grand, world-changing visions, but in the simple, tangible acts of love and service that were within my power to offer.

At first, I resisted. These small acts seemed so insignificant in the face of the enormous challenges we were facing. How could planting a few trees or helping a handful of people make any real difference in the grand scheme of things?

But as I began to engage in these humble acts of service, something shifted within me. I started by planting trees in my immediate surroundings, a simple gesture of care for the earth that had always sustained me. Then, I created a small non-profit project to produce seedlings and support reforestation efforts in my local community.

The scale of my impact was modest—around ten thousand trees per year, a mere drop in the ocean of global environmental challenges. But there was something deeply fulfilling about this work, a sense of alignment and purpose that I had never quite experienced in my pursuit of world-changing ideals.

My efforts soon took on a life of their own. What began a small act of service gradually gained visibility, attracting attention and support from unexpected quarters. Over time, it received international funding, allowing it to grow far beyond what I had initially envisioned. The impact was humbling and inspiring, but it also taught me an invaluable lesson: meaningful work thrives when it is rooted in authenticity, not grand ambitions. This experience shaped my approach to future endeavors, leading me to create and nurture new projects grounded in simplicity and purpose, free from the weight of lofty expectations.

As I engaged in these acts of service, I realized they were not tied to any grand agenda or expectation of recognition. They were simply expressions of my heart's true calling, a way of showing up for life with an open and generous spirit. And that's enough. The actions and their impact, however small or unseen, are not just valuable—they are sacred. Whether or not they change the story on a grand scale is beside the point. What matters is the commitment of my heart and acting according to my deepest values.

Looking back, I can see that my earlier dream, while noble on the surface, was also a product of my own ego and conditioning. It was fueled not only by love, passion, and idealism but also by an unconscious need to prove my importance, to mask the deep existential dread that arises when we confront our insignificance in the face of the vast universe.

It was a beautiful dream, that propelled me toward amazing accomplishments and positive outcomes. My personal narrative led me down an incredible path, resulting in a meaningful impact on many lives. For this, I am profoundly grateful. And yet, in letting go of this dream, I found a new kind of freedom—the freedom to express my genuine desires from a place of grounded presence and self-awareness. I discovered that my small, localized actions, while not world-changing in any grand sense, were far from insignificant. They were a way of honoring the interconnectedness of all life, and taking responsibility for my own role in the larger web of being.

And perhaps most importantly, they brought me a sense of peace and alignment that my earlier pursuit of grandiose ideals could never quite provide. I realized that I didn't need to save the world in order to live a life of meaning and purpose. I simply needed to show up each day with an open heart, ready to be of service in whatever way I could.

My journey has not been an easy one, and there have been times when I have faltered and lost my way. But through it all, I've learned that the path to a life well-lived is often a winding one, full of unexpected detours and revelations.

And so, to anyone who may be struggling to find their own sense of purpose in this turbulent world, I offer this humble piece of advice: let go of the need for grand narratives and world-changing achievements. Instead, focus on the small, daily acts of love and service that are within your power to offer. Trust that when you align yourself with the truth of your heart, you are always exactly where you need to be, doing exactly what you are meant to do.

For it is in these quiet moments of compassion and connection that we mostly contribute to the construction of a better world—one that may not be perfect, but is infused with the grace and resilience of the human spirit, one small gesture at a time.

The Courage to be Real

IN the pursuit of spiritual growth, many of us are drawn to lofty ideals and concepts promising fulfillment and enlightenment. We hear of unconditional love, ultimate freedom, and transcendent states of consciousness, presented as tangible destinations achievable through unwavering dedication and diligent practice.

Sometimes, the pursuit of freedom becomes its own cage. The more we chase an idealized state, the further we drift from the reality of our present experience.

Take, for example, the notion of freedom. In our culture, freedom is often held up as the ultimate goal, the crowning achievement of the human spirit. We're taught to aspire to financial freedom, creative freedom, personal freedom—to break free from the shackles of societal constraints and live life entirely on our own terms.

But have you ever stopped to consider what freedom really means to you? What images and ideas does it conjure in your mind? Perhaps it's the vision of doing whatever you want, whenever you want, free of limitations or responsibilities. Or maybe it's a state of pure, unencumbered bliss, free from all traces of pain, sadness, or anxiety.

Whatever your vision of freedom, a fundamental issue arises: the very act of defining freedom as an ideal to strive for, immediately creates a sense of imprisonment. The moment we envision what freedom should look like, we become acutely aware of how our current reality falls short of this ideal.

If freedom means financial abundance, then financial limitations feel like a prison. If freedom means control over our time and energy, then obligations and responsibilities become chains, weighing us down.

In this way, the pursuit of freedom becomes a self-defeating cycle, a struggle against the present moment in favor of an imagined future always just out of reach. The more we strive for freedom, the more trapped we become in the very concept of freedom itself.

The same pitfalls await us in the pursuit of other spiritual ideals, such as unconditional love. On the surface, the idea of loving all beings equally, without judgment or preference, seems like a noble and enlightened aspiration. But if we look closer, we'll see that the very notion of "unconditional" love is a contradiction in terms.

To love unconditionally means to love without any conditions, without any boundaries or limitations. But the moment we set the intention to love in this way, we're already placing a condition on our love—the condition that it must be unconditional! We're trying to force our love into a predefined mold, to make it conform to a conceptual ideal that is ultimately impossible to achieve.

Love is not something we can manufacture or control to meet abstract standards. It is a natural flow, arising from openness, presence, and deep connection—not from rules or ideals. Furthermore, the idea of loving everyone equally, without boundaries, may be admirable in theory but impractical and even harmful in practice. Healthy love includes the discernment to set boundaries, protect our well-being, and honor relationships that nourish rather than deplete us.

It's easy to profess love for humanity in the abstract, but far more challenging to extend compassion to the difficult people in our lives—the aggressive neighbor, the manipulative coworker, the abusive family member. In such cases, the most loving act may be to love ourselves enough to set firm boundaries, refusing to tolerate harmful behavior.

The issue isn't that unconditional love or freedom are inherently wrong; it's that pursuing them as conceptual absolutes can disconnect us from the living reality of the present moment—the only place where true love and freedom exist.

So what is the alternative? How can we walk a grounded, authentic, and truly liberating path? The key lies in shifting our focus from chasing abstract ideals to cultivating non-judgmental awareness of our inner experience, moment by moment.

Instead of striving for some imagined state of ultimate freedom, we can learn to be present with the reality of our life as it is, with all its challenges, limitations, and opportunities. We can start to accept and even embrace the constraints and difficulties we face, recognizing them as part of our wide and rich human experience.

We can let go of forcing our heart to love unconditionally, embracing and appreciating love when it arises naturally, but also allowing ourselves to experience and accept all of our emotions, including our hatred, anger, and fear. By cultivating a deep presence and awareness of our inner world, we can develop a more realistic and nuanced understanding of love, one that recognizes the inherent complexity of the human experience.

This approach invites compassion not only for others but for ourselves, especially in moments of struggle or emotional pain. It encourages us to honor our boundaries and needs, even when they conflict with others' expectations, recognizing that all emotions, whether joyful or painful, are valid and worthy of our care.

It teaches us to show up fully in our relationships without the pressure to perform or maintain a facade of perfect positivity. Instead, we cultivate self-awareness and acceptance, realizing that our worth is not tied to how well we meet an idealized version of love.

This journey is not about achieving a final, perfect state, but about engaging fully with the messy, complex, and ultimately miraculous process of life. It's about being present with our thoughts and feelings without judgment or resistance and responding to each moment with openness and curiosity.

As we cultivate non-judgmental awareness and authenticity, our experience of life begins to shift in subtle but profound ways. The very things we once perceived as limitations or obstacles can become sources of insight, growth, and even joy.

Organically, our capacity for love and connection deepens and expands, not through the force of will or adherence to abstract ideals, but through the simple, profound act of being fully present. And we discover that the freedom we've been seeking is not some distant goal but the inherent spaciousness of our awareness—the vast, boundless space where all of life unfolds.

Grounding in the Movement of Life

IN the great dance of existence, life reveals itself as a ceaseless flow of change and transformation. From the microscopic world of atoms and cells to the vast expanses of the cosmos, everything exists in a constant state of movement—creation and destruction, growth and decay, emergence and dissolution. Like a boundless ocean of energy and potential, life pulses with the rhythm of birth and death.

As human beings, we are immersed in this vast, ever-shifting landscape of being. It is natural to feel small and vulnerable in the face of such immensity. The sheer scale and complexity of life can be overwhelming, even terrifying, as we confront the fundamental impermanence and uncertainty of our existence.

In our quest for stability and meaning, we often seek refuge in the realm of concepts and ideas. We construct elaborate frameworks of thoughts and beliefs, attempting to impose order and predictability on the chaos of the world around us. These mental structures act as a kind of conceptual scaffolding, offering orientation and purpose in an otherwise dizzying universe.

This capacity for abstract thought and conceptualization has been crucial to our survival and success as a species. It has allowed us to navigate complex social and environmental challenges, to plan for the future, and to create the incredible technological and cultural wonders that define our modern world.

But as essential as these conceptual tools may be, they can also limit our ability to fully engage with the raw, unfiltered reality of life itself. When we become too attached to our ideas and beliefs, too invested in maintaining the integrity of our mental constructs, we risk losing touch with the vibrancy and dynamism of the present moment.

We may find ourselves living more in our heads than in the world around us, more attuned to the static representations of reality we have created than to the fluid, ever-changing reality itself. We may become rigid and inflexible in our thinking, resistant to new experiences and perspectives that challenge our established worldviews.

But as much as we may crave the comfort and familiarity of our conceptual frameworks, life has a way of shaking us out of our mental ruts and reminding us of the inherent fluidity and unpredictability of existence. Whether through sudden changes in our circumstances, unexpected challenges or crises, or simply the gradual erosion of our certainties over time, life has a way of forcing us to confront the limitations of our ideas and beliefs.

And it's in these moments of disruption and upheaval that we have the opportunity to break free from the confines of our conceptual prisons and to rediscover the raw, unmediated reality of life itself. By learning to ground ourselves in the present moment, we can begin to tap into a deeper source of wisdom and resilience that lies beyond the reach of our intellectual understanding.

Grounding in the movement of life requires a willingness to step outside of our comfort zones, to relinquish our attachment to fixed ideas and identities, and to open ourselves up to the unknown and the unpredictable.

When we allow ourselves to fully inhabit the present moment, to engage with life on its own terms rather than through the filters of our conceptual mind, we access a new kind of vitality and aliveness. The world reveals itself with a freshness and wonder that often goes unnoticed, and we marvel at the intricate beauty and complexity we once took for granted. We become more attuned to the subtleties of our own inner experience, learning to navigate the constantly shifting landscape of our thoughts, feelings, and sensations with greater skill and ease.

And perhaps most importantly, we begin to cultivate a deeper sense of connection and intimacy with the world around us, recognizing our fundamental interdependence and interconnectedness with all of life. We see that our individual existence is not separate from the great web of being, but is rather an integral part of the vast, ever-unfolding mystery of the universe itself.

This process is not a one-time event, but a lifelong journey of exploration and discovery. There will always be moments when we find ourselves pulled back into the realm of concepts and ideas, when we lose touch with the immediacy of our experience and become trapped in the static representations of our minds.

But with practice and patience, we can learn to recognize these moments of disconnection and gently guide ourselves back to the present moment. We can cultivate a sense of humor and lightness in our approach, remembering that the journey of life is ultimately a grand adventure, full of twists and turns and unexpected delights.

And as we continue on this path, we may find that our relationship to our concepts and ideas begins to shift in subtle but profound ways. Rather than seeing them as fixed and absolute truths, we may start to view them as useful tools to navigate the complexity of the world, but ones that are always subject to revision and refinement in light of new experiences and insights.

We may discover that our deepest wisdom and creativity arise not from the rigid application of preconceived formulas or strategies, but from a place of open and responsive engagement with the unfolding of life. And we may find that our greatest fulfillment and joy come not from the achievement of specific goals or outcomes, but from the simple, profound act of being fully present in each moment.

We have the chance to embrace the great mystery and wonder of existence itself. We just need to let go of our attachment to our fixed ideas and identities and open ourselves up to the infinite possibilities of the present moment.

While this path may be challenging and uncertain, it's also of incredible richness and depth, offering us the opportunity to experience life in all its raw, unfiltered beauty and intensity. So, let's approach this journey with a curiosity, humor, and open-hearted engagement, knowing that each step we take is an opportunity to discover something new and wondrous about ourselves and the world around us. And let's remember that, despite our fears and uncertainties, we're held in the great embrace of life itself, and our deepest purpose and meaning can be found in the simple, profound act of showing up fully and authentically.

Chapter Four

Your Are Alive: Enjoy the Miracle!

In a small, dimly lit cell within a seventeenth-century Spanish convent, Sister Maria, a young Discalced Carmelite nun, knelt on the cold stone floor. The rough fabric of her habit chafed against her skin as she shifted her weight, the discomfort a constant reminder of her devotion to God. With trembling hands, she reached for the small whip beside her, its knotted cords stained with the blood of countless previous mortifications.

Sister Maria took a deep breath, steeling herself for the pain that was to come. She knew that this suffering was necessary, a means to purge herself of the sinful desires that plagued her mortal body. In her mind, the body was the enemy of the soul, a vessel of temptation and impurity that needed to be tamed through self-inflicted torment.

As she began to flog herself, the sharp sting of the whip tore through her flesh, sending shockwaves of agony throughout her body. Tears streamed down her face, mingling with the beads of sweat that formed on her brow. Each strike was a battle against her own instincts, a war waged between her desire for spiritual purity and the primal urges that threatened to lead her astray.

Sister Maria's mind raced with thoughts of the saints who had come before her, the martyrs who had endured unimaginable tortures for the sake of their faith. She knew that her own suffering paled in comparison to their sacrifices, but still, she persevered, determined to prove her worthiness in the eyes of God.

As the minutes turned to hours, Sister Maria's body grew weak and trembling, the blood from her wounds seeping through her habit and onto the stone beneath her. But even as her physical strength waned, her resolve only grew stronger. She knew that this pain was a small price to pay for the promise of eternal salvation, a means to transcend the limitations of her earthly existence and unite her soul with the divine.

Miles away and centuries apart, in an ancient Indian temple, a young tantric priestess named Kamala prepared for a ritual of a very different nature. The air was thick with the scent of incense and the sound of gentle music, a soothing melody that seemed to emanate from the very walls of this sacred space.

Kamala moved through the temple with a graceful elegance, her body adorned with intricate henna designs and delicate gold jewelry. She wore a flowing red sari, its sheer fabric clinging to her curves in a way that accentuated her natural beauty. As she walked, the bells on her anklets chimed softly, a gentle reminder of the divine feminine energy that flowed through her veins.

In the center of the temple stood her tantric partner, a young man, tall and muscular, with a mane of dark hair that fell to his shoulders. Like Kamala, his body was decorated with sacred symbols and adorned with simple but elegant jewelry.

As Kamala approached him, their eyes locked in a gaze of deep connection and understanding. They knew that the ritual they were about to perform was not merely a physical act, but a means to transcend the boundaries of the self and merge with the infinite.

Slowly, reverently, they began to disrobe, their movements fluid and sensual. As their bare skin touched, a shock of electricity seemed to pass between them, a tangible manifestation of the raw, primal energy that pulsed through the universe.

They explored each other's bodies with a sense of wonder and devotion, each caress an act of worship, each kiss a prayer. As they made love, their minds quietened and their hearts expanded, the boundaries between self and other dissolving in a sea of blissful union.

In that moment, they ceased to be two separate beings and became one with the cosmic dance of creation and destruction, the eternal play of Shakti and Shiva. Their pleasure was not a selfish indulgence, but a means to tap into the very essence of existence, to experience the divine in its most visceral and immediate form.

As they climaxed together, their bodies shuddering in ecstasy, they knew that they had touched something sacred, something that transcended the limitations of the mind and body. They had glimpsed the true nature of reality, the unity that underlies all things, and they emerged from the experience transformed, their souls forever intertwined.

These two stories, so different in their approach to the body and its role in spiritual practice, serve as a powerful illustration of the diverse ways in which we have sought to connect with the divine throughout history.

Tantric practices use the energy of sexual union as a means to transcend the ego and merge with the infinite. Through techniques such as meditation, breathwork, and energy cultivation, the Tantric initiate learns to detach from the constant chatter of the mind and drop into a state of embodied presence. In this space, they begin to perceive the world through a different lens, one that is not filtered through the limited constructs of the intellect, but rather through the direct, unmediated wisdom of the body itself.

In the context of sexual intimacy, Tantric practices take on a particularly profound and transformative power. When two individuals come together in a space of sacred intention and presence, they have the opportunity to merge not just physically, but energetically and spiritually as well. The sexual union becomes a gateway to the cosmic consciousness, a dissolution of the boundaries between self and other, between the individual and the infinite.

In these moments of ecstatic communion, the couple becomes one, their energies intertwining and harmonizing in a dance of divine love and surrender. As they navigate the realm of the gods, their minds dissolve into the vast expanse of consciousness, allowing their bodies to awaken the ancient codes encrypted within their very DNA. The man and woman transcend their individual identities, becoming living embodiments of the divine masculine and feminine principles. They merge into the archetypal forms of *Shiva* and *Shakti*, *Brahma* and *Saraswati*, *Vishnu* and *Lakshmi*—the eternal cosmic lovers whose union gives birth to the universe itself. In this state of divine union, the couple explores realms of pleasure, intimacy, and connection that extend far beyond the boundaries of the physical act, tapping into the infinite wellspring of creativity and bliss that lies at the heart of the existence.

In this state of divine union, the body is revealed not as a limitation but as a sacred gateway to the infinite—a living vessel through which we can experience the profound interconnectedness of all existence. Tantra reminds us that the body is not separate from the spiritual journey but is, in fact, the path itself, a bridge between the material and the divine, where the sacred can be fully embodied and celebrated.

This reverence for the body as a sacred vessel is echoed in many other traditions, including ancient pagan practices. In paganism, the body is seen as deeply intertwined with the rhythms of the natural world, a microcosm of the earth's cycles and energies. Through rituals that honor the changing seasons and the cycles of life, pagan traditions celebrate the interconnectedness of human life with the greater web of existence.

One of the most potent and transformative of these rituals took place at the beginning of the planting season, when the earth was awakening from its winter slumber and the first seeds were being sown in fertile soil. This ritual involved the sacred union of the masculine and feminine principles, embodied in the figures of the Horned God, *Cernunnos*, and the Great Mother Goddess.

During these ceremonies, which often included the sacramental use of psychedelic plants or mushrooms, a chosen Druid would enter a trance state and allow himself to be possessed by the spirit of *Cernunnos*. Adorned with antlers and other symbols of the wild, untamed power of nature, he would become a living embodiment of the God, channeling his primal energy and vitality.

At the same time, a Druidess would undergo a similar process of transformation, aligning herself with the nurturing, life-giving essence of the Great Mother. Through dance, chant, and meditation, she would open herself up to the flow of divine feminine energy, becoming a vessel for the Goddess herself.

As the ritual reached its climax, the Druid and Druidess would come together in a sacred sexual union, their bodies entwined in a dance of ecstasy and surrender. In this moment of intimate communion, they were no longer separate individuals, and instead living conduits for the forces of creation and destruction, life and death, that pulsed through the very heart of nature.

Through their lovemaking, God and Goddess would channel the generative power of the earth, infusing the soil and the seeds with the energy of their union. The human orgasm became a sacred offering, honoring and amplifying the innate sexuality and creativity of the natural world.

For the pagans, these rituals were not mere symbolic reenactments; they were profound acts of embodied magic and transformation. Through these practices, they affirmed the truth that human beings are not separate from the web of life but are active participants in its cyclical dance. By aligning their bodies and spirits with the rhythms of nature and the archetypal energies of the divine masculine and feminine, they honored the body as a sacred vessel—a conduit for the forces of creation, renewal, and interconnectedness. The body, when attuned to the cycles of life, becomes a powerful gateway to transcending the self and connecting with the forces of creation.

This deep connection between the body and the natural world resonates across many traditions, each offering its unique lens on how to honor and integrate the physical self into spiritual practice. While pagan rituals often centered on the rhythms of the earth, other traditions, such as Taoism, turned inward, focusing on the body's internal harmony as a reflection of the cosmos.

In Taoism, the body is revered as a microcosm of the universe, embodying the same balance, flow, and interconnectedness found in nature. Taoist practices emphasize cultivating the life force, or qi, that flows through the body, believing this energy connects us to the rhythms of the cosmos. Through practices like tai chi, qigong, and mindful breathing, Taoists seek to harmonize the body's internal energies with the external world, achieving a state of balance and vitality. The body is not seen as a separate entity but as an essential expression of the Tao, the natural order of existence. By embracing the wisdom of the body, Taoist practitioners unlock a sense of harmony and flow, allowing them to move through life with grace and attunement to the cycles of change.

Similarly, in Sufism, a mystical branch of Islam, the body is seen as a precious gift from God, a means to experience the divine in the physical world. For Sufis, the body is not a barrier to spirituality but a sacred instrument through which the soul can seek union with the Beloved, the ultimate reality that underlies all things. Sufi poets like Rumi use sensual imagery and metaphors to celebrate this union, emphasizing the importance of embracing the physical world as a gateway to spiritual awakening. In this view, the body becomes a bridge between the finite and the eternal, a sacred space where the divine is made manifest.

These traditions remind us that the body is not something to be feared or denied, but rather a sacred tool for spiritual growth and transformation. By learning to embrace and honor our physical selves, we open ourselves up to a deeper understanding of the nature of reality and our place within it.

Shamanic traditions from around the world also offer a profound and reverent perspective on the human body. In these ancient spiritual practices, the body is not merely seen as a tool or vessel, but as a sacred expression of the divine feminine, the Great Mother herself. The body is revered as our first and most intimate home, a microcosm of the vast, interconnected web of life that sustains us all.

For shamans, the body is a delicate and powerful ecosystem, a landscape of energy and consciousness that holds the key to our deepest wisdom and potential. Every sensation, every emotion, every instinct that arises within us is a message from this primal source of life, a guidepost on the path to wholeness and balance.

In stark contrast to this holistic and celebratory view of the body, the Catholic tradition, as exemplified by Sister Maria's self-mortification, has long promoted a vision of the physical self as a source of corruption and sin. The body, with its sensual desires and earthly temptations, is seen as a threat to the purity of the soul, a wild and dangerous force that must be tamed through strict discipline and self-denial.

This dualistic view, which pits spirit against matter, mind against body, has had a profound and damaging impact on the Western culture. It has led to a deep sense of alienation and disconnection from our embodied experience, a fear and mistrust of our natural impulses and desires.

It's not just the Catholic Church that has perpetuated this dichotomy. Many other religious traditions, from certain branches of Islam to some forms of Hinduism and Buddhism, have also promoted a view of the body as an obstacle to spiritual growth, something to be transcended or overcome on the path to enlightenment.

Is this belief a path to liberation, or a form of spiritual manipulation, a way to disempower and control people by severing their connection to their innate wisdom and strength? By convincing us that our bodies are sinful and corrupt, that our desires are shameful and wrong, these institutions rob us of our most potent source of vitality and creativity.

They set us at war with ourselves, fighting against the very essence of who we are. They teach us to mistrust our own intuition, to doubt our own experiences, and to look outside ourselves for guidance and validation. In doing so, they create a population of spiritually and emotionally broken individuals, dependent on external authority for a sense of meaning and purpose.

What if he body held far more than we've been led to believe? What if, by inhabiting our physical selves with presence and awareness, we could access a direct connection to the intelligence of life itself? Could it be that the body—often dismissed as a prison or source of suffering—is, in truth, a gateway to the divine, a sacred vessel of consciousness and creativity waiting to be discovered?

The body holds mysteries we have yet to fully grasp. Across centuries and cultures, it has been revered, denied, celebrated, and condemned—a paradox we carry within our very cells. Yet, more than a battleground or a prison, it's a threshold. Not something to be conquered or transcended, but a visceral poetry, written in flesh and bone, through which existence speaks and unfolds.

To deny the body is to sever ourselves from the raw, unfiltered experience of life. Yet, to fully inhabit it requires courage: the courage to feel deeply, to break open the layers of fear and shame that have hardened over generations, and to reclaim the truth buried in our skin, our breath, our beating hearts. The body is not just ours—it is the cosmos folded into form, the earth's rhythms pressed into flesh. To be alive is not simply to endure its weight but to listen, to move with it, and to let it lead us back to the awe we have forgotten.

Sister Maria's sacrifice and Kamala's ecstasy reveal two sides of the same coin: our longing to transcend, to touch something sacred. But perhaps what we seek is not "out there," beyond us, or above us—it is already here, pulsing in every nerve and vein, waiting for us to stop fighting, stop fleeing, and simply live the miracle we are.

Embracing the Miracle of Your Body

I'm in Lençóis Maranhenses, a desert oasis in the north of Brazil. It's a place of raw, untamed beauty, where the wind and the sand dance together in an endless, mesmerizing waltz. The landscape is a canvas of contrasts—stark white dunes against the deep blue of the sky, crystal-clear lagoons nestled like jewels in the folds of the earth.

Every year, I make a pilgrimage to this place, a ritual of personal alignment. It's a chance to sync up the inner rhythms of my body and spirit with the great, pulsing heartbeat of life itself. Some people might tell you that meditation is all about stillness and relaxation, but for me, the deepest states of mindfulness come when I align my mind with the movement of my body, when I let myself become one with the elemental forces of nature.

Out there in the desert, the wind is the great maestro, constantly sculpting and reshaping the landscape. It's a thing of beauty, the way the dunes and lagoons curve and flow like the lines of a woman's body. And when the sun starts to sink toward the horizon, painting the sky in shades of crimson and gold, it's like the whole world is holding its breath, waiting for the magic to unfold.

I walk in silence, listening to the desert not just with my ears, but with every cell of my being. Each footstep is a drumbeat, a sacred rhythm that echoes through the soles of my feet and up into my bones. The sand rubs against my skin, a rough caress that reminds me of my own aliveness, my own animal presence in this world.

And the wind, oh man, the wind. It's a force to be reckoned with, a wild and untamed thing that whips across the dunes and tugs at my clothes. But it's not just a physical sensation – it's a presence, an intelligence, a voice that whispers secrets from far-off places. When I breathe it in, I can taste the salt of the ocean, feel the memory of rain on my tongue.

As the sun warms my skin and the sweat begins to bead on my brow, I feel a kind of alchemy taking place. The sunlight dances across my body, casting a shimmering glow on the droplets of perspiration that form like tiny, glistening jewels. It's like I'm adorned in a constellation of liquid stars, each one reflecting the brilliant light of the desert sky.

I watch, transfixed, as a single drop of sweat slides down my arm, catching the sunlight like a prism before falling to the thirsty sand below. It's a small offering, a gift of my body's water to this arid landscape, and I feel a sense of communion in the act. The desert receives my offering with silent gratitude, the sand absorbing the moisture like a sponge.

As I continue to walk, sweat and breathe, I feel the boundaries between my body and the desert beginning to blur and dissolve. The sunlight that illuminates the lagoons is the same that illuminates my skin, the same light that sets the dunes ablaze with golden fire. The water that flows through my veins is the same that fills the oases, the same water that cycles endlessly through the earth and sky.

In this moment, I'm not separate from the desert, but an integral part of it. My body is a microcosm of the macrocosm, a reflection of the great, pulsing web of life that encompasses all things. I am the sand and the sky and the shimmering heat, and they are me. We are one and the same, different expressions of the same eternal dance. And that's when the magic really starts to happen. As my mind grows quiet and my body takes over, I feel a kind of expansion happening, a widening of my senses and my awareness. Suddenly, I can feel life coursing through my veins, the steady thump of my heart and the rush of my breath. I can feel the power and resilience of my muscles, the solid strength of my bones.

But it's not just my own body that I'm feeling – it's the body of the world itself. The desert is alive, pulsing with its own rhythms and energy. The lagoons are like great, glittering eyes, reflecting back the light of the sun and the stars. The dunes are like the curves of a lover's body, inviting and mysterious.

And as I sink deeper into this state of embodied presence, I start to realize that there's no separation between the elements, no hard lines dividing sand from water, air from earth. It's all one great, swirling dance of atoms and molecules, a cosmic soup of consciousness and creativity.

My own body is just one node in this vast web of interconnectedness, one fleeting expression of the great mystery of existence. And yet, in that moment, I feel the full power and potential of my own being, the sacred gift of my incarnation.

My mind, which has been the constant companion and narrator of my experience, suddenly falls silent. The endless chatter of thoughts and anxieties, the ceaseless planning and judging and comparing, all of it falls away like a snake shedding its skin.

In that moment of profound stillness, I come face to face with the essence of my own being, the pure, radiant awareness that lies beneath the surface of my mental noise. This awareness is not some foreign entity, not some ethereal spirit that has taken up temporary residence in my body.

No, this consciousness is intrinsic to my being, to the cells and molecules and atoms that make up my physical form. It's the animating force that gives life to my flesh, the intelligence that orchestrates the countless chemical reactions and electrical impulses that keep my heart beating and my lungs breathing.

And in that same moment, I sense that this consciousness is not limited to my own individual being. It's a property of matter itself, a fundamental aspect of the universe present in every particle of matter. It's present in the grains of sand beneath my feet, in the droplets of water that sparkle in the lagoons, in the very air that I breathe.

It's only later, as I start to make my way back to the little village on the edge of the desert, that my mind starts to come back online, to reassert its claim on reality. But even then, the experience lingers, like a half-remembered dream or a whisper from another world.

For a precious, fleeting moment, I touched something vast and unknowable, something that lies beyond the grasp of language or logic. I glimpsed the great, pulsing heart of creation, the source from which all things arise and to which all things return.

In those moments, walking barefoot on the sand and feeling the desert's breath on my skin, I am reminded that the body is far more than a collection of cells and tissues. It is a microcosm of the universe, a reflection of the interconnected rhythms of life itself.

And in that glimpse, I remembered the truth that we so often forget: that life itself is the greatest miracle, the most profound and sacred gift. That to be alive, to have a body and a mind and a heart that can experience the world in all its terror and beauty, is a revelation.

So let me ask you this, my friend: when was the last time you really dropped into the sheer miracle of your own existence? When was the last time you let yourself be awestruck by the simple fact of your own breathing, your own beating heart?

Have you ever truly marveled at the miraculous nature of your physical form? Have you ever taken a moment to contemplate the exquisite complexity and intelligence that animates every cell, every tissue, every organ? The human body is a masterpiece of design, a living work of art that is as beautiful as it is functional. Trillions of cells, each one a marvel of miniature machinery, work together in an intricate dance of cooperation and coordination, ceaselessly laboring to maintain the delicate balance of life.

The body is a tangible manifestation of nature's wisdom, a living testament to the profound intelligence that permeates the universe. From the moment a single cell embarks on its miraculous journey of division and differentiation, to the final breath that marks the end of our earthly existence, the body stands as a constant reminder of the sacred mystery underlying all things. It is a microcosm of the macrocosm, a reflection of the vast, pulsing web of life that binds us all.

More than a mere collection of parts or biological processes, the body is a multidimensional being where the physical, psychological, and spiritual realms converge and intertwine. Within its intricate matrix, instincts, emotions, thoughts, and experiences arise, shaped by and shaping the continuous flow of sensation and perception. It is not just a vessel for consciousness but an inseparable part of it—a repository of memory, a storehouse of ancestral wisdom, and a sacred book upon which the story of our lives is written. Every cell, molecule, and atom carries the imprint of our personal and collective history, echoing the joys, sorrows, triumphs, and tragedies that define us as individuals and as a species.

This ancient wisdom of the body is echoed in modern science. Neuroscientist Dr. Benjamin Libet's groundbreaking experiments revealed that the body often acts before the conscious mind, demonstrating its profound and intuitive intelligence. Libet wanted to explore the moments leading up to a conscious choice—those fleeting instants where thought transforms into action. To do this, Libet devised an experiment that would challenge some of our deepest assumptions about free will and the mind-body connection.

Participants were asked to perform a simple task: press a button whenever they felt the urge. While they focused on this action, Libet monitored their brain activity using advanced equipment. What he discovered was astonishing. A specific spike in brain activity, called the "readiness potential," occurred milliseconds before the participants were even aware of their decision to press the button. In other words, the body initiated the action before the mind caught up to recognize it.

Libet's findings underscore the primacy of the body in our lived experience. They suggest that even our most intimate and personal choices, the ones we attribute to the workings of our conscious minds, are in fact deeply influenced by the subtle cues and impulses that arise from our physical being. This understanding challenges the notion that our conscious mind is the sole arbiter of our experiences and actions, and instead points to a deeper, more embodied source of wisdom and intelligence.

By embracing the central role of the body in shaping our experiences, we unlock a more holistic and profound understanding of what it means to be human. We come to realize that genuine self-knowledge and spiritual awakening are not about escaping the body but about tuning into its subtle language, trusting its innate wisdom, and honoring it with the reverence it so richly deserves.

In this recognition, we may uncover a truth both humbling and extraordinary: the greatest mysteries of the universe, the deepest truths of our existence, are not hidden in some distant, ethereal realm. They reside within the flesh and bone of our being. It's here, in the living temple of the body, that the sacred dance of life happens, in all its breathtaking beauty.

Cultivating a Relationship with Your Body

Do you think your body belongs to you? Or could it be that, in truth, you belong to your body?

We often assume, mistakenly, that our physical form is a mere possession, a vehicle that we own and control. Religions and spiritual philosophies often reinforce this notion, portraying the body as a temporary vessel for the soul, a means of transportation through the earthly realm.

But what if the reality is far more profound than that? What if the body is not just a container for the soul, but an inseparable part of our very essence? Could it be that there is no way to access the depths of our being, the truth of our existence, except through the gateway of our embodied experience?

Every aspect of your reality, every thought, feeling, and sensation, arises within the context of your physical form. Your emotions are not separate from your body, but rather a direct expression of the complex interplay of chemicals, hormones, and electrical impulses that dance through your cells and organs.

Even your psyche, the realm of your innermost self, is not some disembodied entity, but a biological function that emerges from the intricate workings of your brain and nervous system. In a very real sense, everything that you conceive of as "you"—your personality, your memories, your hopes and dreams—is a product of the miraculous creature that is your body.

From this perspective, your body is not just a vessel, but a sacred universe unto itself, a microcosm of the vast intelligence and creativity that permeates all of existence. It is, in a very real sense, the closest thing to the divine that you'll ever encounter in this life.

And yet, how often do you take the time to acknowledge and honor this incredible gift? How often do you pause in your busy life to express gratitude for the countless ways in which your body supports you?

What would it be like to cultivate a deep and loving relationship with your physical form, to treat it not as a servant or a machine, but as a cherished friend and ally? Can you imagine speaking to your body, praying to it, celebrating it as the sacred temple of your being?

We have become so disconnected from our bodies and so deeply entrenched in our minds that we have lost touch with how to truly experience this interconnectedness. We find ourselves lost, grasping for a sense of meaning and connection that seems to elude us at every turn.

We became entangled in intricate webs of thought and interpretation, failing to fully inhabit the present moment. Instead of directly experiencing life, we filter it through the lens of mental constructs, analyzing and judging each moment rather than simply being present with it. This constant mental chatter erects a barrier between us and the raw, unmediated reality of existence, keeping us from truly engaging with the magic of creation unfolding in the now. In essence, we live in our interpretation of each moment, rather than in the moment itself.

We also became addicted to the notion that we must always strive, seek, and grasp for an elusive state of fulfillment or enlightenment. We become fixated on the idea of spiritual attainment, failing to see the inherent wholeness and perfection of each moment. In our quest, we convince ourselves that we must engage in specific practices or rituals, like prayer or meditation, to connect with the divine. Yet, in doing so, we often create an unintended layer of separation, imposing expectations and agendas onto the natural flow of life. True spirituality cannot be forced or controlled; it is a spontaneous awakening, a sudden recognition of the sacred that emerges naturally when we relinquish resistance and allow ourselves to be fully present, free of agenda or expectation.

We often neglect or ignore the body, treating it as an afterthought or an inconvenience. We become so caught up in the pursuit of external goals and distractions that we fail to recognize the treasure trove of wisdom and insight that lies within us. We gaze up at the stars, searching for meaning and purpose in the vastness of the cosmos, while the very ground of our being goes unexplored and unappreciated.

We expend immense amounts of energy and resources seeking knowledge and understanding from outside sources, from experts and authorities who claim to hold the keys to life's mysteries. But all the while, the greatest source of wisdom and guidance lies right beneath our skin, waiting patiently for us to turn our attention inward and listen to it. By tuning into its rhythms and sensations, by honoring its needs and respecting its limits, we can unlock a vast reservoir of untapped potential and creativity. Yet in our modern world, we have become disconnected from this truth, caught up in the illusion of separation between spirit and matter, mind and body. Too often, the body is treated as a mere tool for the mind, valued only for what it can achieve in the pursuit of external goals.

Throughout history, spiritualists from countless traditions—yogis, fakirs, Christian ascetics, and even modern positive thinkers—have sought to assert the supremacy of the mind over the body. From grueling fasts and extended meditation retreats to acts of extreme self-denial and physical mortification, these practices have often aimed to tame, transcend, or even subjugate the body to the will of the mind. The narrative persists: the body is an obstacle to be overcome, a vessel to be disciplined, and the mind, with its lofty aspirations, is the path to enlightenment.

Yet, amid these lofty ideals and intricate theories that elevate the mind as the supreme ruler of our being, there exists a humbling, inescapable truth: for all the claims of mastering reality or unlocking "The Secret," the body inevitably reminds us of its primacy. No matter how disciplined or enlightened one may believe themselves to be, no one can transcend the primal call of nature when the body, in its infinite wisdom, decides it's time to surrender to the most universal human experience: the need to poop.

The body reigns supreme in this material realm, a truth that becomes strikingly clear when contrasted with the fleeting, capricious nature of the mind. While thoughts flicker and fade like fireflies in the night, the body remains a steady, tangible presence. It's the solid ground beneath our feet, the unwavering companion that anchors us firmly in the present moment.

We spend so much of our lives locked up in our heads, chasing after dreams and fantasies, trying to make sense of this crazy, mixed-up world. We get so caught up in our stories and our dramas that we forget the raw, naked truth of our own aliveness.

But the body doesn't lie. The body is always right here, right now, pulsing with the energy of life itself. And when we learn to tune into that energy, to drop out of our chattering minds and into the wisdom of our own flesh and blood and breath, something magical starts to happen.

We start to feel the world differently, to perceive the interconnectedness of all things. We begin to sense the aliveness that runs through everything, from the smallest blade of grass to the mightiest mountain peak. We start to realize that we're not separate from this great web of being, but woven into it, part and parcel of the whole.

It may feel strange or uncomfortable at first, to engage in such an intimate dialogue with your own flesh and blood. But the same consciousness that orchestrates the dance of subatomic particles within your cells is also the source of your emotions, your thoughts, and your deepest longings. Your body is not separate from your mind or your spirit, but rather the very ground from which they arise.

And so, if you truly wish to deepen your connection with the great mystery of life itself, the path may not be one of transcendence or escape, but of radical embodiment. It may be an invitation to dive deeply into the wisdom and intelligence of your physical form, to listen to its many voices and learn its many languages.

For in doing so, you may just discover that the creator you have been seeking all along is not some distant, unknowable entity, but the very life force that animates your being from moment to moment. You may come to see that creation is not something that happened in some far-off time or place, but is an ongoing process that unfolds within you, here and now, with every breath and every heartbeat.

Navigating the journey to forge a sacred relationship with the body is no small feat in a society that frequently undermines its value. In a world where numerous religions and spiritual practices may inadvertently position us against our own flesh, recognizing the divinity within becomes a revolutionary act. The challenge is compounded by the loss or distortion of ancient wisdom that once taught us to venerate the body as an integral part of our spiritual existence. This disconnect leaves many yearning for a sense of holiness in their lives, searching for a creator or a divine experience outside of themselves, not realizing that the sacredness they seek is pulsating within their own bones.

This means cultivating a relationship of deep reverence and gratitude for the miraculous gift of our physical form. It means taking the time to listen to the body's subtle language, to attune ourselves to its needs and desires, and to treat it with the care and compassion it deserves.

So often, we fall into the trap of seeing the body as a problem to be solved, a project to be perfected. We subject ourselves to punishing diets and exercise regimes, not out of love for our own being, but out of a desire to conform to some external standard of beauty or acceptability. We push ourselves to the brink of exhaustion in the pursuit of career success or material gain, ignoring the body's signals of distress and fatigue.

But this approach is ultimately a form of violence against ourselves, a denial of our own inherent worth and wisdom. When we treat the body as a mere object, a tool to be used and manipulated, we cut ourselves off from the very source of our vitality and creativity.

Developing an embodied spirituality means shifting this relationship, to begin to see the body as a beloved friend and ally, a wise and trustworthy guide on the path of awakening. It's to cultivate a sense of curiosity and wonder about the incredible intelligence that animates every cell and every breath, the vast web of consciousness that underlies our physical form.

One powerful way to begin this journey is through the practice of gratitude and dialogue with the body. Take a moment each day to simply sit with your body, to feel its presence and its aliveness. Offer it your thanks for all that it does to support you, for the countless ways in which it works tirelessly to keep you healthy and whole.

And then, begin to listen. Ask your body what it needs, what it desires, what it has to tell you. You may be surprised at the depth of wisdom and insight that arises when you create space for this kind of inner communication.

At first, it may feel strange or even silly to talk to your body as if it were a separate being. But as you practice this kind of mindful attunement, you may begin to sense a profound shift in your relationship to your embodied self. You may start to feel a deeper sense of connection and intimacy with your own being, a greater appreciation for the incredible gift of life that flows through you.

And as you cultivate this sense of reverence and respect for your own body, you may find that it naturally extends outward, to encompass all of life itself. You may begin to see the entire world as a sacred embodiment of the divine, each creature and each element as a unique expression of the great mystery that animates all things.

As you deepen your practice, you may come to understand that the body is far more than just flesh and blood, more than a simple amalgamation of physical parts. It's a reservoir of knowledge, a storehouse of intelligence and power that extends far beyond the confines of your individual self. Through the body, you can access states of consciousness and dimensions of reality that the rational mind cannot even begin to fathom.

Remember that you possess unique resources and gifts that can guide you along the way. These inner wellsprings of wisdom and insight are not always found in the realm of the intellect or the constructs of social conditioning, but often reside in the subtle whispers of your intuition and the deep knowledge of your body.

Wisdom, in its purest form, is not something that we acquire from external sources or teachings, but rather an inherent quality of our very being. It's a natural intelligence that arises from the core of who we are, a deep understanding of life that is not dependent on formal education or spiritual training.

This understanding is not purely theoretical. It comes alive in those who naturally embody a deep connection with their physical selves. One such individual was Fernanda. She was twenty-seven years old when I first welcomed her to Chapada dos Veadeiros. Born in Belém, the capital of the Brazilian Amazon, she had never formally studied any spiritual doctrine or practice. Yet, she possessed a natural wisdom reflected in her unique way of perceiving and navigating life. The ancient knowledge of the Amazonian shamans seemed to flow like water through her young body.

Our first hike together was a four-mile trail leading to a waterfall. The soil was littered with small, sharp rocks, but to my surprise, Fernanda chose to walk the path barefoot. When I suggested that she should wear shoes for protection, she replied with a smile, "I like to walk barefoot when I'm visiting a place for the first time. It's my way of saying to the land that I respect and trust it."

Concerned about her comfort, I pointed out, "But it will hurt." Fernanda's response was both simple and profound: "I like doing things that take me out of my comfort zone. It gives me strength and resilience to better embrace life, with all the hardships it contains."

In that moment, the young shaman (though she never thought of herself as one) taught me two beautiful lessons about our relationship with the body. First, through our actions, we can communicate with life and nature far more effectively than through words alone. By choosing to walk barefoot, Fernanda was engaging in a silent dialogue with the earth, expressing her respect and trust in a way that transcended language.

Second, our relationship with discomfort and pain in the body is not always a form of masochism. Instead, it can be a means of deepening our connection with life itself, teaching us to bear discomfort and pain with an open heart, without immediately seeking escape to our comfort zones. By embracing the challenges and sensations that arise in the body, we cultivate a resilience and adaptability that serves us well in navigating the ups and downs of existence.

Fernanda became my partner, a companion with whom I walk the deserts and valleys of life. We have hiked many trails together since that first meeting. And from that day forward, whenever I set foot on a new path in a place I am visiting for the first time, I do so barefoot, honoring the wisdom she shared with me.

Chapter Five

THE EMOTIONAL FRONTIER

As we delve deeper into the sacredness of the body, we begin to uncover its intimate connection to the essence of our being—our emotions. Just as the body is a vessel for the divine, it is also the theater where our inner lives unfold, where every joy, sorrow, and moment of awe is felt and experienced. Yet, for centuries, emotions have been misunderstood and relegated to the margins of human experience, often dismissed as irrational or secondary to the mind's rationality. In this next exploration, we challenge these long-held assumptions, embracing the profound intelligence of our emotional world and its vital role in shaping our consciousness, identity, and connection to life itself.

We are, first and foremost, sentient beings. Our consciousness is not merely an intellectual faculty, a product of our cognitive abilities, or our capacity for reason and analysis. Rather, it's a physical process, a lived experience that is intimately tied to the sensations and feelings that arise within our bodies.

The understanding of consciousness as an embodied phenomenon challenges the prevailing paradigms that have long dominated both Western and Eastern thought. Across various philosophical and religious traditions, there has been a pervasive tendency to elevate the mind over the body and to prioritize the rational over the emotional.

In the West, this dichotomy can be traced back to the ideas of ancient Greek philosophers like Plato and Aristotle, who saw the rational mind as the highest faculty of the human being, and the emotions as irrational impulses that needed to be controlled by reason. This view was later reinforced by the Judeo-Christian tradition, which often portrayed the body and its desires as sinful and in need of suppression.

Similarly, in Eastern thought, many traditions have emphasized the importance of transcending the physical realm and the world of sensory experiences in order to attain spiritual enlightenment. In Hinduism, for example, the ultimate goal is often seen as the realization of the true self, or atman, which is believed to be distinct from the physical body and its emotions. Buddhism, too, has often stressed the importance of detachment from the world of sensory desire in order to achieve nirvana, or liberation from the cycle of suffering.

While these traditions have undoubtedly produced profound insights and practices to cultivate mental and spiritual well-being, they have also reinforced a certain distrust or denigration of the body and its emotions. The idea that our "true" selves are somehow separate from our physical and emotional experiences has been deeply ingrained in both Western and Eastern cultures, leading to the view that our emotions are something to be controlled, suppressed, or transcended.

But as we delve deeper into the nature of our experiences, we begin to see that the dichotomy between mind and body, between reason and emotion, is just a myth. Our emotions are not some kind of extraneous or unnecessary appendage to our lives, but rather an integral part of who we are and how we make sense of the world around us.

At the most basic level, our emotions are an extension of our senses, a way of interpreting and responding to the constant stream of stimuli that bombards us from all angles. Just as our eyes and ears allow us to perceive the external world, our emotions provide us with an internal guidance system, a way of mapping and navigating the complex terrain of our own inner landscapes. Far from being random sensations, our emotions engage us in a complex and dynamic process of meaning-making, providing us with a way of interpreting the significance of the events and experiences that shape our lives.

This process is not confined to the mind but is deeply rooted in the body. A surge of happiness or pang of grief is not merely a mental state but a visceral, full-body response. Emotions, in essence, are the language of the body—unspoken but deeply felt, the feedback loop that allows us to make sense of the constant stream of sensory information that washes over us in every moment. And it's through this process that we begin to exist, not just as intellectual beings, but as fully embodied, fully sentient creatures.

From birth, emotions guide our perceptions and interactions before rational thought develops. As infants, we engage with the world through feelings rather than concepts, and these feelings structure and shape our earliest experiences. As we grow, our brains develop layers of complexity, all built upon the fundamental structure of our emotional life.

As we grow and develop, our brains undergo a complex process of maturation and integration, with different regions and networks activating at different stages. The earliest parts of the brain to develop are those associated with basic sensory processing, motor control, and emotional regulation, such as the brainstem and limbic system.

It's only later in development, typically around the age of two or three, that the more analytical and conceptual parts of the brain, such as the prefrontal cortex, begin to mature and come into play. This allows us to start making sense of our experiences in more abstract and symbolic ways, and to develop the capacity for language, reasoning, and complex problem-solving.

However, even as we develop these higher cognitive abilities, our emotional brain remains the foundation upon which our mental life is built. Our feelings continue to shape our perceptions, memories, and decision-making processes in profound and often unconscious ways.

As the renowned neuroscientist Antonio Damasio has argued, emotions are essential to our ability to make decisions and to navigate the complexities of social life. In his book "Descartes' Error," Damasio presents a compelling case for the idea that emotions are not separate from reason, but in fact a necessary part of it.

Through his research on patients with brain damage that affected their ability to process emotions, Damasio found that these individuals often struggled to make even simple decisions, such as what to eat for lunch or what clothes to wear. They could still reason logically about their options, but without the emotional feedback that normally guides our choices, they became paralyzed by indecision.

These results reveal that our emotions are a form of intelligence that helps us evaluate and prioritize the information we receive from the world around us. They provide us with a kind of intuitive sense of what is important, valuable, or meaningful, and help us make decisions that are in line with our goals and values.

But emotions do not just shape our individual experiences and choices; they also play a crucial role in our social lives and relationships. They are the connective tissue of human interaction, allowing empathy, bonding, and the navigation of complex social dynamics. Moments of connection—like a smile, a hug, or a spark of chemistry—resonate deeply, grounding our sense of belonging and meaning.

Purpose and meaning, too, are rooted in emotional experience. Passion for a cause, fulfillment in work, or inspiration in creativity are not just mental states but full-body processes that energize and motivate us. In fact, research has shown that people who have a strong sense of purpose and meaning tend to be happier, healthier, and more resilient in the face of stress and adversity. They're more likely to bounce back from setbacks, to find joy and satisfaction in their daily lives, and to feel a deep sense of connection and belonging with others.

All of this points to the idea that emotions are not just a byproduct of our intellectual or cognitive processes, but are actually the foundation upon which our sense of self and our engagement with the world are built. They are the lens through which we perceive and interpret our experiences, the compass that guides us through the ups and downs of life.

Thus, despite our sophisticated intellectual veneer, we are primarily beings of emotion. Earth, named for its land but overwhelmingly covered by water, mirrors our own nature: predominantly emotional, yet in an attempt to stabilize among our inner turbulent and ever-shifting currents, we anchor our sense of identity in the diminutive islands of reason.

This delicate balance is how we exist at the very surface of our being, navigating the shallows while the vast, deep universe of our fundamental nature lies mostly unexplored beneath. We're just beginning to tap into this profound essence, discovering that beneath the superficial layers of calculated thought, exists a rich, mysterious expanse of raw, uncharted feelings and instincts.

Historically, this emotional territory has been misjudged and misinterpreted by both science and religion. We have learned to fear it, mistaking it for something irrational and untrustworthy. Yet, within this realm lies a profound logic and wisdom that defies our intellectual understanding. The intelligence that resides within the core of our emotional system is not a product of rational analysis or logical deduction, but rather a primal, intuitive wisdom intrinsic to the very depths of our being. However, the wisdom of our gut will always challenge our intellect, for attempting to intellectualize it is like trying to contain the vast expanse of the ocean within a single glass of water.

The idea of surrendering to our emotions can be a frightening prospect. We often feel a deep-seated need to control our inner world, to bend our feelings to the will of our rational mind. Yet, no matter how hard we try, we cannot truly escape or dominate our emotional nature. Our emotions are an intrinsic part of who we are. Attempting to constantly run away from or suppress our emotions is ultimately an illusion, a futile attempt to deny the fundamental reality of our existence.

The alternative, then, is to embrace a different approach: to surrender to the intelligence of our emotions and learn from them. This doesn't mean becoming a slave to every passing feeling or whim, but rather developing a relationship of trust with our emotional world—one where we can silence our minds, shed our judgments, and awaken our hearts to feel. In this state of silence, curiosity, and humility, deep wisdom may begin to reveal itself, enlightening the sanctuary of our consciousness.

The Essence of Emotional Intelligence

PICTURE a vast ocean, its surface shimmering with the play of light and shadow. The gentle waves dance to the rhythm of the wind, creating a mesmerizing display of beauty and tranquility. Yet, beneath this serene exterior lies a world of untold depths, a realm where ancient currents swirl and hidden caves guard mysterious treasures.

In many ways, our emotional lives are like this ocean – a landscape of profound complexity and power, where the visible surface belies the intricate currents of feelings and impulses that churn beneath. Just as the ocean's depths remain largely unexplored, so too do the inner workings of our emotional selves often elude our conscious understanding.

This is the essence of emotional intelligence – not a matter of intellectual mastery, but a process rooted deep within the unconscious mind. It's a dance that unfolds independently of our awareness and consent, a secret language that speaks to us through the subtle whispers of our intuition and the powerful surges of our feelings.

We humans have evolved an extraordinary capacity for sentience – the ability to not only feel our emotions but to observe and make sense of them. This self-reflective awareness is a gift that allows us to navigate the complex currents of our inner lives, to understand the ebbs and flows of our moods, and to glean wisdom from the storms of our passions.

Yet, for all our emotional acuity, we are not the masters of our own feelings. Our emotions are not mere playthings of the intellect, to be molded and manipulated at will. They are wild and untamed, rising and falling like the tides, often without warning or permission. We may feel the heat of anger coursing through our veins, the ache of sadness weighing heavy on our hearts, or the flutter of joy lifting our spirits to soaring heights – but these experiences are not within our control.

We've developed an increasingly sophisticated intellect – a tool that allows us to probe the mysteries of the universe, to unravel the secrets of nature, and to create marvels of technology and art. We've learned to use our minds to navigate the external world, to solve problems and overcome challenges, and to build the grand edifices of civilization.

Yet, it's the wisdom that springs from the core of our being, moving the primal waves of our emotions, what pulls the strings of our thoughts and actions. Though the intellect is powerful and proficient, it remains a humble servant to this deeper intelligence within us.

Consider a typical day at the office. You arrive in the morning, ready to tackle your to-do list and make progress on your projects. The sun is shining, you've had a great workout, and you're feeling energized and optimistic. Your mind is sharp, your thoughts are clear, and you approach your work with a sense of enthusiasm and purpose.

In this state of positive emotion, challenges feel like opportunities, setbacks are merely temporary obstacles to be overcome. Your colleagues' quirks and foibles are endearing rather than irritating, and you find yourself approaching interactions with patience, humor, and grace. The day unfolds smoothly, productively, and you leave the office feeling satisfied and accomplished.

Now, let's rewind the clock and imagine the same day, but with a different emotional backdrop. Perhaps you've had a restless night, plagued by worry and self-doubt. You wake up feeling groggy and irritable, your mind clouded by negative thoughts and anxieties. As you trudge into the office, everything seems to conspire against you – the traffic is terrible, your coffee is cold, and your inbox is overflowing with demands and complaints.

In this state of emotional distress, the very same tasks and interactions take on a completely different character. Suddenly, challenges feel like insurmountable barriers, setbacks are catastrophic failures that confirm your worst fears about yourself. Your colleagues' idiosyncrasies are grating and intolerable, and you find yourself snapping at them or withdrawing into sullen silence.

The day drags on, each minute feeling like an eternity of frustration and struggle. By the time you leave the office, you're exhausted, demoralized, and convinced that nothing you do makes a difference.

These two scenarios illustrate the profound power of emotion in shaping our experience of reality. Objectively, the events of the day may be exactly the same – the same tasks, the same people, the same environment. Yet, the subjective experience of those events is drastically different, filtered through the lens of our emotional state.

In both scenarios, our reasoning worked to reinforce our emotional state, rather than operating as an independent, objective entity. When we were in a positive mood, our mind naturally focused on the opportunities and silver linings behind the challenges, using logic to construct a narrative of resilience and growth.

Conversely, when we were emotionally distressed, our intellect was hijacked by our negative feelings, scrutinizing our colleagues' personalities to highlight their worst flaws and interpreting setbacks as catastrophic confirmations of our deepest insecurities.

Instead of approaching the day with neutrality, our rational mind was influenced and shaped by our emotional landscape, weaving a coherent story that aligned with and amplified our prevailing mood. This demonstrates how our emotions and thoughts are deeply intertwined, with our logical faculties often serving as a tool for our feelings to create meaning and justify our subjective reality.

This seamless interplay between emotion and thought reveals a powerful truth: our logical minds often act in service of our emotional core. Yet, despite this inherent connection, societal norms have long resisted this integration, favoring logic over emotion and discouraging us from fully embracing our emotional experiences.

From a young age, we are taught to value rational thinking and to view emotions as irrational, untrustworthy, or even shameful. This conditioning creates a deep-seated resistance to our emotional experiences, leading us to fight against or attempt to control our feelings rather than learning from them.

Until our intellect stops fighting our emotions, there can be no true integration between these two essential aspects of our being. We must shatter the illusion that we can command everything with our brain alone, recognizing that our emotions are not obstacles to be overcome but vital sources of wisdom and guidance. Only by letting go of our resistance and embracing our emotions with openness and curiosity can we begin to learn from them and harness their transformative power.

It requires us to confront and let go of deeply ingrained patterns of resistance and avoidance. But as we begin to trust in the intelligence of our emotions and to listen to their guidance, we open up to a more authentic and fulfilling way of being in the world.

It is often said that emotions are messy, inconvenient, or even dangerous—forces to be managed, suppressed, or ignored. But what if the very chaos we fear holds the key to a profound truth? What if our emotions, in all their unpredictability and intensity, are not weaknesses but the raw material of wisdom itself? To live fully, we must stop trying to outsmart or outrun our feelings and instead plunge headfirst into their depths.

For in those depths, we might discover that our emotions are not obstacles to reason but their original architects, weaving meaning and purpose into the fabric of our lives. Like the ocean currents beneath the shimmering surface, our emotions are vast, mysterious, and essential to the rhythm of our existence. Only when we stop resisting their pull can we learn to navigate their tides—and in doing so, find the courage to embrace the uncharted waters of our humanity.

Breaking the Mental Barrier: Emotions in Their Pure Form

I've spent most of my life deeply entrenched in what I believed to be a quest for knowledge. Yet, looking back, my pursuit of understanding had often been a refuge—a way to shield myself from the chaos of my emotions. My intellect had become my fortress, a place where I could analyze, categorize, and control the world around me. But over time, I began to sense the trap I had built for myself. The same structures that had offered me safety now confined me, keeping me disconnected from the raw, unmediated truths of my emotional nature.

The journey I embarked upon was one of deconstruction—breaking down the mental scaffolding that had obscured my emotions and held them captive. It was a painstaking process, requiring me to confront the walls I had built and the stories I had told myself about what it meant to feel. I began to see my emotions not as chaotic forces to be controlled, but as an untamed wilderness—vast, unpredictable, and deeply uncomfortable to navigate. They didn't fit neatly into the structures I had spent years building; instead, they challenged me to confront parts of myself I had long avoided. This wasn't a language I could simply learn—it was a terrain I had to survive, a raw and unfiltered reality that demanded I surrender my need for control.

It was during this pivotal time, as I unraveled my defenses and sought to set my emotional self free, that I met Denise Maia. She was a witch of extraordinary depth and insight, a woman who would come to shape not only my understanding of emotion but the very foundation of my being. Denise was both a guide and a challenger, pushing me to explore dimensions of intuition, feeling, and the intricate language of the soul that I had long ignored. Our connection, both spiritual and deeply personal, became a fifteen-year partnership—equal parts transformative and turbulent—that would redefine my relationship with myself and the world.

I vividly remember one of our early experiences together, an event that entirely changed my relationship with my emotions. It was an early morning in Cruzeiro do Sul, a small town in the Amazon where the *Ayahuasca* vine grows abundantly. Denise had been tirelessly speaking since evening, her words flowing like a river of wisdom, guiding me into a new realm of understanding.

She spoke of the fundamental nature of reality, describing the universe as a vast, interconnected web of energy, where everything is entangled in a cosmic dance of creation and destruction. In this realm, she explained, the boundaries between mind and matter, between the observer and the observed, begin to blur and dissolve.

Moving quickly between different topics, she arrived in the nature of time, describing it as both a prison and a liberator, the orchestrator of all the rhythms and frequencies that structure the manifested existence.

"Everything in the universe has a frequency," she explained. "And every frequency is rhythmic, pulsating with the heartbeat of creation. Time, then, is not some external force imposed upon us, but an intrinsic part of the structure of every manifested thing."

Yet, she cautioned, for us as human beings, time can often feel like a prison, a relentless march toward an inevitable end. "We are born, we age, and we die," she said softly, "all to the ticking of the cosmic clock. In this sense, time is the reaper, the great leveler that reminds us of our own impermanence."

But then, shifting perspective again, Denise invited me to consider time from a quantum realm. "In the world of subatomic particles," she explained, "time as we know it ceases to exist. Past, present, and future coexist as one single, unified whole, a state of pure potentiality waiting to be collapsed into tangible reality."

She spoke of the relativity of time, and how time can stretch and contract depending on the observer's frame of reference. "In the quantum field," she said, "every memory, every experience, every potentiality that ever was, is, or will be, can be accessed in the same eternal moment. It's all there, waiting to be tapped into by those who know how to navigate these realms."

Denise then reminded me about the role of the shaman in preserving the delicate balance of the forest. "When a species in the forest starts to become extinct," she said, her voice taking on a tone of reverence, "the shaman must travel through the dimensions of time to bring it back. They must navigate the quantum field and weave them back into the manifested reality of the present moment."

She described this process as a way of honoring the interconnectedness of all life and ensuring the continued vitality of the ecosystem. "The shaman understands that time is not a barrier, but a doorway," she explained. "By traversing the boundaries of past, present, and future, they can heal the wounds of history and ensure a balanced and thriving future for all beings."

She then turned to the concept of karma, describing it as a force that can stagnate the soul, trapping it in the dimensions of time where the karmic event occurred. "To truly liberate ourselves," she insisted, "we must reclaim all the scattered pieces of our being, re-absorbing not only the memories but the atomic energy trapped in the quantum field. This is the work of the shaman, to retrieve the fragments of their soul left behind in the corridors of time."

Denise emphasized that only by completing this process of soul retrieval can the shaman truly awaken and unleash their full power. "When all aspects of the self are reunited and integrated," she said, her voice filled with a quiet intensity, "the shaman becomes a conduit for the very forces of creation. They are able to tap into the infinite reservoir of energy and wisdom that underlies the veil of reality, and use it to heal, to transform, and to manifest their deepest intentions."

As I listened, I felt a strange sensation wash over me, as if the boundaries of my own temporal existence were beginning to blur. Denise fixed me with her penetrating gaze and said, "You may think you are doing this work now, but remember your dream last night? The one with the shaman smoking his pipe, absorbing you with each inhalation?"

I nodded, a chill running down my spine as I recalled the vivid imagery.

"Do you think he exists in the past?" she asked, a knowing smile playing at the corners of her mouth. "No, this is an incarnation of you that is already in the future, absorbing you right now, even as we speak. The boundaries of time are far more fluid than we often realize, and your future self is already drawing upon the experiences and insights you are gaining in this very moment."

My mind reeled at the implications, the dizzy realization that the linear narrative I had always assumed was my life might just be one thread in a vast, multidimensional tapestry of existence. The more I tried to grasp it, the more it seemed to slip away, like trying to hold water in the palm of my hand.

"Are you finding it scary to think you are just a fragment of someone's past, being absorbed?" Denise asked, her eyes filled with a deep understanding. "Know that you actually are trapped in the past, condemned to live and exist there. Look at the stars. The light you see takes thousands, millions of years to get here. Some of the stars we see don't even exist anymore. We're looking at the past. It's the same with everything you experience as reality. There's a gap between the moment when things happen and the time the brain takes to process what your body absorbs through your five senses and creates a holographic image of it. The every-moment reality you perceive as now is always something that has already happened, and you're always one step behind in the line of time."

As the night evolved, Denise explored these and many other mind-bending concepts, each revelation building upon the last, creating a body of understanding that challenged everything I thought I knew about the nature of reality. Yet, just when I felt I had grasped a fundamental truth, she would pivot to another perspective, equally compelling, that seemed to contradict what had come before.

It was like peering through a kaleidoscope of knowledge, each turn revealing a new pattern, a new way of seeing the world. The more I tried to follow her with my rational mind, the more I felt like I was chasing shadows, attempting to grasp the ineffable with the clumsy tools of language and logic.

For hours I tried to follow and grasp it with my mind, like assembling a vast, intricate puzzle where each piece was a fragment of knowledge. But as I fit them together, the resulting image was not a coherent picture but a chaotic world of fractals, each one leading to an infinite regression of complexity. It was around 4am when I felt the weight of this mental struggle reach a breaking point. Something within me cracked, and I sensed the immaterial membrane that had kept my consciousness confined within the limits of my intellect starting to splinter and give way.

In that moment of surrender, as the boundaries of my mind dissolved, a new clarity emerged. It was as if a veil had been lifted, revealing a reality I had never before perceived. The realization washed over me: my intellect, for all its power and importance, was also a constraining force, filtering my experience of the world through a narrow aperture. By stepping beyond its borders, I had accessed a new kind of freedom.

From that day forward, the elements of my subjective world took on a completely different meaning. Emotions, sensations, and intuitions that I had previously processed through the lens of my rational mind now spoke to me directly, bypassing the need for intellectual interpretation. Colors and sounds took on a new vibrancy and depth, communicating their essence in a language that transcended words. Most astonishingly, I discovered that my gut had the capacity to listen, to perceive truths that my brain alone could not grasp. And so, I began to cultivate this new way of hearing, attuning myself to the wisdom of my body.

As I explored this uncharted terrain, I began to understand each feeling's nature, reason, and purpose on a level that transcended intellectual comprehension. Beneath the surface of my emotions, I encountered a vast, systemic intelligence – the same intelligence, I realized, that coordinates every process of my body and psyche, from the beating of my heart to the firing of my neurons. This intelligence was not separate from my emotions, but rather their very source and substance.

This realization was a turning point in my journey of self-discovery, opening up a whole new realm of understanding and exploration. It became clear to me that our emotions are a source of deep wisdom and guidance.

Each emotion, I discovered, speaks its own distinct language and follows its own internal logic—a unique way of interpreting and responding to the world. By attuning myself to this emotional intelligence and learning to trust its guidance, I unlocked a deeper, more intuitive understanding of life. This shift allowed me to navigate challenges and seize opportunities with greater authenticity and clarity.

Anger, for example, which I had often tried to suppress or rationalize away, revealed itself as a powerful ally in setting healthy boundaries and standing up for my values. By allowing myself to fully feel and express my anger in constructive ways, I discovered a new sense of strength and resilience within myself.

Sadness, too, took on a new depth and meaning. Rather than trying to push away or "fix" my sorrow, I learned to sit with it, to allow it to wash over me and reveal its hidden gifts. In the depths of my grief, I found a profound capacity for empathy and connection, a softening of the heart that allowed me to be more present and compassionate with myself and others.

Even fear, which had often paralyzed me in the past, became a teacher and a guide. By learning to befriend my fear, to listen to its warnings without being overwhelmed by them, I was able to tap into a greater sense of courage and clarity in the face of uncertainty.

Continuing to explore this new landscape of emotional intelligence, I began to see how it was intricately connected with every aspect of my being – from my physical health to my relationships and my creative expression. The more I trusted in the wisdom of my emotions, the more I felt a sense of integration and wholeness, a coming home to myself.

Yet, these words are but a humble attempt to articulate the magnitude of what cannot be translated into words, for my emotions are infinitely more to me. Each one is a living source brimming with life and wisdom, and a portal to a dimension of my soul that defies the confines of language. They are the silent narrators of a story that can only be felt, a resonant truth that dwells beyond the reach of mere words—a truth that demands presence rather than explanation.

It is through this presence that the journey of emotional intelligence reveals itself, not as an act of conquest but as a process of communion. This path invites us to meet our feelings with openness and stillness, to let them flow through us unimpeded by judgment or resistance. In embracing this sacred dialogue, we come to understand that our emotions are not barriers, but profound gateways to the soul—portals to the vast, uncharted landscapes of our inner being.

And in the quiet depths of these emotions, we find a profound truth: that we are not isolated islands of thought and reason, but part of a greater ocean of life, where every wave of feeling is a ripple in the fabric of existence. To embrace this truth is to reclaim the fullness of our humanity, to reconnect with the primal intelligence that moves through every cell of our bodies and every beat of our hearts.

This journey begins with surrender—letting go of defenses, silencing the fortress of the mind, and allowing ourselves to feel without reaction or resistance. In that stillness, emotions dissolve like rivers flowing into the ocean, leaving behind the quiet, resonant wisdom of the soul.

The Emotional Architecture of Our World

OUR emotions exert a profound influence on every aspect of our existence. From the personal to the societal, from the scientific to the spiritual, the currents of our emotional lives shape the very foundation of our world.

Consider, for a moment, the grand edifices of human civilization – the towering skyscrapers, the bustling cities, the intricate networks of commerce and communication that span the globe. It's tempting to view these structures as the product of pure rationality, the triumph of logic and planning over the chaotic forces of nature. But to do so is to overlook the fundamental role that emotions have played in their creation and maintenance.

At the heart of every human endeavor, from the most mundane to the most ambitious, lies a complex web of emotional drives and desires. The need for safety and security, the yearning for connection and belonging, the thirst for power and status – these are the hidden engines that propel us forward, the invisible architects of our individual and collective realities.

Take, for example, the realm of scientific research. On the surface, it may appear to be a purely rational pursuit, guided by the impartial laws of empiricism and the cold light of reason. But scratch beneath the veneer of objectivity, and you will find a roiling sea of emotions – the passion and curiosity that drives researchers to pursue their questions, the frustration and despair that accompanies setbacks and failures, the elation and pride that comes with breakthrough discoveries.

Indeed, studies have shown that emotions play a crucial role in the creative process, from the initial spark of inspiration to the persistence required to bring ideas to fruition. A 2015 study published in the journal "Frontiers in Psychology" found that emotions like joy, love, and interest were strongly associated with creativity and innovative thinking, while emotions like fear and anger could also serve as powerful motivators for problem-solving and risk-taking.

Similarly, the worlds of art, music, and literature are suffused with emotional resonance. The greatest works of human expression are not merely intellectual exercises, but profound outpourings of the heart – the joy and sorrow, the ecstasy and anguish, the love and loss that define the human condition. They speak to us on a level that transcends the merely cognitive, tapping into the deep well of feeling that connects us all.

Even the seemingly rational domains of politics and economics are, at their core, driven by emotional forces. The ideologies and policies that shape our societies are not the product of pure reason, but of the hopes, fears, and aspirations of the people who create and sustain them. The ebb and flow of markets, the rise and fall of nations – these are the manifestations of the collective emotional currents that surge beneath the surface of our world.

Religion, too, is rooted in the soil of emotion. The great spiritual traditions of the world are not merely sets of abstract beliefs and practices, but profound expressions of the human heart's deepest longings – for meaning and purpose, for connection and transcendence, for solace in the face of suffering and death. They offer a framework to navigate the turbulent waters of our emotional lives, and to find peace and meaning amidst the chaos.

As we move forward in our exploration of the emotional dimensions of our being, it's essential that we approach this terrain with both courage and humility. We must be willing to confront the uncomfortable truths that lie buried within us, to face the shadows of our own psyche with honesty and compassion.

In the chapters that follow, we will delve into some of the most challenging and often misunderstood emotions that shape our world. By developing a constructive relationship with these emotions, harnessing their power and wisdom for the greater good, we can begin to chart a new course for ourselves and our society.

This journey invites us to step beyond the boundaries of our familiar patterns and beliefs, questioning the assumptions and narratives that have guided us thus far. Through cultivating emotional intelligence, we can learn to navigate the complexities of our inner lives with greater autonomy and creativity.

As we venture into the uncharted territories of our own hearts, we open ourselves to a deeper understanding of life. There is a vibrancy and beauty that can only be accessed through embracing our deepest emotions. Let's step through these doorways, honoring the emotional truths of our existence, and create a world enriched by the full spectrum of our humanity.

CHAPTER SIX

FACING YOUR FEARS

Fear is a paradox—it has both preserved our species and imprisoned our minds. While it once kept us alive, today it often holds us back from fully living. Rather than a force to be conquered, fear can be a threshold, guiding us to where courage is most needed.

Throughout history, fear has served as a kind of societal glue, binding communities together in the face of adversity. It has galvanized action, driven innovation, and shaped the rise and fall of civilizations. From the ancient fears of wrathful gods and natural disasters to modern anxieties over global pandemics, climate change, and political unrest, fear has consistently dictated the contours of our collective experience. It is both the architect of our highest aspirations and the author of our darkest chapters.

Yet, fear is not simply a collective phenomenon—it's deeply personal. It whispers in our ears, painting the world in hues of threat, shaping how we perceive ourselves and others. It lurks in the shadows of our minds, feeding on uncertainty, and grows in the fertile soil of our imagination. The human mind, ingenious in its capacity to create, also crafts countless fears—both real and imagined—that influence our choices and define our lives.

As we peel back the layers of fear, we uncover its profound interplay with power. Fear has long been wielded as a tool of control, a means by which rulers, governments, and institutions have shaped the behavior of individuals and societies. Whether through the specter of war, economic collapse, or existential threats, fear has been used to consolidate authority and maintain order. But it has also sparked resistance, fueled revolutions, and inspired acts of courage that defy oppression.

The modern age has not diminished the potency of fear; it has amplified it. In a world saturated with information, where every corner of the globe is just a click away, fear spreads faster than ever. The media, technology, and political systems have created an ecosystem in which fear thrives, magnifying our insecurities and feeding our collective anxieties. Fear is no longer a fleeting emotion but a constant presence, shaping our identities, our relationships, and our sense of reality.

Fear is more than an obstacle—it is a mirror, reflecting our deepest vulnerabilities and untapped potential. Within it lies an opportunity for profound transformation.

This is the ultimate paradox of fear: it can be a prison or a path to liberation. To embrace fear is to acknowledge its grip, to feel its weight without being crushed by it, and to use it as fuel for growth. Fear holds a profound truth about what it means to be human: it exposes the fragility of our existence while reminding us of our capacity for courage and resilience.

Fear is not an enemy to be conquered but a guide that shapes our instincts and ensures our survival. Far from being a tyrant, it is a teacher. We can move beyond the instinctive urge to flee or fight and instead learn to face it with open eyes and an open heart. In doing so, we may discover that fear, far from being a tyrant, is a teacher.

Ultimately, fear is the greatest revealer of who we are and who we could become. It strips away our illusions and forces us to reckon with the raw, unfiltered reality of life. And in that reckoning, it offers us a choice: to be consumed by it or to rise because of it. Fear does not define us—how we respond to it does.

The Anatomy of Fear

DESPITE its undeniable power and pervasive influence, fear remains a taboo subject, an inconvenient truth that we prefer to sweep under the rug. We live in a society that prizes courage and confidence, that sees fear as a weakness to be overcome rather than a natural part of the human experience. We are told to "face our fears," to "conquer our doubts," to "be brave" in the face of adversity. But in doing so, we often fail to acknowledge the complex role that fear plays in our lives, the ways in which it shapes our choices and our actions, often without our conscious awareness.

This reluctance to confront fear head-on has consequences that reach far beyond the individual. When we refuse to acknowledge the power of fear and try to suppress or ignore it, we create a society that is ill-equipped to deal with challenges and uncertainties. We become more susceptible to manipulation and control, more likely to fall prey to the divisive tactics of those who would seek to exploit our fears for their own gain. And we become less able to find common ground, to build bridges of understanding and empathy that can help us overcome our differences and work toward a shared vision of the future.

In the rich tradition of Hinduism, there is a divine triad that represents the cyclical nature of the universe: Brahma, the creator; Vishnu, the preserver; and Shiva, the destroyer. Each of these deities plays a crucial role in the cosmic dance of existence, ensuring that the world is constantly born, sustained, and reborn in an endless cycle of transformation. But what if we were to look at this triad not as separate entities, but as facets of a single, all-encompassing force? What if, in the realm of human emotions, there was one god that embodied all three aspects of creation, maintenance, and destruction? That god, I would argue, is none other than fear itself.

Fear is the spark that ignites the fire of creation. It's the force that drives us to innovate, to push beyond our limits and explore uncharted territories. Just as Brahma breathed life into the cosmos, fear breathes life into the human spirit, compelling us to create, to build, and to transform the world around us.

Imagine the world of our early ancestors. They lived in a time of great danger, where every shadow could conceal a predator, and every rustle in the underbrush could signal a deadly threat. It was in this world that fear first began to work its magic, drawing people together in the face of a common enemy. Huddled around the flickering light of a fire, they found comfort in each other's presence, knowing that together, they stood a better chance of survival.

But fear did more than just bring people together. It also sparked the first glimmers of human ingenuity. Faced with the constant threat of starvation and attack, our ancestors were forced to think creatively, to push the boundaries of their minds in search of new solutions. From sharpened sticks to stone axes, they crafted the first rudimentary weapons, tools that would help them hunt, defend themselves, and carve out a place in a hostile world.

As time passed, fear continued to shape the course of human history. The fear of starvation drove our ancestors to abandon their nomadic ways and settle in agricultural villages, where they could cultivate crops and ensure a steady supply of food. The fear of disease and of the natural elements spurred the development of science, as people sought to understand and control the forces of nature that threatened their survival.

And then there was the fear of each other. In a world where violence and chaos were always just a heartbeat away, people sought to create systems of law and justice, mechanisms of social control that could keep their evil instincts in check. From the first codes of Hammurabi to the intricate legal systems of today, these structures have been essential to the maintenance of civilization, ensuring that even in the face of our darkest impulses, we can find a way to live together in relative peace and harmony.

Fast forward to the present day, and we can see the same forces at work. The COVID-19 pandemic has brought fear back to the forefront of our collective consciousness, reminding us of the fragility of our world and the importance of working together in the face of a common threat. Across the globe, people came together to pool their resources, their knowledge, and their creativity in the fight against this invisible enemy. From the development of new vaccines to the adoption of new technologies and ways of working, we witnessed the power of fear to drive innovation and change on a scale that would have been unimaginable just a few short years ago.

But fear is not just a creator; it's also a preserver. Just as Vishnu maintains the delicate balance of the universe, fear maintains the delicate balance of our societies and individual lives. It's the force that compels us to adhere to the rules and norms that hold our world together, the invisible that orchestrates the symphony of civilization.

On a larger scale, fear acts as a powerful collective force, compelling individuals from diverse backgrounds, ideologies, and perspectives to adhere to a shared set of rules and norms. It's the great equalizer, transcending personal beliefs and biases, and ensuring that everyone, regardless of their status or position, operates within the same framework of social order.

This becomes especially clear when we look at the State, that ultimate wielder of fear, capable of shaping entire societies through its authority. Whether it's a dictatorship ruling with an iron fist or a democracy cloaked in the guise of liberty, the State uses fear as its most effective tool. The threat of punishment—be it fines, imprisonment, or even the death penalty—keeps the machinery of society running smoothly, ensuring people toe the line

Fear often drives people to follow rules and keeps employees clocking in—not solely out of a sense of duty or passion, but because of the consequences they wish to avoid. In this way, fear acts as a stabilizer, maintaining the order of our lives and the structure of our societies.

Indeed, it's this innate fear that forms the very foundation of our political systems and the existence of nations themselves. Without the fear of reprisal, without the threat of force to maintain order and stability, the delicate structure of society would quickly collapse. Governments would crumble, borders would dissolve, and the world as we know it would descend into chaos. It's only through the collective, often subconscious, influence of fear that the institutions that form the bedrock of our societies stick together.

Fear is not just a theoretical concept; it's a visceral, tangible force that we have all felt in the depths of our being. Think about the last time you were consumed by rage, your blood boiling and your vision narrowing to a pinpoint of fury. Maybe someone cut you off in traffic, or maybe your boss berated you for a mistake that wasn't your fault. In that heated moment, you may have felt an overwhelming urge to lash out, to unleash your anger upon the world. But something held you back, something more powerful than mere reason or morality. It was fear, plain and simple—the fear of legal consequences, the fear of losing your job, the fear of irreparably damaging your relationships. This primal emotion, hardwired into our very being, keeps us from succumbing to our basic instincts and tearing apart the delicate web of society that we have spent millennia weaving.

And yet, just as Shiva destroys in order to make way for new creation, fear can also be a destructive force. When fear is allowed to run rampant, unchecked by reason or compassion, it can lead us down a path of darkness and despair. History is littered with examples of how fear, when wielded by those in power, can lead to unspeakable atrocities and the erosion of our very humanity.

This destructive force is often amplified by political propaganda, a tool used to manipulate collective fears and justify oppression. Leaders exploit anxieties by dehumanizing perceived enemies and framing violence as necessary for security. In Nazi Germany, propaganda turned fear of the "other" into justification for genocide. During McCarthyism in the United States, fear of communism led to the suppression of civil liberties and the destruction of lives. Similarly, in the Israeli-Palestinian conflict, narratives on both sides perpetuate cycles of fear and retaliation, deepening division and suffering. In such climates, fear is not merely an emotion—it becomes a weapon that fractures societies, erodes moral responsibility, and perpetuates endless violence.

The cycle of fear-driven violence and manipulation leaves deep scars on humanity, shaping societies and individuals in profound ways. Yet, for all its devastating effects, fear is not inherently evil—it is a complex force capable of both destruction and transformation. Its misuse and misunderstanding have fueled atrocities, but its potential for insight and growth remains untapped for many.

The destructive power of fear isn't confined to grand historical events or societal upheavals; it seeps into the fabric of our everyday lives, shaping our thoughts, choices, and relationships. Fear can manifest in the hesitation to voice an opinion during a meeting, paralyzing us with the dread of judgment or rejection. It can whisper doubts that stop us from pursuing dreams, convincing us that failure is inevitable or that we're not enough. Fear sows mistrust between friends, estranges loved ones, and keeps people locked in toxic environments, afraid of the uncertainty that comes with change. This quiet yet pervasive force creates invisible walls around us, trapping us in cycles of avoidance and self-doubt. In these moments, fear doesn't just hold us back; it erodes our sense of agency, leaving us disconnected from our potential and from the meaningful connections that could enrich our lives.

And so, we find ourselves in a world where fear is not just a singular force, but a trinity of creation, preservation, and destruction. Yet, for all its power and omnipresence, fear remains a deeply misunderstood and often maligned emotion. In a world of facade heroes fueled by marketing and propaganda, fear is frequently seen as a sign of weakness, a shameful secret to be hidden away and never spoken of. As a result, our relationship with fear is often one that exists primarily in the shadows of our subconscious, influencing our thoughts and actions in ways we may not even be aware of.

Fear is not something to be overcome, but an essential part of the human experience. By acknowledging its presence, we reclaim the power it holds.

In this world, we are all acolytes of the god of fear, whether we realize it or not, and whether we like it or not. We are all engaged in the eternal dance of creation, maintenance, and destruction, playing our parts in the grand cosmic drama of existence. And just as the gods of the Hindu triad work together in harmony to keep the universe in balance, so too must we learn to work with our fear, to use it as a tool for growth and transformation, rather than allowing it to consume us.

As we navigate this complex landscape, we must reflect on how this powerful emotion manifests in our own lives. Which aspect of fear is playing a central role in your life? Is fear a creative force that propels you to innovate and find ingenious solutions? Is it a preserving instinct that compels you to adhere to rules and fight fiercely to safeguard what you cherish most? Or is it the destructive impulse that causes you to perceive your fellow humans as rivals or foes, and shuts your mind to fresh ideas and collaborative efforts?

Fear has played all its roles in my life, from the creative to the preserving to the destructive. It has been a constant companion, shaping my choices and directing my path in both subtle and profound ways.

None of us can escape fear. It's an essential component of our psychic structure, inherent to our DNA, a primal force that shapes our lives in ways we may never fully understand. Trying to rid ourselves of fear is a futile endeavor, a battle that we are destined to lose. Instead, we must recognize that fear is a shared human experience, a thread that binds us all together.

Fear is a fascinating creature, a magical entity whose tentacles reach into every corner of our lives, influencing our thoughts, our actions, and our relationships with others. It's a raw, primal force to be respected and harnessed, not dismissed.

Some Good Reasons to Panic

FEAR is not just a fleeting emotion, a momentary response to danger or uncertainty. It's a deeply intelligent force, a logical and reasonable reaction to the very nature of existence. To live is to be constantly at risk, navigating a world filled with real and imagined threats. From the moment we draw our first breath to our last heartbeat, we are engaged in a never-ending dance with fear.

The world we inhabit is a perilous place, fraught with challenges that have haunted humanity since the dawn of time. From the earliest days of our species, when we were but hairless apes scrambling for survival in a world filled with teeth and claws, these threats have loomed large in our collective consciousness.

Fear, in its essence, is a survival mechanism, honed by millions of years of evolution. It alerts us to danger, urging us to take action to protect ourselves. But beyond immediate threats, fear taps into deeper, more existential anxieties. It shapes our decisions, our relationships, and our sense of self.

Understanding our fears requires delving into their origins and acknowledging their profound impact on our lives. As we explore the most basic human fears, we uncover the ways they have shaped our behaviors, decisions, and societal structures. These primal fears, rooted deeply in our evolutionary past, continue to influence us in ways both subtle and significant.

The first among these fears is the specter of starvation, etched into our very DNA through countless generations of struggle and hardship. For hundreds of thousands of years, when we were fragile creatures navigating a world of towering beasts and merciless elements, hunger was a constant companion. Our ancestors lived on the knife's edge of survival, never knowing if the next hunt would succeed or if a withered crop might bring oblivion.

Though the immediate threat of starvation belongs to the distant past, the fear it instilled remains deeply embedded within us. Compared to the vast stretch of human history spent in scarcity, the marvels of modern agriculture and the abundance it has brought are but a fleeting chapter. Today, most of us have access to more resources than our ancestors could have imagined. Yet the specter of scarcity continues to haunt us, its primal dread passed down through countless generations. We instinctively hoard resources, amassing far more than we need, as if shielding ourselves from an ancient ghost.

Ironically, this very fear now perpetuates the cycle of starvation. Our drive to accumulate and jealously guard resources, even as others go without, has created a global imbalance. Some have far too much, while others struggle to secure life's most basic necessities. The same fear that once kept us alive now threatens to tear us apart.

This fear of scarcity traps many of us in a constant state of anxiety and stress, perpetually worried about the future and bracing for the worst. It drives us to overprotect what we have, making us too afraid to take risks or pursue our passions. Over time, this primal fear can lead to stagnation and regret, as we focus so intently on survival that we forget to truly live.

Even those who have achieved immense wealth and success are not immune. I've seen millionaires living in misery, consumed by selfishness and miserliness, clinging to their possessions with a dragon-like ferocity. So afraid of losing their treasure, they fail to enjoy it. True abundance, they forget, lies not in what we keep, but in what we share.

Overcoming such a deeply ingrained fear is no small task. It requires a deliberate, long-term shift in mindset—from hoarding to generosity. We must challenge ourselves to give freely, whether it's our time, resources, or kindness. By recognizing the abundance already present in our lives and developing gratitude, we can shift our focus to the wealth of experiences, relationships, and opportunities around us.

True security doesn't come from amassing more but from building communities rooted in support and trust. The more we share, the richer our lives become. Wealth isn't measured by what we possess but by the positive impact we have on others.

Yet, the fear of starvation is only one of the many elements shaped by our primordial brain. Alongside it screams another deeply rooted fear—the fear of isolation. While scarcity reflects our physical need for survival, isolation touches on our profoundly social nature as human beings. Unlike these tangible fears, the fear of the unknown is more abstract, yet it profoundly influences our psyche and behaviors.

From the moment we are born, utterly dependent on our caretakers for survival, we begin to dread the prospect of being alone. In humanity's earliest days, when our ancestors lived in close-knit tribes and clans, rejection—and the isolation that followed—was a death sentence. To be cast out, cut off from the safety and resources of the group, was a fate worse than any other.

Today, while our survival no longer hinges on our social bonds in quite the same way, the fear of rejection still haunts us. We go to great lengths to fit in, conforming to the expectations and norms of our peers, often at the expense of our authenticity.

Think about the masks we wear and the personas we craft to navigate social complexities. How much of ourselves do we conceal? How often do we suppress or distort our true nature in the desperate quest for acceptance? The fear of isolation drives us to mold ourselves into forms that aren't genuine, sacrificing authenticity on the altar of belonging.

From early childhood, this primal fear shapes us. Vulnerable and dependent, we dread abandonment and mold ourselves to meet the expectations of those around us. As we grow, the desperate need to belong intensifies. In adolescence, caught between childhood and adulthood, we grapple with internal changes while trying to find our place in the world. The fear of being an outcast becomes overwhelming, pushing us to experiment with roles and masks in a frantic search for validation.

As young adults, the pressure doesn't ease. Anxiety about fitting into society drives us to adopt increasingly elaborate facades, aligning with societal standards while burying our true selves under layers of conditioning. In relationships, we might silence our needs to avoid conflict. Within families, we take on specific roles—like the responsible one or the peacekeeper—to maintain harmony. At work, we conform to corporate culture, suppressing our opinions to fit in and advance our careers. Over time, these masks become second nature, blurring the lines between pretense and authenticity.

Eventually, the personas we've created overshadow our genuine nature. The true self becomes a distant memory, buried beneath the constant demands of our crafted facades. Robert Fisher's *The Knight in Rusty Armor* poignantly captures this struggle. In his story, a knight becomes indistinguishable from the armor he wears, embodying the tension between our authentic selves and the roles we present to the world. As Fisher writes: "As time went on, the knight became so enamored of his armor that he began wearing it to dinner and often to bed. After some time, he didn't bother to take it off at all. Gradually his family forgot how he looked without it."

The more we disconnect from our true selves, the weaker and more vulnerable we become. This disconnection creates a profound sense of isolation—not just from others, but from our own being. Living in the husk of the character we play, we drift aimlessly, lacking the anchor of authenticity that gives life meaning and direction. This state of isolation is more debilitating than external separation because it severs us from the core of who we are.

Reclaiming our legitimacy requires embarking on a journey of self-discovery and self-acceptance. We must start by listening to our inner voice, honoring our true feelings, desires, and values. By embracing our unique qualities and letting go of the need to conform to external expectations, we begin to shed the weight of the masks we've worn for so long.

Creating environments that nurture our true selves is equally essential. Surround yourself with people who appreciate you for who you genuinely are. Take small, courageous steps to express your true self in daily life—whether through your work, relationships, or personal pursuits. Each step strengthens your connection to your inner being, transforming the fear of isolation into a powerful sense of belonging.

The fear of isolation has shaped us so profoundly that most of us don't even know who we truly are. We wear masks so often, mold ourselves so thoroughly to fit societal expectations, that our real selves become a distant memory. Yet, this loss of self is just a drop in the vast ocean of our ignorance. Beyond the isolation lies an even greater fear—one that emerges when we begin to sense how little we truly understand about ourselves and the world. We live amidst paradoxes and mysteries that defy comprehension, and their weight unsettles us deeply.

This primal fear of the unknown, of confronting the uncharted depths of our psyche and existence, can be paralyzing. It keeps us tethered to familiar, yet unfulfilling, roles and patterns, mistaking predictability for security. It is the dread of being adrift in a vast, unfathomable universe—a primal response to the boundless mystery that lies at the heart of being human.

Life itself is an enigma, a puzzle that defies resolution. We are born into a vast and complex world that operates according to principles we can only faintly grasp. Every discovery reveals the immense ocean of our ignorance, reminding us that our accumulated knowledge is but a speck in an infinite universe. From the earliest days of human consciousness, as our ancestors huddled around flickering fires, staring into the impenetrable dark, the mysteries of existence have haunted us. Who are we? Why are we here? What is the nature of reality? These questions remain as unanswered today as they were millennia ago.

To avoid the terror of being adrift in this sea of uncertainty, we cling to the familiar. We grasp at the scraps of knowledge and understanding we've managed to gather, treating them as life rafts in a storm-tossed ocean. We construct stories and ideologies in a desperate attempt to impose order on the chaos. Yet, beneath our confidence and wisdom, we know these constructs are fragile barricades against the unyielding mystery that surrounds us.

In this state of existential fear, we become vulnerable to even the most absurd beliefs. Ideologies or doctrines promising clarity and certainty can be irresistible, no matter how irrational or harmful. Charismatic leaders offering simple solutions exert a magnetic pull on those desperate for an anchor in the chaos. By aligning ourselves with their ideas, we find a fleeting sense of belonging and purpose.

However, this illusory safety comes at a steep cost: the surrendering of critical thought, the relinquishing of personal agency, and the severing of connection to our genuine self. These fragile islands of certainty are little more than mirages, offering momentary respite while leaving us stranded in deeper existential fear. As Erich Fromm observed in Escape from Freedom: "Modern man is still anxious and tempted to surrender his freedom to dictators of all kinds, or to lose it by transforming himself into a small cog in the machine, well fed, and well clothed, yet not a free man but an automaton." Faced with the existential dread of confronting our own depths, many of us choose to sacrifice our autonomy and individuality, seeking refuge in the illusory safety of conformity and submission.

Though we may try to deny it, to push it to the back of our minds and carry on as if we had it all figured out, the truth is that we are all wanderers in a strange and inscrutable world, fumbling our way through the darkness with only the faintest glimmer of light to guide us.

But the vastness of the unknown, though daunting, also holds endless potential. In confronting our fears and acknowledging our uncertainties, we find the seeds of transformation. Moving from the familiar to the uncharted, we're challenged not only to navigate the darkness but to uncover the light within it—an opportunity to reshape our relationship with fear and embrace the possibilities it conceals.

How many possibilities lie waiting in the vast expanse of the unknown? If we learn to sit with discomfort, we might unlock the door to these possibilities. Can you feel this fear — the way it creeps into your thoughts and influences your actions? Can you perceive the fragility of your mental constructs and the inherent fear of being adrift in the chaos of the unknown? Recognizing and embracing life's uncertainties is liberating. Unburdened by the heavy armor of false certainty, we can live more genuinely and expansively and explore the mysteries of the unknown with curiosity and wonder.

The ultimate aspect of the unknown, the one that is most daunting and universal, is death. This final frontier looms over us all, sparing no one—rich or poor, mighty or meek. From the moment we draw our first breath, we are set on a journey that leads to an inevitable end. Whether long or short, this journey carries us toward the same inescapable destination.

It's this certainty, this undeniable reality, that gives rise to humanity's most primal and pervasive fear. From the moment we first become aware of our mortality, we're haunted by the specter of our own demise. This knowledge—that our time on Earth is finite—colors our thoughts and actions with urgency and unease. It's the unspoken dread that lurks beneath the surface of our lives, the shadow that follows us wherever we go, reminding us of the fragility and impermanence of everything we love and fight for.

Throughout history, humanity has gone to extraordinary lengths to deny or transcend the reality of death. We have built empires and monuments, created art and literature, founded religions and philosophies—all

in an effort to leave a mark that will endure beyond our brief span of years.
endure beyond our brief span of years.

The fear of death is profoundly unsettling because it conflicts with our deep-seated desire for survival and continuity. To cope, we often engage in behaviors that seek to deny or diminish its inevitability. Social psychologists Jeff Greenberg, Tom Pyszczynski, and Sheldon Solomon explored this phenomenon through Terror Management Theory, showing how reminders of mortality often drive us to bolster self-esteem, defend our value systems, and cling to rigid beliefs. Their studies reveal how this fear influences actions—from prejudice and nationalism to the idolization of charismatic leaders promising certainty in a chaotic world.

These reactions highlight the fear of death's destructive potential. It leads us to seek safety within narrow identities, alienating those who challenge our worldview. It fuels bigotry, extremism, and division, often at the cost of empathy and rationality. In trying to deny our mortality, we risk losing the very qualities that make us human.

Beyond its social impacts, the fear of death also fuels an obsession with safety and control. We go to great lengths to protect ourselves, often sacrificing freedom, innovation, and the richness of life in the process. The irony is that in our attempts to outrun death, we diminish the quality of the life we are trying to preserve. By clinging to false certainties, we cut ourselves off from the beauty of impermanence and the transformative potential of the unknown.

In the face of this stark reality, we are left with a choice. We can succumb to the paralysis of fear, retreating into a life of stifling safety and predictability, forever haunted by the specter of our own fragility and mortality. Or we can embrace the audacity of life, charging headlong into the unknown with the knowledge that our time is fleeting and precious.

But neither of these extremes, on their own, offer a solid ground for a productive and purposeful existence. To live well, to live fully and authentically in the face of fear, requires a delicate balance. It's necessary to temper our daring with prudence, our caution with courage. We must learn to dance with our fear, to harness its energy and intensity without being consumed by it.

For fear, when understood, is not our enemy. It's an intrinsic part of the human experience, a force that reminds us of what is at stake and urges us to act. To deny our fear is to deny our nature, but to let it rule us is to surrender our potential. Instead, we can learn to coexist with fear, listening to the wisdom it offers while refusing to let it dictate the terms of our existence.

So let's be gentle with ourselves in the face of fear, treating it as a companion rather than an adversary. Fear walks beside us from our first breath to our last, and in its presence, we are united with every other human being. In this shared vulnerability lies an opportunity for connection and compassion.

The path forward, then, is one of integration and acceptance. While we may not have the power to choose our feelings or dictate the fears and anxieties that arise within us, we do have the choice in how we react to these feelings and respond to the primal terrors pulsing through our veins.

By skillfully steering our boat, we can channel the primal energy of our fears to keep us safe without limiting us, motivating us to grow rather than trapping us in obsolete patterns of suffering.

A New Approach to Fear

FEAR is an inevitable part of the human experience, but must it define our lives? Is a life dominated by fear and insecurity the only possibility for us, or is there another way? Can we find the courage to face our fears, to explore the uncharted territories of our own being, and to discover a deeper source of strength and resilience within ourselves?

Perhaps the answer lies in reimagining fear—not as an adversary to be defeated but as a teacher and guide. What if, instead of running from fear, we learned to listen to it, to uncover the wisdom it holds and use it as a force for growth and self-discovery?

Though fear serves a purpose, its roots often extend into the unexamined depths of our childhood psyche. Early fears, shaped by the uncertainties and traumas of our formative years, can cast long shadows across our lives.

Our psyche, in its wisdom, has developed intricate mechanisms to shield us from emotions that threaten to overwhelm our sense of stability. When feelings become too intense—too raw, too painful, or too destabilizing—our mind instinctively encapsulates them, locking them away in the labyrinthine depths of our subconscious. This process, often referred to as repression, acts as a protective barrier, allowing us to function in the face of trauma or distress.

Imagine a child who experiences profound fear or rejection; the mind, unable to process the intensity of these emotions, tucks them away into hidden corners of the psyche. These emotions, though out of sight, are far from gone. They linger, shaping our behaviors, thoughts, and reactions in subtle but powerful ways. Like seeds planted in the shadows, they grow silently, influencing how we navigate relationships, respond to stress, and perceive the world around us. The very things we sought to escape in our childhood continue to exert their influence over us, shaping our thoughts, our emotions, and our choices in ways we may not even realize.

It takes a profound act of courage to summon the strength to open these doors, to step into the darkness and face the specters that await us there. The voice of fear may whisper in our ear, its icy breath sending shivers down our spine, urging us to turn back, to retreat into the familiar comfort of our carefully constructed personas. But if we can find the valor within ourselves to press on, to confront these fears head-on, we may discover that the monsters of our imagination are nothing more than echoes from our past.

In this world we are all frightened children walking in the guise of adults, our hearts heavy with the weight of our own insecurities. We look around us and see a sea of masks, each one carefully crafted to hide the vulnerability that lies beneath it. Some seek solace in material possessions, surrounding themselves with the trappings of success and status. Others don the cloak of arrogance, wielding their bravado like a shield against the world. Still others retreat into the safety of the known, never daring to venture beyond the confines of their comfort zones.

But beneath each of these facades, an uncomfortable truth remains: we're all afraid. We're all grappling with the same fundamental doubts and uncertainties, the same existential questions that have haunted humanity since the dawn of consciousness. The question is not whether we feel fear, but rather how we choose to confront it.

Our society, in its relentless pursuit of an illusory sense of control, has sought to banish fear from our collective consciousness. We are told that to feel afraid is to be weak, that to acknowledge our insecurities is to invite judgment and ridicule. But in our efforts to deny the existence of fear, we have only driven it deeper into the shadowy recesses of our psyche, where it festers and grows, feeding on the energy of our resistance.

The path to a life lived in alignment with our deepest truth lies not in the denial of our fears, but in the willingness to face them. By embracing our insecurities, by acknowledging them as natural and inevitable parts of the human experience, we can begin to transmute their energy, transforming them from obstacles into allies on our journey of self-discovery.

As we learn to integrate our fears and insecurities into the wholeness of our being, something remarkable begins to happen. We start to emanate a different energy, a vibration of authenticity and trust that touches the lives of those around us in profound and unexpected ways. By communicating from the depths of our being, by speaking from the heart rather than the mask, we invite others to do the same, creating ripples of connection and healing that extend far beyond our individual lives.

Of course, this path is not always an easy one. It requires a willingness to step outside the bounds of the familiar, to risk vulnerability and exposure in a world that often feels harsh and unforgiving. There will be those who feel threatened by our authenticity, who seek to drag us back into the realm of pretense and self-doubt. But if we can summon the strength to stay true to ourselves, we may find a new sense of freedom and peace as we learn to embrace and accept our own vulnerability.

Imagine, for a moment, the dullness of a life devoid of fear – a flat, monotonous existence, stripped of the exhilarating highs and lows that make us feel truly alive. Without the tension and suspense that fear brings, without the rush of adrenaline and the pounding of our hearts, we would be little more than walking corpses.

As we begin to cultivate a friendship with our fear, we start to see it in a new light. By making peace with our fear, we take a crucial step toward accepting ourselves in our entirety, embracing the full spectrum of our human nature.

So let's not be afraid to face our fears, to embrace our insecurities as the precious gifts that they are. Let's summon the courage to open the doors of our being, to step into the shadows and face the monsters that reside there. It's only by confronting our deepest wounds, by bringing the light of awareness to the darkest corners of our psyche, that we can truly begin to heal, to grow, and to step into the fullness of our potential.

May we find the strength to be gentle with ourselves, to approach our fears and insecurities with the loving kindness they deserve. May we learn to see our vulnerabilities not as weaknesses, but as portals to a deeper understanding of ourselves and the world around us. And may we all find the courage to keep shining the light of our truth in a world that so desperately needs it.

For the greatest gift we can give to ourselves and to each other is the gift of our own wholeness, the gift of our own radiant, unbridled humanity. And as we learn to embrace all that we are, fears and insecurities included, we may just discover that the key to true freedom, to true joy and fulfillment, lies not in the absence of fear, but in the willingness to love and accept ourselves exactly as we are.

Chapter Seven

THE QUIET STORM

My heart pounds relentlessly, each beat crashing against my chest like it's trying to escape. Breathing feels like pulling air through a clogged straw—labored and suffocating. A tight band squeezes my chest, making every gasp an effort. My lungs burn, and for a moment, it feels like my own body has turned against me, staging a protest I can't quite reason with.

I close my eyes, hoping for calm, but it's a trap. Behind my lids, worries explode like fireworks, each one bigger and brighter than the last. Worst-case scenarios march through my mind, vivid and uninvited, like a horror movie marathon no one asked for. My hands shake, a cold sweat drips down my back, and I feel like I've been tossed into the world's cruelest ice bath.

A wave of nausea churns in my stomach, threatening to upend everything. The room tilts and spins, and for a second, I'm sure I'll collapse. Reaching out for something solid, my fingers grab at nothing, leaving me adrift in the chaos. My skin tingles with prickly heat, and I tug at my shirt collar, desperate to escape the invisible weight crushing me.

Through it all, my voice mutters softly, *please, please, please...* A mantra, a plea, a desperate attempt to summon some kind of relief. It feels ridiculous, like trying to bargain with a storm. But then, slowly, the storm begins to quiet. My chest loosens, my breath slows, and the shaking ebbs away. The world comes back into focus, though everything feels muted and far away.

I'm left drained, as if I've just run a marathon I never signed up for. Anxiety, that relentless foe, has had its moment—leaving me shaken, exhausted, and reluctantly impressed by its sheer persistence.

As the fog of panic lifts, I begin to recognize my old companion, anxiety. The haunting monster who inhabits the depths of my inner chambers, the one who has knocked me down so many times. The one who challenges my reason, reducing it to rubble, and rendering all my emotional intelligence theories as useless as ashes scattered in the wind.

It's striking how isolating anxiety can be. It's like a siren's call, luring us into the depths of the loneliest parts of ourselves, forcing us to confront the traumas and fears we so desperately try to sweep under the carpet. However, despite its isolating nature, anxiety is a universal emotion, an inherent part of the human experience that touches every one of us, uniting us in the cold emptiness of our loneliness.

Anxiety has many faces. For some, it's the gentle flutter of butterflies in the stomach before a first date, a reminder of the excitement and possibility that comes with new beginnings. But for others, it's an all-consuming terror that strikes without warning, leaving them gasping for air and clutching their chest, convinced that they're on the brink of death itself.

This feeling is the constant worry that gnaws at the edges of the mind, the endless stream of "what ifs" and worst-case scenarios that play out like a horror movie on repeat. It's the sense of impending doom that lurks just beneath the surface, the feeling that disaster is always just one misstep away.

For far too many, anxiety is a constant companion, a shadowy presence that follows them through every waking moment. It colors every interaction, every decision, every aspect of their lives. It's the voice in their head that whispers *you're not good enough, you'll never succeed, everyone is judging you*. It's the force that keeps them trapped in a cycle of avoidance and isolation, too afraid to step outside their comfort zone, too ashamed to admit they need help.

And then there are those for whom anxiety is a full-blown assault on the senses, a tidal wave of panic that crashes over them without warning, leaving them feeling like they're drowning on dry land. These are the people who live with the crippling fear of social situations, the ones who experience panic attacks so severe that they become prisoners in their own homes. They are the ones who are told to just "snap out of it," to "toughen up," to "stop being so dramatic." As if it were that easy.

Anxiety can be a debilitating force, one that robs people of their joy, their confidence, their very sense of self. It's a thief in the night, stealing away the moments that make life worth living. And for far too many, it's a burden they carry alone, too ashamed or afraid to reach out for help.

The pharmaceutical industry claims that anxiety is a medical condition, one that affects millions of people worldwide. And just like any other medical condition, it requires treatment and support.

Quick fixes and magic pills to numb your innermost human struggles. Benzodiazepines to soften the edge, antidepressants to lift the veil of despair. And for some, these medications can be a lifeline, a way to regain some sense of control over their lives.

But the sheer scale of the problem is staggering. In 2024, the global anxiety disorder and depression treatment markets are valued at over 21,51 billion dollars. And it's only expected to grow in the coming years, fueled by a world that seems to be spinning faster and faster, a world where uncertainty and fear have become the norm.

It's a sobering thought, isn't it? That so many people are struggling with this invisible beast, that so much money is being poured into trying to keep it at bay. And yet, for all the advancements in medicine and technology, for all the talk of self-care and mindfulness, anxiety remains a stubborn and pervasive force in our lives.

Is anxiety merely a demon lurking in the depths of our minds, feeding on our vulnerabilities and aiming to destroy us? Or is there more to it? What lessons can we learn from our anxiety? Can we harness its power for good? In this chapter, we will delve deeply into the multifaceted nature of this emotion, examining its origins in the complex interplay between our conscious and unconscious minds. Ultimately, we'll explore its potential to illuminate the deepest recesses of our being. Through this exploration, we may discover that anxiety, similar to fear, is not an enemy to be defeated but a powerful catalyst for personal growth and creative expression.

Through the lenses of great thinkers like Freud and Jung, we'll trace anxiety's origins and start to recognize it not as an alien force, but as the expression of our deepest struggles. We'll shed light on the existential challenges that anxiety brings to the surface—the unavoidable realities of death, freedom, isolation, and the search for meaning. And we'll explore how, by turning toward these ultimate concerns with curiosity and courage, we can develop a more authentic and purposeful relationship with ourselves and the world around us.

As we navigate the evolution of anxiety from the primal fears of our ancestors to the unique pressures of the digital age, we'll consider how the complexities of modern life may be amplifying our collective unease. But we'll also recognize that, ultimately, the roots of our anxiety lie not in the external circumstances of our lives, but in the uncharted depths of our own psyche.

Rather than merely understanding anxiety on an intellectual level, let's take a deeply personal odyssey to the core of what makes us human. Let's drop the safeguards of our intellectual constructions and dive with our heart and senses into the untapped reservoir of life and creativity that resides at the core of our anxiety.

Together, let's step into the heart of anxiety with the curiosity of explorers and the courage of adventurers. For it's only by fully engaging with the uncharted landscapes of our inner world that we can hope to discover the treasures that lie hidden within, and to unleash the boundless creativity and potential that is our birthright as human beings.

Freud, Jung, and the Nature of Anxiety

THE word "anxiety" has its origins in the ancient Latin word "anxietas," which meant a state of agitation or distress. The Romans used this term to describe the unease that often preceded important events, such as battles or public speeches. They recognized anxiety as a natural human experience, one that could be both motivating and debilitating.

But it wasn't until the late 19th century that anxiety began to be studied as a psychological phenomenon. Enter Sigmund Freud, the father of psychoanalysis and one of the most influential thinkers of the modern era. Freud was fascinated by the inner workings of the human mind, and he devoted his life to exploring the hidden depths of the psyche.

In his groundbreaking work "The Problem of Anxiety," published in 1926, Freud delved deep into the nature of anxiety and its roots in the unconscious mind. He proposed that anxiety was a signal of danger, a warning from the ego that something threatening was lurking in the depths of our psyche.

For Freud, anxiety was not just a symptom to be treated, but a key to unlocking the mysteries of the human experience. He believed that by understanding the origins of our anxiety, we could gain insight into the deepest recesses of our being and ultimately find a path to healing and self-discovery.

Freud's theories were nothing short of revolutionary. He proposed that our psyche was composed of three distinct elements: the id, the primitive and instinctual part of our mind that operates on the pleasure principle; the ego, the rational and reality-based part that mediates between the demands of the id and the constraints of the outside world; and the superego, the moral and ethical part that acts as a kind of internal judge, holding us to the standards of behavior we have internalized from our parents and society.

Freud suggested that these three elements were in constant tension with one another, with the id seeking immediate gratification, the superego demanding moral perfection, and the ego trying to find a workable balance between the two. And he argued that anxiety arose when this delicate balance was threatened, when the ego felt overwhelmed by the conflicting demands of the id and the superego.

Imagine that you're standing at a party, surrounded by familiar and unknown faces. The music pulses in the background, a rhythmic heartbeat to the evening's festivities. Yet, amidst the laughter and the clinking of glasses, a subtle tension that begins to coil within you. It's as if you're on a stage where every word you speak and gesture you make is under the invisible scrutiny of an unseen audience. This is the stage where the id, ego, and superego play out their timeless drama.

Your id whispers seductively, urging you to abandon caution and indulge in the night's pleasures without a second thought. It seeks the thrill of immediate satisfaction, the lure of an easy laugh or the fleeting warmth of a stranger's glance. Yet, no sooner does this desire arise the superego sternly rebukes it, imposing a rigid framework of should and shouldn't, echoing the moral and ethical codes instilled upon you since childhood. It warns of the judgments that might follow any misstep, the silent condemnations that could tarnish your social image.

Trapped in the tumultuous crossfire of these opposing forces, the ego—the vigilant guardian of your individuality—endures a relentless battle within the maze of social dynamics. It's like a tightrope walker, delicately balancing above an abyss, with the id's raw, primal desires on one side and the superego's strict, moral judgments on the other. Each carefully measured step reveals the ego's intense effort to move through this maze with a grace that seems just out of reach. The anxiety you experience is not just an echo but a loud cry from this inner struggle, signaling the ego's exhaustive attempt to maintain a semblance of harmony in the chaotic landscape of your psyche.

This relentless overthinking becomes a torture, a series of *what-ifs* and *should-haves* that chain you to a wheel of endless contemplation, robbing you of the freedom to simply exist, to be spontaneous. It's a maddening cycle, where every potential misstep morphs into a specter of humiliation and regret, each decision a potential minefield of social faux pas. The frustration and tension mount, a crescendo of psychic agony, as you're ensnared in the web of your own thoughts, desperate for release, for a moment of unguarded authenticity.

Amid this internal maelstrom, the ego is also tasked with a Herculean feat: to veil this turmoil under a mask of tranquility, to project an image of serenity to an unsuspecting world. It's a performance of Olympian proportion, where the slightest crack in the facade could betray the tempest raging within. The fear of exposure, of revealing the raw, unvarnished truth of your struggle, adds another layer of anguish to the ego's burden.

Thus, you navigate the social sphere, encased in an armor of feigned ease, while inside, an unseen but deeply felt battle rages. The ego's plight is one of profound isolation, a silent journey through the dark valleys of the mind, where the search for balance is both elusive and essential. This is the ego's trial by fire, a journey through darkness in search of a light that flickers just out of reach, the eternal hope for a peace that remains stubbornly, painfully, beyond grasp.

Freud would say that this anxiety is not just a personal ordeal but a universal human experience. It arises in moments of decision, at the crossroads of desire and duty, where the possibility of failure looms large. It's a reminder of the stakes involved in the act of living, of the constant negotiation between our deepest impulses and our highest ideals.

But Freud also offered a silver lining. He argued that by confronting our anxiety, by seeking to understand its roots and its messages, we could achieve greater self-awareness and psychological growth. He believed that the journey through anxiety was not a path to be shunned but embraced, for it leads to the discovery of our genuine selves, beyond the masks we wear and the roles we play.

As we venture deeper into the labyrinth of the psyche, guided by the torches of Freud's insights, we encounter a diverging path, illuminated by the profound reflections of Carl Gustav Jung. If Freud's journey into anxiety reveals the tensions within the self, then Jung's exploration opens a door to a broader, more mystical landscape where anxiety is not just a personal challenge but a call to a deeper, more universal journey of the soul.

Jung, standing at the crossroads of the conscious and the unconscious, perceived anxiety not merely as a symptom of conflict within the psyche but as a pivotal signal from the depths of what he termed the collective unconscious—a vast, shared reservoir of human experiences and archetypes that transcends individual existence. In this expansive view, anxiety becomes a messenger, beckoning the individual to embark on a journey of individuation, a process of integrating and reconciling the disparate parts of the self, both known and unknown.

Imagine yourself in a dense, ancient forest, the canopy above a tapestry of stars, the path underfoot shrouded in mist. This is the realm of the collective unconscious, where every shadow and light, every mysterious sound, speaks of ages past and stories untold. Your anxiety in this place is a reflection of the unknown that lies within and around you, a sign that you are on the cusp of discovering realms of your being that have remained hidden, awaiting recognition and integration.

As you navigate this forest, the id and the superego become actors in a much larger drama, with archetypes—the Hero, the Shadow, the *Anima* and the *Animus*—joining the cast. Your journey is no longer just about balancing primal desires and moral judgments but about reconciling the many aspects of your identity with the broader narratives of humanity itself. The anxiety you feel is the tension of this reconciliation, the growing pains of expanding beyond the ego to touch the edges of a universal self.

Jung's insight casts anxiety in a transformative light, as a necessary companion on the path to self-realization. It's no longer an adversary to be vanquished but a guide, leading you through the dark woods to a clearing where all parts of the self can come together in harmony. Here, in the heart of the forest, you find a sacred space where the personal and the collective, the conscious and the unconscious, meet and meld.

The ego, once beleaguered by its role as mediator and mask-bearer, finds a new purpose in this space. It becomes a bridge between worlds, a vessel for the integration of the shadow with the light, the personal with the collective. The anxiety that once felt like a burden now becomes a source of power, a wellspring of creative energy and insight, fueling your journey toward wholeness.

In this grand narrative, the social anxieties and internal conflicts that once seemed so overwhelming are reframed as part of a larger, more meaningful process of growth and discovery. The party, with its cacophony of voices and clashing wills, becomes a microcosm of the greater psychological and spiritual challenges we face as we seek to understand ourselves and our place in the world.

Jung, like Freud, sees in anxiety not just a challenge but an opportunity—an invitation to embark on the greatest adventure of all, the exploration of the self. But where Freud emphasizes the personal history and inner conflicts that shape our anxieties, Jung opens the door to a world where those anxieties connect us to the universal human experience, offering us a chance to engage with the deepest mysteries of existence and emerge not just healed but transformed.

The Courage to Face Ourselves

AS we've explored the intricate landscape of anxiety, guided by the illuminating insights of Freud and Jung, it's tempting to hope that their theories might offer us a clear path to healing, a way to finally conquer the fears and doubts that plague us. But while their ideas provide invaluable tools for understanding the complex workings of our psyche, they are not a panacea for our struggles with anxiety.

Indeed, to truly grapple with the profound role that anxiety plays in our lives, we must be willing to let go of the notion that there is a simple solution or cure. The works of Freud and Jung, for all their brilliance, do not promise a quick fix or a straightforward path to peace of mind. Instead, what they offer us is something far more valuable: an invitation to embark on a journey of self-discovery, to explore the deepest recesses of our being and to engage with the fundamental questions of existence.

Anxiety, seen through this lens, is not merely a problem to be solved but a gateway to a richer, more real way of being. It's a signpost pointing us toward the uncharted territories of the self, urging us to venture beyond the narrow confines of our conscious mind and to engage with the vast, mysterious landscape of the unconscious.

To embark on this odyssey, we must approach our anxiety with a spirit of humility and openness, like a curious explorer standing at the edge of an uncharted wilderness. Rather than seeking to anesthetize or vanquish our fears, we must learn to listen to them with the attentive ear of a wise counselor, striving to discern the hidden truths they whisper. We must cultivate the courage to sit with our doubts and uncertainties, to welcome them as valuable companions on our journey of self-discovery, and to engage them with a compassionate and inquisitive heart.

In this sense, our anxiety becomes a guiding light illuminating the shadowed corners of our psyche, inviting us to explore the uncharted depths of our being. With each step, each breath, each gentle encounter with our deepest fears, we peel back the layers of our conditioned selves, shedding the masks we have worn, until we stand authentic and vulnerable before the mirror of our own truth. It's in this space of genuine self-reflection, where the boundaries between self and fear become permeable, that we may catch a glimpse of the profound insights that reside at the core of our being, the transformative wisdom that emerges from embracing our anxiety as a path to self-understanding.

It's a delicate balance, this act of holding our anxiety close yet not letting it overwhelm us. This isn't a pursuit fueled by ambition, to turn anxiety into a triumphant tale of overcoming, but rather an acknowledgment of the intricate dance we must perform. Battling to eliminate anxiety entirely often proves to be a Sisyphean task. The true path lies in understanding that anxiety, when listened to with compassion and curiosity, can illuminate aspects of ourselves that need attention. It's about harnessing the whispers of our worries to move toward a more profound self-awareness and embracing the transformative journey that can lead us to a deeper acceptance of who we are.

At the heart of our struggle with anxiety lies a fundamental truth: it is often a reflection of the deepest, most existential concerns that we grapple with as human beings. These are the immutable, implacable aspects of life that we often try to deny or push away, which our anxiety inevitably brings to the surface.

As the psychotherapist Dr. Irvin Yalom notes in his book "Existential Psychotherapy," there are four ultimate concerns that every individual must confront: death, freedom, isolation, and meaninglessness. These are the inherent challenges of the human condition, the unavoidable realities that we must all face in our own way.

Our anxiety, then, can be seen as a manifestation of our struggle with these ultimate concerns. The fear of death, of our own mortality and the inevitability of loss, can trigger a deep-seated anxiety that colors our entire existence. The burden of freedom, of the overwhelming responsibility that comes with shaping our own lives and destinies, can be a source of profound unease and self-doubt.

Moreover, the experience of isolation, of the fundamental separateness that divides us from others, can give rise to a pervasive sense of loneliness and disconnection. And the search for meaning, for a sense of purpose and significance in a vast and often inscrutable universe, can be a wellspring of existential angst and uncertainty.

Yalom states that confrontation with the reality of existence is painful but ultimately healing. It's in the personal experience of these ultimate concerns that one finds the power to change, to move beyond the constrictions of neurosis into a new realm of self-awareness and inner freedom.

In other words, by turning toward our anxiety with a spirit of openness and curiosity, by acknowledging and exploring the deep-seated fears and concerns that underlie it, we can begin to develop a more genuine and meaningful relationship with ourselves and the world around us.

By cultivating a willingness to engage with these challenges we can begin to develop a greater sense of resilience and self-understanding. We can learn to navigate the ups and downs of our own emotional landscape with greater equanimity and grace.

Some psychoanalysts consider anxiety to be the only real emotion, distinct from others in its origin and nature. While emotions like joy, sadness, anger, and fear are often seen as direct responses to external stimuli and immediate situations, anxiety arises from within, from the complex interplay of our inner world.

Anxiety is not merely a reaction to the challenges we face in the external world, but a manifestation of the deeper psychological dynamics that shape our inner experience. It's the product of the ongoing dialogue between our conscious and unconscious minds, the result of the conflicts and tensions that exist within the very structure of our psyche.

In this sense, anxiety can be seen as an emotional bedrock, a fundamental aspect of our psychological structure that underlies and influences all other emotional experiences.

In a world where religions and spiritual gurus often speak of connecting with the universal love that defines our humanity, there's a more grounded and realistic path to self-discovery and personal growth. This path doesn't rely on lofty ideals or esoteric practices, but rather on a simple yet profound act of self-love: the willingness to explore the depths of our being by bearing witness to our anxiety and learning from it.

While the idea of embracing our anxiety may seem counterintuitive or even frightening, it's in fact an act of self-worth and courage. It requires us to confront the parts of ourselves that we may prefer to keep hidden, to shine a light into the darkest corners of our psyche. It demands that we be willing to feel the discomfort, the uncertainty, the vulnerability that comes with truly seeing ourselves.

But it is precisely in this willingness to face our shadows that we develop the capacity to really love ourselves. By refusing to turn away from our existential anguish, by welcoming our most profound struggles and vulnerabilities, and by wholly embracing these tormenting aspects of our human condition, we direct our love not toward an idealized image of ourselves, but to the raw and genuine essence of who we truly are.

From Saber-Toothed Stress to Digital Distress: The Evolution of Anxiety

UPON the ancient canvas of the Earth, our species emerges as a mere smudge in a corner—infants of evolution, our presence spanning just 200,000 years against the backdrop of a planet that has seen life unfurl across its surface for over four billion. In the vast expanse of geological epochs, humanity's time is a fleeting whisper, a momentary pause between the inhale and exhale of the Earth's slow breath.

Yet, within this brief passage of time, humanity has undergone a metamorphosis so profound it defies the imagination. From the earliest days, when our survival hinged on the keenness of our senses and the swiftness of our limbs, we have traded the sharp acuity of smell for the subtlety of speech, the raw power of muscle for the finesse of the mind. Our physical prowess may have waned, replaced by a reliance on tools and technology, but this loss pales in comparison to the extraordinary expansion of our cognitive horizons. The human brain has blossomed in complexity, crafting languages, cultures, and technologies that extend our reach far beyond the immediate grasp of our senses. Intuition and physical strength have given way to creativity, strategy, and an unparalleled ability to manipulate our environment. This trade-off has not merely changed us; it has catapulted our species into a new realm of existence, redefining what it means to be human.

Imagine a journey across these colossal stretches of time. Transport one of our ancestors from one hundred thousand years past into today's frenetic world, and the sheer shock of our concrete forests and digital streams might very well snuff out their life before nightfall. These first humans, skilled in the silent language of nature and the rhythm of the stars, would find no solace here, their survivalist instincts outmatched by the bewildering complexity of our age.

Conversely, catapult a modern human into the untamed wilderness of the past, and the dissonance would be equally lethal. Stripped of technology, the lifelines of our current existence, how many of us would greet the dawn? Without the armor of civilization, our knowledge is rendered impotent against the raw, predative forces of a world where the earth pulses with untamed life.

Beneath the same stars that once guided our ancestors through dense, uncharted forests, modern humans navigate a labyrinth of concrete and steel, their paths illuminated not by the celestial bodies but by the cold, artificial glow of screens. Where once the threat of predators set our hearts racing with a primal fear for survival, today's incessant barrage of notifications sends anxiety coursing through our veins, keeping us perpetually on edge. The tiger lurking in the shadows has morphed into the relentless pressure of deadlines, the expectation to be ever-available, ever-productive, turning the workplace into a jungle where only the most adaptable survive.

In the warmth and safety of your modern dwelling, a world away from the harsh, inhospitable caves of your forebears, you find yourself nestled in the soft embrace of a comfortable bed. The fridge is stocked with food, and the idea of a wild beast breaching the sanctity of your home to prey on you is nothing more than a distant echo of a primal fear. Yet, in this cocoon of modernity, it isn't the gentle touch of dawn's first light or the serene melody of bird song that ushers you into consciousness. Instead, the abrupt wail of an alarm clock shatters the quiet of the early hours, a stark contrast to the natural awakening of ages past. As your hand reaches out, guided by muscle memory, to silence the electronic intruder, you're met with the blinding glow of your phone's screen. A torrent of notifications floods your vision—urgent emails from work, breaking news stories, updates from social media—a digital deluge that ignites a familiar knot of anxiety in the pit of your stomach.

You drag yourself out of bed, your body still heavy with exhaustion, and stumble into the bathroom. As you brush your teeth, your mind is already racing with the day's impending challenges: the project deadline looming on the horizon, the stack of unpaid bills on the kitchen counter, the argument you had with your partner the night before.

This story is not unique; it is a common story in the annals of modern life. In a world that is constantly accelerating, where the pressures of work, family, and social obligations collide in a dizzying whirlwind, anxiety has become a ubiquitous presence, a shadow that follows us wherever we go.

Gone are the days when our ancestors faced the primal threats of the wild—the saber-toothed tigers and the unforgiving elements that honed our stress response over millennia. Today, our tigers take a different form: the relentless ping of email notifications, the ever-growing list of tasks and deadlines, the constant pressure to do more, be more, achieve more.

In the modern era, the specter of falling behind in a relentlessly productive society ignites the same primal alarm that once signaled the presence of a predator lurking in the shadows. The critical difference lies in the frequency of this threat; while our ancestors faced sporadic physical attacks, the modern world presents an incessant, unyielding menace that stalks us through our daily lives. The dread of losing one's footing on the career ladder, of becoming obsolete in a system that favors the swift and the adaptable, conjures a fear as visceral and all-consuming as any that our forebears confronted in the untamed wilds.

As the world hurtles forward at an ever-increasing pace, propelled by the breakneck speed of digital innovation, our collective capacity to adapt is tested like never before. In the past, a single technological advancement might have reshaped society over the course of generations; today, these same innovations can overhaul entire industries in the span of a few short years. With breathtaking swiftness, the skills and knowledge that were once prized can become redundant, swept away by the relentless tide of progress. The modern job market, a kaleidoscope of constant change, reflects this stark reality. In the previous century, the half-life of a job skill was estimated to be around 25 years; today, that number has plummeted to a mere five years, and continues to shrink. This rapid acceleration leaves us scrambling to stay relevant, grappling with the unsettling knowledge that today's expertise may be little more than digital detritus in the ever-evolving narrative of human endeavor.

Here you are, at the epicentrum of this digital revolution, with AI taking over. As you navigate your morning commute, inching through gridlocked traffic, your phone buzzes incessantly with messages from your team. There's a crisis at work, a client is unhappy, and suddenly your carefully planned day is thrown into chaos. You grip the steering wheel tighter, your jaw clenched, as a wave of stress washes over you.

In the office, the pressure only intensifies. You are bombarded with a barrage of demands—from your boss, your colleagues, your clients. The phone rings off the hook, the emails flood in, and you find yourself pulled in a dozen different directions at once. You struggle to focus, your mind constantly jumping from one task to the next, never able to fully immerse yourself in any one thing.

As the day wears on, your anxiety levels continue to rise. You skip lunch, too busy to take a break, and by mid-afternoon, you're running on fumes. Your neck and shoulders ache from hunching over your computer, and a dull headache throbs behind your eyes.

But even as you finally leave the office, the weight of work refuses to relinquish its grip on your psyche. The unfinished tasks, the deadlines looming overhead like a gathering storm, and the pressure of the run, the pervasive feeling that if you don't hurry, you'll be left behind—all of these thoughts cling to your stomach, making it nearly impossible to relax. In a bid for solace, you turn to your mobile device, seeking a solution in the glowing promise of the screen.

Social media, that wondrous invention promising connection and validation, beckons with its siren song. Yet, as you scroll, an unsettling sensation creeps in—a subtle weight you barely notice at first. Each polished snapshot of someone else's vibrant, successful life seems to highlight your own shortcomings. The smiling faces and tales of achievement subtly whisper: You're falling behind.

In the glow of your screen, comparison tightens its grip, feeding on insecurities you thought you'd left behind. What begins as a quest for connection leaves you adrift in self-doubt, wondering if you'll ever truly measure up to the lives so carefully crafted on your feed.

At home, you're greeted by a sink full of dirty dishes, a pile of laundry waiting to be folded, and a partner who is equally stressed and exhausted. You snap at each other over minor irritations, both too drained to have a real conversation. As you lie in bed that night, your mind is still racing, replaying the day's events, worrying about tomorrow's challenges.

In such a world, anxiety is a close companion that can slowly erode our sense of self, our ability to connect with others, and our capacity for resilience and growth. When we're constantly operating in survival mode, always bracing for the next crisis or challenge in a world where competition is the rule, it can be hard to find the space for introspection, for creativity, for the kind of deep, nourishing relationships that make life feel worth living.

It's important to recognize that life in this modern world is, in many ways, truly amazing. We've achieved feats that would have been unimaginable to our ancestors, conquering countless threats to our existence. In the past, a simple cavity could have spelled the end of a life, a minor infection could have wiped out entire communities. But today, we have at our disposal a vast array of medical knowledge and technology, allowing us to treat and cure diseases that once devastated populations.

Similarly, we have built sophisticated food industries that keep us fed and nourished, even in the face of global challenges. We have created systems of law enforcement and public safety that, while imperfect, offer a level of protection and security that our forebears could scarcely have dreamed of. The list of our accomplishments is long and impressive, a testament to the ingenuity and resilience of the human spirit.

And yet, for all of these triumphs, we find ourselves more anxious than ever before. Despite the marvels of modern medicine, the abundance of our food supply, and the relative stability of our societies, we remain haunted by the pervasive feelings of isolation, meaninglessness, and vulnerability.

Perhaps our anxiety is not a reaction to the external world but a reflection of the turmoil within. Consider, for a moment, the possibility that the frenetic pace of modern life—the relentless pressure to achieve, compete, and consume—is not the root cause of our anxiety, but a symptom of it. What if the world we've built, with all its stress and strain, is merely a mirror reflecting the fears and insecurities we harbor within?

Could it be that our obsession with success, our constant need to prove ourselves and outdo others, stems from a deep-seated fear of failure, of not being enough? Might our relentless pursuit of material goods and status symbols be an attempt to fill a void within ourselves, to numb the pain of our own existential doubts?

And what of our increasing isolation and disconnection, the growing sense that we are all alone in the world, even as we are more connected than ever before? Could this, too, be a reflection of our own internal struggles, a manifestation of our fear of vulnerability and intimacy?

These are not easy questions to confront, and there are no simple answers. But as we grapple with the complexities of modern anxiety, it's crucial that we begin to look beyond the surface, to delve into the deeper psychological and spiritual dimensions of our experience.

For in the end, the truth may be that while we have indeed conquered many of the external threats to our existence, we have yet to fully confront the demons that lie within. We have built a world of incredible technological sophistication, but we have not yet learned to master the intricacies of our own hearts and minds.

In this sense, we are like children stumbling through a landscape of emotional and psychological complexity, armed with tools that we barely understand. The same technological marvels that have allowed us to reshape the external world, to conquer disease and hunger and explore the farthest reaches of space, have also given us unprecedented power to influence the inner world of our own psyche.

But like children wielding weapons of great destructive potential, we often use these tools recklessly, without fully comprehending their impact on our minds and souls. We create social media platforms that offer the illusion of connection, but that can also amplify our insecurities and anxieties. We develop algorithms that are designed to capture our attention and keep us engaged, but that can also manipulate our emotions and distort our perceptions of reality.

In this sense, the very technologies that have the potential to help us mature and evolve, to deepen our self-understanding and expand our empathy, can also be used to construct elaborate prisons for the mind. They can reinforce our biases and prejudices, feed our fears and doubts, and trap us in cycles of addiction and compulsion.

This, then, is the great challenge of our age—not merely to build better machines or more efficient systems, but to cultivate a deeper understanding of ourselves and our place in the world. To recognize that the root of our anxiety lies not in the external circumstances of our lives, but in the internal landscape of our own psyche.

Only by turning our attention inward, by confronting our fears and insecurities with compassion and clarity, may we begin to find a new way forward—a path that leads not to more stress and strain, but to greater peace, purpose, and fulfillment.

Turning Anxiety into an Ally

IN the labyrinthine depths of our psyche, where the primal and the civilized collide in an eternal dance, anxiety emerges as a powerful force, a testament to the complex interplay of our innermost struggles and contradictions. It is the voice of our wild, untamed nature, the roar of the beast within, forever straining against the chains of social convention and self-restraint.

As we navigate the treacherous waters of modern life, it is all too easy to become lost in the maze of our own neuroses, to mistaken the protective shell of our social persona for the totality of our being. But the more we cling to this facade, the more we disconnect from the raw, pulsating energy that lies at the core of our existence, the more we invite anxiety to take up residence in the shadowed corners of our mind.

For anxiety is not, as we so often assume, an enemy to be vanquished, a demon to be exorcised from our psyche. It is, rather, a vital part of our humanity, a powerful catalyst for growth and transformation. Just as the intense pressure and heat generate the planet's lifeblood magma, our deepest internal pressures give rise to the force of anxiety—a potent mixture of creative and destructive power, stirring up both fear and awe within us. Anxiety is a force of creation and destruction, a source of both terror and wonder.

To truly harness the power of anxiety, we must first learn to embrace it, to sit with the discomfort and the fear, to allow ourselves to be consumed by the flames of our own intensity. This is no easy task, for the heat of anxiety can be searing, the pain of confronting our deepest fears and insecurities almost unbearable.

In the face of an anxiety crisis, connecting with our innermost selves can feel like trying to swim upstream through a raging waterfall. The torrential currents of fear and doubt threaten to sweep us away, pulling us further from the tranquil depths of our being. Yet, the more we avoid plunging into these turbulent waters, the more we try to escape or numb the chaos within, the more powerful the currents become, and the harder it becomes to establish a connection with our deeper selves. That's why it's essential to start with small steps, taking moments amidst the chaos to pause and, instead of reacting, simply be present. By gradually acclimatizing ourselves to the tumultuous flow of our emotions, we can slowly build the strength and resilience needed to navigate the treacherous waters of our psyche and emerge on the other side.

As you stand on the precipice of your own psyche, it's crucial to recognize that the biggest mistake in approaching anxiety is attempting to do so solely through the mind. Anxiety is born in a realm far more ancient and powerful than our rational thoughts, a primal force that demands a different set of tools for exploration.

The great geniuses of human history, the artists, thinkers, and visionaries who have left an indelible mark on our world, were often tormented by their own inner turmoil. Yet, their power never stemmed from conformity or normality, but rather from their willingness to embrace the chaos within and channel it into creative expression.

Take, for example, Vincent van Gogh, whose vibrant, swirling brushstrokes and vivid colors were a direct reflection of his own tortured psyche. Or consider the haunting, evocative poetry of Sylvia Plath, whose words were forged in the fires of her own struggles with depression and anxiety. These individuals, and countless others like them, understood that the key to unlocking their true potential lay not in suppressing their inner turmoil, but in harnessing it as a source of creative energy.

To follow in their footsteps, we must cultivate a new relationship with our anxiety, one that is rooted in curiosity, compassion, and creative exploration. Rather than trying to analyze or rationalize our fears, we must can engage with them on a more intuitive, visceral level.

This might mean picking up a paintbrush and allowing our emotions to flow onto the canvas in a burst of color and movement, or putting pen to paper and letting our thoughts and feelings pour out in a stream of consciousness. It could involve dancing with wild abandon, letting our bodies express the energy and intensity that words cannot capture, or immersing ourselves in music that resonates with the depths of our being.

But the path of creative expression is not limited to the traditional arts alone. For some, the key to unlocking their inner power may lie in the realm of physical pursuits, in pushing their bodies to the limit and discovering the strength and resilience that lies within.

This could mean taking up a martial art and learning to channel the fire of anxiety into focused, disciplined movement. The intense physical demands of these practices can provide a powerful outlet for pent-up energy, while the mental discipline required can help cultivate a sense of inner calm and clarity.

For others, the rush of endorphins and the sense of accomplishment that comes from pushing oneself to the brink in a sport like running, swimming, or cycling can be a transformative experience. The rhythmic pounding of feet on the pavement, the surge of adrenaline as one breaks through to a new level of performance, can be a way to alchemize anxiety into a source of power and vitality.

Even the simple act of taking a walk in nature, surrounded by the beauty and majesty of the natural world, can be a form of creative connection with one's inner landscape. The fresh air, the quiet solitude, the opportunity to disconnect from the constant chatter of the mind and reconnect with the wisdom of the body and the earth, can be a powerful balm for the soul.

The key is to find a creative outlet that allows us to engage with our anxiety in a way that feels authentic and meaningful to us, one that bypasses the limitations of our rational mind and taps into the raw, primal power of our emotions. Whether through art, music, dance, sports, or any other form of expression, the goal is to create a space where we can confront our fears, explore our depths, and emerge stronger, wiser, and fully alive.

This process is not about achieving perfection or mastery, but rather about the journey of self-discovery and transformation. It's about learning to be present with ourselves, to embrace the full spectrum of our emotions and experiences, and to use them as fuel for our own growth and evolution.

As we engage with our anxiety in these creative and meaningful ways, we may find that our relationship with it begins to shift. Rather than seeing it as an enemy to be fought or a weakness to be overcome, we may start to recognize it as a valuable ally, a source of insight and inspiration that can guide us toward a deeper understanding of ourselves and the world around us.

And as we continue on this path, we may discover that the very act of creative expression becomes a form of healing, a way to integrate the disparate parts of ourselves and find a sense of wholeness and purpose that transcends the limitations of our fears and doubts.

So, from one anxious person to another, let us embrace the full range of creative possibilities that life has to offer, and let us use them as tools to explore the vast, uncharted territory of our own psyche. Let us run, dance, fight, and create our way through the darkness, knowing that each step brings us closer to the light of our own true nature, to the boundless potential that lies waiting to be unleashed within us all.

Anxiety has been my constant companion, a shadow that has played me like a puppet on a string. It has frozen me in moments when action was crucial, and it has propelled me forward with reckless abandon when patience would have been the wiser choice. I've tried countless methods to rid myself of this unwanted passenger, but all my efforts were in vain.

In 2020, I found myself at a crossroad, a juncture where the paths of my past and future intersected. My son, now grown and independent, no longer needed my constant guidance. My marriage had run its course, ending in divorce. And after a fifteen-year chapter of spiritual and material work in Curitiba, I felt the urge to close the book and embark on a new adventure, to travel the world and see what lay beyond the horizon.

Yet, the world had other plans. The pandemic's iron grip limited my options, and I found myself in Alto Paraíso, a quaint town nestled in the heart of Brazil's Chapada dos Veadeiros. There, the savannah and the tropical forests intertwine, their beauty nourished by the crystalline waters that dance through rivers and cascade down waterfalls. This hidden gem, discovered by wandering hippies in the 70s, had become a mecca for free spirits, gurus, and seekers from all corners of the globe.

Amidst the tranquility of nature, I thought I had found my paradise. My days were a gentle rhythm of yoga, breathwork, and dance, followed by hours tending to the food garden, bathing in the rivers, cooking wholesome meals, indulging in the occasional pot, trekking through the lush landscapes, losing myself in quiet contemplation, reading, and resting. It was the manifestation of a dream I had nurtured since my twenties, when I flirted with the hippie lifestyle.

But as the weeks turned into months, a restlessness began to stir within me. The idyllic peace that had once seemed so inviting now felt like a stifling cage. My old friend, anxiety, began to whisper in my ear once more. Its call awakened a realization that had been dormant within me: I craved tension, the spark of creation, the thrill of unfolding new possibilities within myself. I needed challenges, movement, and the dance of anxiety that fueled my growth.

I tried to ignore and silence this insistent voice, hoping the serene surroundings would eventually quell the unease. Yet, the more I resisted, the louder it grew, transforming my moments of peace in nature into a personal hell. The angst gnawed at me, an unrelenting void in my stomach that demanded attention. It was only when I began to direct this restless energy that I found my flow. Not the idyllic and harmonious state of peace I had envisioned, but a vibrant, anxious, and tumultuous creative drive.

This period became one of intense creation and transformation. For three years, I made Alto Paraíso my home, but my time there was far from the peace and love story one might imagine. I channeled my restless energy to turn my online business into a real company: The Vessel. I wrote and filmed online journeys, crafted masterclasses, and kept myself in a state of constant creation, fueled by a blend of enthusiasm and anxiety. In embracing my anxiety, I harnessed its power to create beautiful and meaningful work, discovering that sometimes, our greatest discomforts can be the catalyst for our most profound achievements.

Eventually, the whispers of change grew too loud to ignore, and I bid farewell to Alto Paraíso, seeking a place that could nourish other facets of my creativity.

For me, every creative endeavor is a tightrope walk between the euphoria of inspiration and the anguish of obsession and anxiety. But through this journey, I've come to understand that anxiety is not my enemy, but a part of who I am. I've learned to embrace it, to let the boundaries blur until the line between bliss and anxious obsession dissolves, leaving only the raw, pulsing energy of creation in its wake.

Chapter Eight

FROM FRUSTRATION TO PERSONAL POWER

The world is on fire, and we are the kindling. With each passing day, the flames of hatred, division, and suffering seem to burn ever brighter, threatening to consume us all in their relentless blaze. And yet, amidst the chaos and the pain, there is a glimmer of hope, a spark of possibility that whispers to us from the depths of our own being.

It's the voice of frustration, that great and terrible force that lies coiled within the heart of every man and woman, waiting to be unleashed upon the world. For too long, we have been taught to fear this power, to suppress and deny it, to hide from the truth of our own anger and pain. But what happens when we learn to embrace it instead? What if we were to see frustration not as an enemy, but as a guide and a teacher?

This is the question that has haunted me for years, driving me to delve into the darkest recesses of the human psyche in search of answers. It has led me to some uncomfortable places, forcing me to confront the shadow sides of my own nature and the world around me. But it has also opened me up to a much deeper perspective on life, revealing transformative ways of thinking and living that have the power to profoundly reshape my own existence and potentially the lives of others.

In the pages that follow, I invite you to join me on this journey of discovery, to step into the fire of your own frustration and see what lies on the other side. Along the way, you will encounter a cast of characters as diverse as they are compelling, each one a reflection of the myriad of ways in which frustration shapes our lives and our world.

From the tortured artist grappling with the limitations of their craft to the spiritual seeker yearning for enlightenment, from the activist fighting for justice in a world of oppression to the lover navigating the treacherous waters of desire and heartbreak, these stories will serve as our guides and our companions, illuminating the path forward through the darkness.

Together, we will explore the depths of our own anger and pain, the wounds that lie buried beneath the surface of our lives, waiting to be acknowledged and healed. We will confront the ways in which frustration has been used as a weapon of control and manipulation, a tool to keep us small and docile in a world that seeks to crush our spirits.

But we will also discover the transformative power of frustration, the way in which it can serve as a catalyst for growth, creativity, and change. We will learn to harness the fire of our own anger and use it as a force for good to bring light into a world that often feels shrouded in darkness.

Through a thoughtful blend of storytelling, philosophy, and personal reflection, we will uncover the universal truths that lie at the heart of the human experience, the common threads that bind us all together in this great and mysterious dance of life.

Together, let's step into the fire of our own frustration and see what lies on the other side. Let's embrace the full spectrum of our humanity, from the soaring heights of joy and ecstasy to the darkest depths of sorrow and despair.

And let's never forget that it is through the crucible of frustration that we are forged into the strongest, most resilient versions of ourselves. For in a world that often feels like it's tearing itself apart, it's only by embracing our own inner fire that we can hope to light the way forward, to build a future that is more just, more compassionate, and more alive than anything we have ever known.

The Inevitable Frustration of the Multifaceted Self

ACT I begins and a king, resplendent in crown and royal robes, stands at the center of his throne room. A crowd of merchants, farmers, scholars, and priests surrounds him, vying for his attention.

The merchant steps forward, his silk robes rustling as he bows low before the throne. "Your Majesty," he begins, his voice dripping with honey, "I implore you to lower the taxes on my goods, so that I may expand my trade and bring prosperity to the kingdom." The king nods thoughtfully, stroking his beard as he considers the request.

But before he can respond, the farmer pushes his way to the front of the crowd, his weathered face etched with worry. "Sire," he pleads, his voice trembling, "my crops have failed, and my family is starving. I beg you, please provide us with food and aid, so that we may survive the winter." The king's heart goes out to the poor man, and he vows to do whatever he can to help.

Next comes the scholar, eyes blazing with intensity behind his glasses. "My liege," he declares, his voice ringing with conviction, "I have made a great discovery, but I need your support to bring it to fruition. Grant me the resources I need, and I will make our kingdom the envy of all others." The king is touched by the scholar's passion.

But the priest, his robes billowing as he strides forward, has a different vision. "Your Highness," he intones, his voice deep and sonorous, "the people are losing their way. We must double down on our efforts to enforce morality and piety, to ensure the kingdom remains a bastion of virtue in a sinful world." The king, a devout man himself, nods in agreement, even as he feels a twinge of unease.

And so it goes, on and on, each petitioner presenting a different request, a different vision of what the kingdom should be. The king listens patiently to each one, trying his best to find a way to satisfy everyone. He lowers taxes for the merchant, but raises them on the farmer to pay for the scholar's research. He provides aid to the farmer, but cuts funding for the priest's moral crusade. He supports the scholar's discovery, but imposes strict regulations on its use to appease the priest.

As the king makes his final decision, the stage lights dim, and the petitioners fade into the shadows. The curtain falls, leaving the audience to ponder the complexities of the king's predicament and the impossible task of pleasing everyone.

The curtain rises on Act II and a new day dawns upon the kingdom. The king once again takes his place upon the throne. The faces that greet him are all too familiar – the same petitioners from the previous day, their expressions now twisted with frustration and discontent.

The king realizes that the decisions he made, though well-intentioned, have sparked a fresh wave of grievances and complaints.

The merchant is the first to step forward, his once-honeyed words now laced with venom. "Your Majesty," he spits, "the regulations you imposed on my trade have ruined me. I thought you were a friend to commerce, but now I see that you are nothing more than a fickle tyrant."

The farmer is next, his eyes blazing with anger. "Sire," he cries, "the aid you provided was a mere pittance, and the taxes you raised have left me destitute. I came to you for help, but you have only made my suffering worse."

The scholar pushes his way to the front, his face flushed with indignation. "My liege," he seethes, "the restrictions you placed on my work have stifled my genius. You claim to support progress, but your actions betray your true nature."

And finally, the priest, his voice trembling with righteous fury. "Your Highness," he thunders, "your lack of commitment to the moral crusade has allowed sin and depravity to flourish in the kingdom. You have failed in your sacred duty, and the people will suffer for your weakness."

The king tries to respond, to explain the impossible choices he faced, but his words are drowned out by the clamor of the crowd, their anger and disappointment pressing down on him, suffocating him.

And then, just when it seems that things couldn't get any worse, a new group of petitioners arrives, their demands even more urgent and contradictory than before. The king's head spins as he tries to keep up, to find some way to please everyone, but he knows in his heart that it is an impossible task.

As the day wears on, the king's desperation grows. He can feel himself being pulled in a thousand different directions, his very sense of self unraveling under the constant onslaught of conflicting demands.

When the scene reaches its climax, the stage begins to spin, faster and faster, the petitioners blurring into a dizzying whirlwind of color and noise. The king clutches his head, overwhelmed by the chaos, and speaks a single line – a question that echoes through the theatre like a thunderbolt:

"Who am I?"

The stage falls silent, the petitioners frozen in place. The king looks out at the audience, his eyes haunted, his voice barely a whisper.

"I don't know anymore. I've tried to be everything to everyone, but in the end, I've lost myself. I'm no longer a king, but a hollow shell, a puppet dancing on the strings of the desires that surround me."

He rises from his throne, his movements slow and heavy, as if the weight of the world rests upon his shoulders. He takes off his crown and holds it out in front of him, staring at it as if seeing it for the first time, just to let it fall with a clatter. The king then turns and walks slowly offstage, his head bowed, his steps faltering.

As the king's tale draws to a close, we find ourselves pondering the deeper implications of his struggle. The king's dilemma, it becomes clear, is not merely a story confined to the realm of fiction but a powerful metaphor for the human condition itself. Just as the king grappled with the impossible task of satisfying the conflicting demands of his petitioners, we all must navigate the treacherous waters of our own psyches, each of us a ruler of our own inner kingdom.

In our relentless pursuit of inner peace and harmony, we often find ourselves, like the king, desperately striving to appease the multitude of voices within us. We cling to the illusory belief that if we can just discover the perfect combination of actions and compromises, we can silence the internal discord and attain a state of sublime equilibrium, unencumbered by the unsettling pangs of frustration. However, as the king's struggle poignantly illustrates, this is a futile endeavor, a quixotic quest to grasp the intangible. For frustration is not a problem to be solved, but rather a natural, intrinsic and necessary element of the human experience.

Through this lens, the king's struggle assumes a new layer of depth. His attempts to placate his petitioners, to forge a compromise that would satisfy all, can be interpreted as a metaphor for our own efforts to quell the internal discord that arises from the competing demands of our psyche. Like the king, we too are assailed by a cacophony of inner voices, each one vying for dominance and recognition.

Yet, in the grand theater of the human psyche, frustration commands the spotlight, a principal actor in the unfolding narrative of our lives. It's an omnipresent force, an understudy lurking in the shadows, poised to take center stage at a moment's notice. We may fantasize about a life unshackled from its grasp, a utopian existence where every desire is satiated and every aspiration realized, but such a life is a mere chimera, a gossamer illusion that evaporates in the harsh light of reality.

At the core of our being, a fundamental truth resides: we are not monolithic entities, but multifaceted beings, harboring a legion of contradictory voices within. Like an orchestra populated by disparate instruments, each playing its own distinct melody, our minds are a discordant symphony of competing desires, each one vying for primacy and expression. The stoic philosopher may seek tranquility and detachment, while the hedonist craves pleasure and indulgence. The altruist yearns to serve others, while the egoist demands self-gratification. These internal characters engage in an interminable tug-of-war, leaving us feeling stretched and fragmented, like a garment pulled taut from all directions.

As the conductor of this mental symphony, we are faced with the Herculean task of bringing harmony to the discord. Each decision we make is an act of prioritization, a value judgment that elevates one voice above the others. Yet, no matter how adroitly we navigate this internal landscape, there will always be parts of ourselves that feel neglected, unheard, and unfulfilled. Frustration, then, is the inescapable byproduct of our psychological complexity, the price we pay for the richness and depth of our inner worlds.

Some may attempt to quell the internal uprising by appeasing every voice, striving to be all things to all people, including themselves. But this is a fool's errand, a path that leads only to greater frustration and disillusionment.

Take, for example, the aspiring entrepreneur who dreams of starting her own business. One voice within her whispers enticingly of the freedom and fulfillment that come with being her own boss, painting a vivid picture of a life untethered from the shackles of a nine-to-five job. Yet, another voice, stern and cautionary, warns of the risks and uncertainties that line the path of self-employment, urging her to cling to the stability of a steady paycheck.

As she grapples with this internal tug-of-war, she may find herself paralyzed by indecision, unable to take the leap into entrepreneurship for fear of disappointing her risk-averse side, yet equally incapable of fully embracing the corporate world lest she betrays her adventurous spirit. She may try to appease both voices by starting a side hustle while maintaining her day job, only to find herself stretched thin and exhausted, frustrated by her inability to fully commit to either path.

To make matters worse, as she pours herself into her work, hunched over her laptop for hours on end, other voices begin to clamor for attention. A part of her, longing for love and companionship, chastises her for neglecting her personal life, insisting that she should be going out on dates and nurturing her romantic prospects. Another voice, acutely aware of her physical well-being, nags at her to hit the gym and take better care of her appearance, warning her that her sedentary lifestyle will take its toll. And then there's the voice of wanderlust, the part of her that yearns to break free from the daily grind and embark on a wild adventure, urging her to throw caution to the wind and use her hard-earned savings to travel the world and seek out new experiences.

When these voices join the fray, each one vying for supremacy, she feels pulled in a thousand different directions, her mind and body stretched to the breaking point. The task of finding balance and harmony in this internal cacophony fells like an impossible feat. She finds herself questioning her every move, second-guessing her decisions, and doubting her ability to ever find a path to satisfy all the aspects of her being.

Or consider the father torn between his roles as a provider and a nurturer. One part of him, deeply rooted in traditional notions of masculinity, insists that his primary duty is to ensure his family's financial security, even if it means long hours at the office and missing out on precious moments with his children. Another part, however, yearns to be a more present and engaged parent, to forge deep emotional bonds with his kids and play an active role in their lives.

In an attempt to satisfy both impulses, he may try to squeeze in quality time with his family whenever he can, perhaps by reading bedtime stories over Skype from his hotel room during business trips or rushing home from work just in time to catch the end of his son's soccer game. But despite his best efforts, he can't shake the gnawing sense that he's falling short on both fronts, a feeling that intensifies when his boss complains about his dwindling productivity, or his son begins to act out in school.

As he struggles to find a balance between his work and family life, other conflicting desires begin to surface, adding to his internal turmoil. A part of him, yearning for personal growth and intellectual stimulation, urges him to enroll in a graduate program or take on new challenges at work, even if it means sacrificing even more time with his loved ones. Another voice, craving the adrenaline rush of adventure and physical exertion, whispers seductively of early morning surf sessions and weekend rock-climbing trips, tempting him to carve out space for his own passions and pursuits.

While these competing desires swirl within him, he begins to feel like a man divided against himself, torn between his various roles and responsibilities. He may try to appease all these voices, carefully scheduling his time, allocating a few hours here and there for each pursuit, but the result is a fragmented and unsatisfying existence.

The more he tries to be everything to everyone, including himself, the more he feels he's failing on all fronts—a mediocre employee, a distracted father, a neglectful partner, and a stunted version of himself. The weight of his own expectations, coupled with the demands of the world around him, becomes a crushing burden, leaving him feeling perpetually inadequate and unfulfilled.

Even the seemingly mundane act of deciding what to have for dinner can become a source of frustration when our internal voices clash. The health-conscious part of us may advocate for a salad, while the comfort-seeking part lobbies for pizza. The adventurous foodie within us may crave trying that new Ethiopian restaurant, while the creature of habit argues for sticking with our tried-and-true Chinese takeout spot.

As we stand frozen in the grocery store aisle, paralyzed by indecision, we may be tempted to laugh at the absurdity of it all. Here we are, blessed with an abundance of choices, and yet we find ourselves frustrated by our inability to make a simple decision about what to eat. Even the most trivial aspects of our lives can become battlegrounds for our conflicting desires, leaving us stuck and unsatisfied.

Of course, the real punchline is that even if we do manage to make a decision—if we finally muster the courage to quit our job and start that business, or if we find a way to be both a breadwinner and an involved parent, or if we choose the salad over the pizza—our satisfaction is likely to be short-lived. As soon as one desire is fulfilled, another springs up to take its place, leaving us once again grappling with the inevitable frustration of being a multifaceted human being in a complex world.

It's like playing a game of whack-a-mole with ourselves, wielding the mallet of willpower to silence one desire, only for another to take its place. The harder we try to keep up, the more frenzied and drained we become, until we're left overwhelmed by the endless demands of our own wanting.

But perhaps there's a different way to approach this game—one that involves putting down the mallet and simply observing the moles as they pop up and recede. Instead of trying to suppress or satisfy every desire, we can simply let them be, trusting that they will eventually run their course and make way for new ones.

Such a task demands a level of self-awareness and acceptance that many of us find difficult to attain, along with a willingness to endure the discomfort of unfulfilled desires. It is far from satisfying, as it forces us to confront the harsh reality that life does not cater to our every whim and that we cannot have all we desire. Yet, the alternative — trying to eliminate frustration by appeasing every volatile desire — only leads to even greater suffering.

The Illusion of Modern Fulfillment

LET us move from the micro to the macro, from our inner spectacle to the theatre of modern life and, as the curtain rises we'll find an environment meticulously crafted to dazzle and entice. The backdrop is a glittering stage made of curated social media feeds, each one a window into a world of seemingly endless possibilities and perfection. The air hums with the siren song of advertisements, promising joy and fulfillment just a click away. And in the spotlight, the self-help gurus take their bows, their voices ringing out with the tantalizing promise of transformation and achievement.

As the audience, we find ourselves drawn into this mesmerizing show, our eyes wide with wonder and our hearts full of yearning. We see before us a vision of life as it could be, a highlight reel of triumph and success that seems to hold the key to our deepest desires. And as we watch, we can't help but feel a growing sense of inadequacy, a nagging suspicion that we are falling short of this shimmering ideal.

Everywhere we turn, we are bombarded with messages that seem to confirm our worst fears. The images that flood our screens and the words that echo in our ears all seem to say the same thing: that we are not enough, that we are missing out on the life we were meant to live. And so we find ourselves caught in a never-ending cycle of striving and self-improvement, always chasing after the elusive promise of happiness and fulfillment.

This dynamic is one of the very pillars that structure modern society, an integral part of the cultural air we breathe. From the workplace to our personal relationships to the realms of spirituality and self-improvement, we are constantly bombarded with messages that reinforce the idea that we are inadequate, that we need to be fixed or transformed to be worthy of love and acceptance.

And here, we begin to see the insidious nature of the system, the way in which our very frustration and dissatisfaction are used against us. The glossy images and slick promises that surround us are not just a harmless distraction, but a deliberate manipulation, a way of keeping us trapped in a cycle of endless consumption and striving.

At the heart of this manipulation lies a simple but powerful lie: the idea that happiness and fulfillment are just one purchase or one achievement away. We are told that if we can just acquire the right product, attain the right status, or transform ourselves in just the right way, we will finally find the joy and contentment we crave.

But this promise is a shimmering illusion that recedes further into the distance the more we chase after it. Each time we make a purchase or reach a milestone, we feel a fleeting sense of satisfaction, a momentary rush of pleasure and validation. But inevitably, the glow fades, and we find ourselves right back where we started – frustrated, dissatisfied, and searching for the next fix.

The elusive nature of lasting happiness is not merely a product of subjective experience or anecdotal wisdom. Rather, it is a phenomenon deeply rooted in the human psyche, one that has been the subject of rigorous scientific inquiry. At the forefront of this research is the concept of the Hedonic Treadmill, a theory that highlights our remarkable resilience in maintaining overall levels of well-being, despite life's tumultuous highs and lows.

This idea is supported by robust evidence from the field of psychology. In a study titled "Lottery winners and accident victims: Is happiness relative?", researchers Brickman, Coates, and Janoff-Bulman provided striking evidence of our psychological elasticity. They discovered that lottery winners, initially buoyed by their unexpected fortunes, saw their happiness levels return to their original state within a year. Conversely, individuals who had endured severe accidents resulting in permanent disabilities experienced a notable dip in happiness but gradually returned to their prior emotional baseline.

It shows that long-term happiness is surprisingly immune to dramatic shifts in fortune. This resilience stems from "hedonic adaptation," a psychological mechanism through which we adjust to significant changes, whether beneficial or detrimental. Consequently, our overall happiness levels stabilize, neutralizing the intense emotions triggered by initial events.

Ongoing studies in this area consistently affirm these observations, demonstrating that while specific life events can temporarily disrupt our emotional equilibrium, we typically revert to a consistent level of well-being. This body of research underscores the vital importance of cultivating happiness from within, focusing on enriching personal relationships, engaging in meaningful growth, and finding deep fulfillment, rather than seeking it through superficial or material means.

It's within this context that the alluring narratives of modern consumer culture often miss the mark. The endless cycle of consumption, fueled by the illusion that happiness can be bought or achieved through the next purchase or achievement, perpetuates the chase after an ever-receding mirage.

And it's here that the manipulation reaches an even more pernicious level, bringing the myth of the hero into play – that archetypal figure who embodies all the qualities we feel we lack. In the stories we are told, the hero is brave, strong, and decisive, able to overcome any obstacle and achieve any goal through sheer force of will and determination. The hero is a shining example of what we could be, if only we were good enough.

But the hero myth sets an impossible standard, a bar that is always just out of reach. No matter how much we strive and struggle, we can never quite measure up to the idealized image of perfection that the hero represents. And so we are left feeling perpetually inadequate, forever falling short of the impossible expectations set for us.

This dynamic plays out in every arena of our lives. In the workplace, we're held up to the standard of the tireless, endlessly productive employee, expected to give everything we have and then some in pursuit of the company's bottom line. In our personal relationships, we're bombarded with images of perfect, fairy-tale love, a romantic ideal that leaves no room for the complexities and challenges of real human connection.

And even in the realm of spirituality, where one might expect to find solace and acceptance, we are often met with more of the same. Whether it's through the rigid dogma of organized religion or the New Age promises of enlightenment and transcendence, we are sold a vision of spiritual perfection that is unattainable, that denies the fundamental truth of our human fallibility and imperfection.

Modern ambition sells us the illusion that more effort leads to more fulfillment. Yet, the pressure to optimize every moment—to be successful, well-rounded, and endlessly productive—often leads to exhaustion instead. Burnout isn't a sudden collapse; it's a slow erosion, where fatigue is mistaken for perseverance and joy is lost in the chase for the next goal.

The pursuit of 'having it all' becomes a treadmill—each victory immediately replaced by another target, leaving no time to reflect or appreciate what's already been achieved. Instead of fueling purpose, this cycle drains it, turning ambition into a burden rather than a path to meaning.

This obsession with unattainable standards drains our energy and fosters a culture of competition. In a world that glorifies individual achievement, we're pushed to see others not as companions, but as rivals—fueling disconnection rather than fulfillment.

From the cutthroat world of business and finance to the ruthless social hierarchies of high school and beyond, we are taught that success means rising above others, that happiness is a zero-sum game in which one person's gain is another's loss.

But even if we do manage to claw our way to the top of the heap, even if we achieve the kind of success and status that the world tells us we should want, we are still left with a gnawing sense of emptiness and unease. For there will always be someone richer, someone more beautiful, someone with a more perfect life than ours. The goalposts of success are always shifting, always receding just beyond our grasp, leaving us forever chasing after an illusory ideal. We are left exhausted and disillusioned, forever seeking a sense of fulfillment that remains just out of reach.

Perhaps the greatest tragedy is that in buying into this system, in allowing ourselves to be pitted against one another in a never-ending battle for status and success, we miss out on the very things that make life truly meaningful – the simple joys of connection and community, the sense of purpose that comes from working toward a common goal, the deep satisfaction of knowing that we are part of something larger than ourselves.

What if we could learn to see through the myth and, instead of constantly striving to measure up to an impossible standard, we chose to embrace our own unique paths and celebrate the progress we make along the way?

Imagine the freedom that would come from letting go of the need to constantly compare ourselves to others, from the exhausting pursuit of an idealized version of success. What if we could learn to find meaning and value in our own journeys, to appreciate the beauty and richness of our imperfect, messy humanity?

This is not to say that we should abandon our dreams or resign ourselves to a life of mediocrity. But what if we could learn to pursue our goals from a place of intrinsic motivation, rather than external pressure? What if we could define success on our own terms, based on what truly matters to us, rather than what society tells us we should want?

When we focus on being true to ourselves, on honoring our own unique gifts and passions, we open ourselves up to a world of possibilities. We begin to see that there are infinite paths to fulfillment, infinite ways to make a meaningful contribution to the world. We learn to find joy in the journey itself, rather than fixating on some distant, idealized destination.

And perhaps most importantly, we begin to cultivate a sense of compassion and connection, both for ourselves and for those around us. When we let go of the need to constantly compete and compare, we create space for genuine relationships and communities to flourish. We start to see our fellow human beings not as rivals to be beaten, but as companions to be cherished and supported.

Learning to celebrate our unique journeys may be the greatest act of rebellion against a system that seeks to keep us forever striving and never arriving. By choosing to embrace our own imperfect humanity, we reclaim our power and agency, and we open ourselves up to a life of true authenticity, purpose, and joy.

The Shifting Goalposts of the Mind

IN the depths of our minds lies a peculiar mechanism that shapes the contours of our lives in ways we seldom fully comprehend. It lurks beneath the surface of our conscious awareness, quietly pulling the strings of our desires and aspirations, orchestrating the intricate dance of our hopes and dreams. It's the source of our eternal restlessness, the wellspring of our insatiable longing for something more. The voice that whispers in our ear, urging us onward and upward, forever in pursuit of the next goal, the next achievement, the next milestone on the winding path of life.

At first glance, this incessant drive might seem like a blessing, a powerful motivator that propels us toward growth and self-improvement. After all, without the spur of ambition, without the hunger for success, where would we be? Surely, we would be condemned to a life of mediocrity, forever languishing in the stagnant waters of complacency.

And yet, upon closer examination, this same force can take on a more sinister character. For in its relentless pursuit it leaves us perpetually unfulfilled, forever grasping at a sense of contentment that remains just out of reach.

Picture the aspiring entrepreneur we encountered earlier, who once grappled with the conflicting desires of stability and passion. Imagine that, through a combination of grit, determination, and sheer force of will, she has managed to overcome the myriad of obstacles in her path and build a thriving business from the ground up.

On the surface, her life seems like a testament to the power of the human spirit, a shining example of what can be achieved through hard work and unwavering commitment. She oversees a bustling office with nearly a hundred employees, each one a vital cog in the machine of her success. Her days are filled with the heady rush of high-stake negotiations and critical decision-making, the thrill of watching her vision come to life.

But beneath the polished veneer of her accomplishments, a subtle shift begins to take place. At first, it is barely perceptible, a faint whisper of unease that she can easily dismiss as the natural jitters of a high-pressure role. Yet, as the weeks turn into months, and the months into years, the whisper grows louder, more insistent, until it becomes a constant companion, a lingering shadow that follows her through the halls of her own creation.

It's the weight of responsibility, the crushing realization that the fate of so many livelihoods rests squarely on her shoulders. In the early days of her entrepreneurial journey, this responsibility felt like a badge of honor, a symbol of her own power and agency. But now, it feels like an albatross around her neck, a burden that grows heavier with each passing day.

She begins to long for the simplicity of her former life, the predictable rhythms of a nine-to-five job with a steady paycheck and the promise of weekends and holidays. Now, the boundaries between work and life have blurred beyond recognition, and she finds herself tethered to her phone at all hours, always on call, always on edge.

As the pressures of her role mount, she begins to feel like a prisoner in her own life, trapped by the very dreams she once held so dear. The corner office that once seemed like the ultimate symbol of success now feels like a gilded cage, a lonely perch from which she can only watch as the world passes her by.

And so, after years of pouring her heart and soul into her business, she makes a decision that shocks everyone around her. She walks away, leaving behind the empire she has built and the identity she has crafted, in search of something more elusive, more meaningful.

At first, there is a sense of exhilaration, a feeling of lightness and freedom that she hasn't experienced in years. She travels the world, meets new people, and immerses herself in experiences that she never would have had time for in her previous life. But as the novelty starts to wear off, a familiar sense of restlessness begins to creep in, a nagging feeling that she has left something important behind.

She finds herself second-guessing her decision, wondering if she made a mistake in giving up everything she had worked so hard to achieve. The grass, which had seemed so much greener from the other side of the fence, now appears patchy and wilted, and she begins to long for the sense of purpose and direction that her work once provided.

It's a tragic irony, a cruel twist of fate that seems to underscore the fundamental inadequacy of the human condition. We're creatures of contradiction, forever caught between the poles of our own desires, always chasing after a sense of fulfillment that remains just out of reach.

In moments like these, we may catch a glimpse of the true nature of this mechanism of our psyche, the insidious way in which it keeps us forever chasing after a satisfaction that remains elusive. It's like a cosmic sleight of hand, a metaphysical bait-and-switch that keeps us running on the hamster wheel of our own desires.

As the philosopher Alan Watts so eloquently put it, "The only way to make sense out of change is to plunge into it, move with it, and join the dance." This sentiment resonates deeply with my own experience, as I've found myself caught in a perpetual cycle of change and adaptation, forever seeking a sense of home and belonging in a world that feels increasingly transient and impermanent.

I consider myself a focused, constant, and determined person, even stubborn at times. I take great pleasure in my work and find immense joy in the sanctuary of my home. And yet, I've lost count of the number of times I've found myself setting up a new home in a different corner of the world. From the outside, it may sound exciting, a life filled with adventure and novelty. But the reality is often far more complex and painful.

Each move represents a massive investment of time, energy, and resources. The process of finding a new place to live, whether it involves purchasing, renting, or even constructing a home, is exhaustive. And then there are the countless hours spent furnishing and decorating, transforming an empty space into a reflection of my personality.

With each move also comes the task of creating a new life, building new social circles and establishing new routines. It requires patience, resilience, and adaptability, as I navigate the inevitable feelings of isolation that come with being a stranger in a strange land.

And yet, despite all these efforts, there inevitably comes a moment when the place I once cherished begins to feel confining—when the walls seem to close in, and the horizon calls with the allure of something new and uncharted. It's a feeling I know all too well: a quiet restlessness that grows beneath the surface until it erupts into an irresistible longing for change.

After countless moves and reinventions, I've realized that home is not a physical space but a state of being—one rooted in embracing the transitory nature of life. On one hand, there is a certain freedom in accepting it, in embracing the idea that every experience is a temporary gift to be savored and enjoyed while it lasts. It allows me to live more fully in the present moment, to invest wholeheartedly in the people and places that cross my path, without the burden of expectation or attachment.

But there is also a profound sense of loss that comes with this realization, a grief for the roots that will never be planted, the connections that will inevitably be severed by time and distance. It's a pain that I've come to know intimately, a dull ache that pulses beneath the surface of even my happiest moments.

Faced with this existential dilemma, I found myself at a crossroad. I could choose to detach, to move through the world as light as a ghost, leaving no trace and making no commitments. Or, I could choose to lean in, to embrace the ephemeral nature of existence and pour my heart and soul into every fleeting moment, knowing that it may all be gone tomorrow.

In the end, I chose the latter path. I chose to love deeply, even knowing that my heart would be broken. I chose to build homes, even knowing that I would eventually have to leave them behind. I chose to invest in communities, even knowing that I may one day have to say goodbye.

It's a choice that requires some courage. While it may not provide the illusion of permanence or stability that I so often crave, it offers something far more valuable – a chance to be fully present, fully engaged, and fully alive in every moment.

For perhaps the true measure of a well-lived life is not the length of our stay in any one place, but the depth of our presence while we are there.

This lesson is not unique to my own experience. Each of us faces unavoidable frustrations and trials. Whether it's the deep ache of heartbreak, the bitter taste of failure, the abandoned dreams sacrificed for the roads we've taken, or the daunting realization of our own mortality—these are the harsh truths of life, the toll we pay for the profound depths of human consciousness.

Despite these challenges, we are far from powerless. We hold the power to choose how we respond, how we steer through the stormy seas of our lives. We could choose to battle relentlessly against the current, to shut our hearts tightly to avoid the vulnerability of love, to stifle our dreams for fear of failure, or to succumb to a sense of nihilism in the face of life's brevity. Or, we could take a bolder, more liberating path: to open ourselves up, to let go of our fears, to embrace the raw and unpredictable current of the now with courage and zeal. In doing so, we invite a life of rich textures and profound truths, navigating our existence with a vibrant spirit of adventure and an open heart.

This is the profound lesson that frustration can teach us, the essential wisdom concealed within our difficulties. It encourages us to accept the inevitability of pain, to recognize it as an intrinsic element of our life's journey. By acknowledging and embracing frustration, we discard the futile pursuit of perfection, strip away the facades we maintain, and stand exposed and open to the core realities of our existence.

This acceptance is not resignation but an active engagement with life, a way to deepen our understanding and expand our horizons. Can you reconsider your own unavoidable frustrations, the challenges and obstacles that seem to stand in the way of your happiness and fulfillment? What would it mean to stop fighting against them, to accept them as an integral part of your journey?

What would it look like to embrace the reality of your life, with all its pain and all its beauty, and to pour your heart into every moment, knowing that it is a precious and fleeting gift?

In embracing this path, you may uncover a sense of freedom and lightness that defies expectation. Within you lies a reservoir of resilience and strength, waiting to rise. And beneath the surface of your struggles, there is a profound beauty—a hidden treasure that is your birthright as a human being.

For in the end, it is not about avoiding pain or frustration, but about finding the courage to face them. It is about weaving grace and wisdom into the fabric of every moment, embracing the light and the shadow, the ecstasy and the agony. In this acceptance, you discover the true depth and richness of what it means to be alive.

The Pressure Cooker of Piety

FRUSTRATION, like a shapeshifter, can morph into various forms, each with its unique challenges and opportunities for growth. Among these, sadness and anger stand out as two of its most potent and transformative manifestations.

Sadness, with its heavy, leaden weight, can settle upon the soul like a thick fog, obscuring the light and casting a gray pallor over the world. If left unacknowledged, it can slowly solidify into the unyielding cement of depression, trapping us in a state of stagnation and despair.

However, if approached with a spirit of acceptance and curiosity, sadness can become a wise and gentle companion on the path to wisdom. In the quiet introspection of our sorrow, we may discover hidden truths about ourselves and the world around us. By embracing the pain and allowing it to wash over us, we create space for profound personal growth. The tears we shed can become the nourishing rain that helps our inner garden flourish, even in the darkest of times.

On the other hand, frustration can also ignite the flames of anger, a powerful and often misunderstood emotion. Anger, like fire, can be both destructive and transformative, depending on how it's channeled and expressed.

When left unchecked and unintegrated, anger can consume us from within, burning away our peace of mind and leaving us charred and brittle. When directed outwards without mindfulness, it can unleash a firestorm of damage that inevitably reverberates back to us, creating a cycle of suffering and conflict. This vicious cycle, fueled by unresolved frustration, traps us in a state of perpetual anguish and turmoil.

Yet, when approached with wisdom and skill, anger can become a formidable ally in the journey of personal growth. It can help us set healthy boundaries, asserting our value and worth in the face of challenges and obstacles. Anger can fuel our courage and willpower, propelling us forward through adversity and helping us overcome both internal and external barriers. It can burn away the constraints that hold us back, forging us into stronger, wiser, and more resilient individuals.

Across the spectrum of sacred writings and doctrines, anger is frequently viewed as a destructive and unwelcome force. This sentiment is not reserved solely for instances where anger is directed at an adversary; it's a broad admonition against the emotion itself, highlighting its potential to disrupt peace and cause harm.

The scriptures and teachings from various faiths consistently convey a message about the perils of anger. Christian doctrine often identifies anger as a sin indicative of humanity's flawed nature. Judaism views anger as particularly harmful, both spiritually and ethically. The Talmud suggests that anger causes one to lose their wisdom and prophetic abilities, likening an angry person to an idolater, which underscores the deep spiritual repercussions of this emotion.

Similarly, in Islamic teachings, the Prophet Muhammad emphasized the importance of controlling anger, likening uncontrolled temper to holding a burning coal. Followers are encouraged to seek Allah's refuge when angered and to respond with forgiveness and patience.

Hindu philosophy also warns against the dangers of anger, as outlined in the Bhagavad Gita. It describes a cascade effect where anger leads to delusion, followed by a loss of memory, which in turn erodes the ability to discriminate right from wrong, ultimately leading to self-destruction. In Buddhist philosophy, anger is identified as one of the three root poisons—alongside ignorance and desire—that are fundamental causes of human suffering.

These ideas convey a resounding consensus across various teachings: anger, regardless of its cause or intention, is inherently problematic and should be avoided and transcended. The message is clear—spiritual growth requires rising above the disruptive waves of anger, nurturing a state of inner peace and balance that remains undisturbed by life's inevitable fluctuations.

Throughout history, religious institutions have leveraged the ideals of love and compassion as formidable instruments to shape societal norms and maintain order. Advocating for forgiveness, patience, and non-retaliation, these institutions have played a significant role in regulating the behavior of the masses and keeping aggression in check.

On one level, this emphasis on love and non-violence has undoubtedly had a positive impact, helping create more stable and harmonious communities. In a world where unchecked anger and aggression could easily tear societies apart, the religious message of restraint and compassion has served as an important counterbalance, promoting greater peace and understanding between individuals and groups.

Yet, paradoxically, these very messages of peace have, at times, been co-opted to sanction some of the most egregious acts of violence and oppression throughout history. Positioned as the ultimate moral authorities, religious institutions have often been able to manipulate the masses into accepting or even participating in atrocities that utterly contradict the core values of love and compassion they preach.

In this regard, the religious suppression of anger has often functioned as a double-edged sword. While it has contributed to social order and stability, it has also served to bottle up deep-seated resentments and frustrations, creating a pressure cooker of unresolved emotions. When these pent-up feelings are finally unleashed, they can erupt with devastating consequences, fueling cycles of conflict and retribution.

The religious directives against anger are usually not absolute. Most spiritual traditions permit, and sometimes even advocate, the expression of anger under specific circumstances, especially when directed against perceived adversaries of the faith.

This selective sanctioning of anger reveals a troubling double standard. While followers are admonished to suppress their own frustrations and resentments, they are simultaneously encouraged to channel their rage against those deemed enemies of the faith. This hypocrisy creates a dangerous moral loophole, allowing anger to be weaponized in service of religious agendas.

The Hebrew Bible contains many instances of divinely commanded violence against Israel's foes. For example, in the Book of Numbers (Numbers 31:2), God instructs Moses to enact revenge on the Midianites, leading to a brutal campaign of slaughter and enslavement, sanctioned by divine authority. Similarly, in the Book of Psalms, the prophet declares, "Blessed is the one who seizes your infants and dashes them against the rocks" (Psalm 137:9), a chilling endorsement of violence against the enemies of God's chosen people.

The historical narrative continues with the conquest of Canaan, as described in the Book of Joshua, where the Israelites, following divine commands, engage in a merciless war aimed at annihilating the indigenous Canaanite populations, leaving "nothing that breathes" (Joshua 11:11). This campaign of genocide and ethnic cleansing, carried out with cold, calculated efficiency, stands as a chilling reminder to the perils of religious zealotry and the dehumanization of the "other."

Another somber chapter in religious history, the Crusades, painted the world in blood. Christian armies, blessed by the Catholic Church and spurred by promises of spiritual glory, marched to reclaim the Holy Land from Muslim rule. Led under the guise of divine love and rewarded by the promise of heaven, these soldiers inflicted profound suffering, slaughtering untold numbers of innocent men, women and children. Pope Urban II's proclamation at the Council of Clermont in 1095 ignited this bloody conflict, proclaiming: "Let those who have been accustomed unjustly to wage private warfare against the faithful now go against the infidels and end with victory this war which should have been begun long ago."

Equally grim was the Inquisition, an institutionalized ordeal of severe interrogation and punishment that targeted heretics and apostates. Orchestrated by the Catholic Church to safeguard doctrinal purity, this operation was marked by extreme cruelty. Tomás de Torquemada, the notorious first Grand Inquisitor of the Spanish Inquisition, epitomized this brutality with his severe persecution of Jews, Muslims, and other deemed heretics. His words offer a glimpse of the horrors perpetrated by the inquisitors in the name of God: "There is only one crime I am guilty of... being too merciful! When you were my prisoner, I should have spent more time with you in the torture chamber... so you could really understand the meaning of pain."

Religious righteousness also left its mark in the New World. The conquest of the Americas was characterized by a deadly blend of fervent religious zeal and ruthless violence. Spanish conquistadors, sanctioned by the Church and driven by a mandate to convert indigenous populations to Christianity, unleashed a wave of genocide and enslavement upon the native peoples. The cross and the sword, it seemed, were two sides of the same coin. The conqueror and chronicler Bernal Díaz de Castillo candidly revealed the dual motives behind the conquest, stating, "We came here to serve God, and also to get rich."

In more recent times, the persecution of the Rohingya Muslims in Myanmar has cast a dark shadow over the image of Buddhism as a religion of peace and non-violence. In 2017, the Myanmar military, with the support of Buddhist nationalists, launched a brutal campaign of violence against the Rohingya, a long-persecuted ethnic minority. The atrocities committed—rape, torture, murder, and the burning of villages—shocked the world and shattered the myth of Buddhist exceptionalism.

In each of these cases, the core messages of love and compassion central to many religious teachings have been distorted to rationalize acts of severe violence and oppression. The very institutions that proclaimed the supremacy of love and warned of the perils of anger were the ones who showed the most ruthless spirit of intolerance and destruction. Time and time again, we see a disturbing pattern: while anger may be generally discouraged, there are times when it is not only permitted, but actively encouraged. The enemy of the faith must be confronted, defeated, and exterminated, no matter the cost.

This manipulation of anger can be likened to a spring-loaded trap, carefully set and held under tension until the opportune moment. Just as a hunter may conceal a trap, waiting patiently for their prey to stumble into its jaws, so too do those in power keep the anger and frustration of their followers in check, allowing these volatile emotions to build and fester until they can be unleashed with devastating force against a designated target.

For those bearing the burden of years of repressed frustration—born from the religious suppression of their sexuality and fundamental emotions—the designated adversary offers not just an opportunity for guiltless cathartic release, but also a sense of meaning and purpose. In the embrace of a worldview that grants these primal urges a rightful place, their raw rage is distilled into a force that feels both just and necessary.

This manipulation of frustration and anger, however, is not confined solely to the realm of religion. The same tactics can be seen at play in the world of politics and ideology, where leaders and movements seek to harness the rage of their followers for their own purposes.

In the communist revolutions of the 20th century, for example, the frustration and anger of the working class was carefully cultivated and directed against the bourgeoisie, the capitalist class that was seen as the enemy of the people. The language of class struggle and revolution was used to justify the most brutal acts of violence and repression, from the gulags of the Soviet Union to the killing fields of Cambodia.

Similarly, in the democratic movements of the modern era, anger has been weaponized to fuel the fires of nationalism and xenophobia. Political leaders on both the left and the right have sought to exploit the fears and frustrations of their followers, channeling their rage against immigrants, minorities, and other perceived threats to the social order.

Just as religious authorities may define certain groups as enemies of the faith, so too do political leaders paint their opponents as enemies of the state, traitors to the cause, or threats to the very pillars of society. And once these enemies have been identified, the trap is set, waiting only for the right moment to be sprung. The frustrations of the people, left to simmer for so long, are finally given an outlet, a target upon which to vent their pent-up anger and resentment.

The parallels between religious and political manipulation of frustration and anger are striking, and they speak to a deeper truth about the nature of power and control. Those who seek to wield power over others have always understood the potency of anger as a tool for shaping behavior and mobilizing the masses.

To break free from this vicious cycle, we must recognize the ways in which our own anger and frustration are being manipulated and controlled. We must be willing to question the narratives that seek to paint others as enemies, to look beyond the simplistic dichotomies of us versus them.

Only by cultivating a deeper understanding of our own emotions we can hope to build a world that is free from the tyranny of the spring-loaded trap. A world in which these powerful feelings are not weapons to be wielded by the unscrupulous, but tools for positive change and personal growth.

It demands that we sit with our frustration, that we explore the roots of our anger, and that we find healthy and constructive ways to channel these intense energies. But if we can learn to transmute our frustration into a catalyst for transformation, we may yet find a way forward. We may discover that, within the crucible of our struggles and setbacks, lies the key to unlocking a brighter, more compassionate future.

In this future, frustration is not a wellspring of shame or weakness, but a powerful teacher, pointing us toward the changes we need to make. Anger is not a destructive force to be feared or suppressed, but a potent fuel for positive action. And love, far from being the antithesis of these emotions, is the guiding light that helps us channel them toward their highest purpose.

Embrace Your Anger

THE video of George Floyd's final moments, captured on a bystander's smartphone, sent shockwaves around the world. For an excruciating eight minutes and forty-six seconds, the world watched as Floyd, a forty-six-year-old Black man, lay pinned to the ground by a white police officer's knee on his neck. Floyd's desperate pleas for air—"I can't breathe"—were met with cold indifference from the officer, Derek Chauvin, who maintained his deadly hold even as Floyd's body went limp.

As the video went viral, it ignited a powder keg of anger and frustration that had been building for centuries. The image of Floyd's lifeless body became a symbol of the systemic racism and police brutality that had long plagued communities of color in America. It was a harsh reminder that, even in the twenty-first century, Black lives were still treated as disposable by those in power.

In the days and weeks that followed, that anger poured out onto the streets in a wave of protests and demonstrations that swept across the country and around the globe. Under the banner of "Black Lives Matter," millions of people of all races and backgrounds came together to demand justice for Floyd and countless other victims of racist violence.

The anger that fueled these protests was not the destructive, uncontrolled rage that so many religious teachings warn against. Rather, it was a righteous anger, a holy fury born of centuries of oppression and injustice. It was the justifiable frustration of a people who had been pushed to their breaking point, who could no longer tolerate the daily indignities and violence inflicted upon their communities.

And yet, even in the midst of this anger, there was a sense of purpose and discipline. The protests were largely peaceful, with participants marching, chanting, and holding vigils in a show of solidarity and determination. When violence did erupt, it was often in response to provocations from police or counter-protesters which was quickly condemned by movement leaders.

Through their anger, the protesters achieved what had once seemed impossible. They forced a national reckoning on race and policing, with lawmakers and leaders across the political spectrum acknowledging the need for systemic change. They pushed for the arrest and prosecution of the officers involved in Floyd's death, with Chauvin eventually convicted of murder. And they inspired a new generation of activists and organizers, who continue to fight for racial justice and equality.

The story of the Black Lives Matter shows us that, when channeled thoughtfully and directed toward a just cause, anger can be a catalyst for profound social and political change.

And while anger can be a potent catalyst for change on a societal level, we don't need to always wait for a wave of collective outrage to begin making a difference in our own lives and communities. Each of us has the power to listen to our own frustration, to identify the ways in which we are being held back or oppressed, and to start taking small, incremental steps toward change.

These baby steps might seem insignificant at first, but they can quickly add up to something much larger. By speaking out against injustice when we see it, by supporting those who are marginalized or oppressed, and by working to educate ourselves and others about the issues that matter most to us, we can begin to chip away at the systems and structures that perpetuate inequality and suffering. In doing so, we channel our frustration into a constructive force for transformation, rather than letting it ferment into a toxic brew of resentment and despair.

Consider the issue of climate change, for example. It's easy to feel anger and despair when confronted with the sheer scale of the problem, to believe our individual actions are insignificant in the face of such a massive global crisis. Yet, this frustration can be a powerful motivator if we choose to channel it constructively. By making small, meaningful changes—walking or biking instead of driving, reducing meat consumption, or supporting sustainable businesses—we take tangible steps toward addressing the crisis.

These actions may seem minor, but they are expressions of our anger transformed into determination.

Or take the issue of homelessness. Anger at the injustice of poverty can easily lead to feelings of helplessness or apathy, but it can also spark a commitment to action. Volunteering at a shelter, donating essentials, or simply offering a kind conversation to someone experiencing homelessness are small acts with profound impact. Through these actions, we not only address immediate needs but also challenge the stigmas and stereotypes that perpetuate homelessness. In doing so, our anger becomes a force for empathy and connection, helping to build a more compassionate and inclusive society.

And just as anger, can be harnessed for good in the most diverse spheres of our world and society, so too can it serve as a powerful force for personal growth and transformation. In our own lives, we all face limitations and obstacles that can leave us feeling stuck, helpless, and deeply frustrated. Whether it's a dead-end job, a toxic relationship, or a self-defeating habit, there are times when we may feel like we're banging our heads against a wall, unable to break free from the patterns that hold us back.

But it's in these moments of frustration that we often find the spark of motivation we need to create real change. By allowing ourselves to feel the full force of our anger, to sit with it and examine it closely, we can begin to identify the root causes of our discontent. We can ask ourselves what we truly want, what we are willing to fight for, and what steps we need to take to get there.

This process is not always comfortable. It requires us to confront parts of ourselves that we may prefer to ignore, to take an honest look at our own limitations and shortcomings. But by doing so, we open ourselves up to the possibility of real transformation. We find the courage to take risks, to step outside our comfort zones, and to pursue our deepest desires and aspirations.

When we allow ourselves to feel the full depth of our discontent, we create space for something new to emerge. We begin to see beyond the limitations of our current circumstances, to tap into a deeper sense of purpose and meaning.

We find the strength to stand up for ourselves and for others, to speak our truth even when it feels risky or uncomfortable. And we develop the resilience to keep going even in the face of setbacks and challenges, knowing that each obstacle we overcome brings us one step closer to our goals.

In this way, anger becomes not a hindrance but a gift, a powerful ally in our quest for meaning, purpose, and fulfillment. And as we learn to embrace it, to use it as fuel for the fire of our own transformation, we begin to see that even the greatest frustrations of our lives can be sources of growth, creativity, and positive change.

When we think of anger, we often associate it with violence and destruction—a fist slammed on the table, harsh words spoken in the heat of the moment. But this is only the most superficial manifestation of this complex and multifaceted emotion. At its core, anger is a powerful force for change, a fire that burns within us, urging us to act and fight for what we believe in. And when this anger is tempered by love, when it is channeled not into blind rage but into a passionate commitment to justice and compassion, it becomes something truly transformative.

This is the anger that fuels the spiritual warrior, the activist, the revolutionary. It is the anger that propelled Martin Luther King Jr. to stand up against the forces of racism and oppression, the anger that inspired Mahatma Gandhi to lead a nonviolent resistance against British colonialism. It is the anger that burns in the hearts of all those who refuse to accept the status quo, who dare to dream of a better world and who are willing to fight for it with every fiber of their being. This is the anger that changes lives, that topples empires, that rewrites the course of history. And it all begins with a single spark, a moment of **frustration** that ignites the recognition that things cannot go on as they are, that we have the power and the responsibility to make a difference.

What are the places where you feel stuck, frustrated, or unfulfilled? What are the injustices that make your blood boil? What are the dreams and aspirations that keep you up at night, the goals that seem always just out of reach? Whatever they may be, know that your anger is not a weakness to be suppressed or ignored, but a powerful ally in your quest for meaning and purpose.

Embrace your anger, let it be the voice of your deepest frustration. Allow it to fuel your passion and determination. Use it to propel you forward, to take bold and decisive action in the direction of your dreams. And when you encounter obstacles and setbacks along the way, as you inevitably will, don't let them douse your fire or dampen your spirit. Instead, let them temper your anger into an even stronger, more resilient force. See them as opportunities to test your resolve, to strengthen your commitment, and to prove the depth of your conviction to yourself and the world.

Remember, the path of transformation is not a leisurely stroll in the park. It's a fierce and unrelenting fight, a daily battle against the forces of inertia and the weight of the status quo that try to keep you stuck in frustration. But it's a fight worth fighting, not because of some promised land of eternal bliss on the other side, but because it is in the very act of struggling that we discover our true strength.

It's in the heat of the battle, when we're pushed to our limits and forced to dig deeper than we ever thought possible, that we catch a glimpse of the fire that burns within us. And it's in honoring that flame, in staying true to our anger and our passion even in the face of adversity, that we find a sense of aliveness and purpose that goes beyond mere happiness.

So don't shy away from the fight, don't shrink from the challenges that lie ahead. Embrace them, welcome them, and let them be your teachers and your guides. For it is only by walking through the fire of our own frustration that we can emerge on the other side, tempered and transformed, ready to set the world ablaze with the light of our passion.

You can take that first step today, no matter how small or insignificant it may seem. Set a goal, make a plan, and begin to take action. Identify the source of your deepest frustration and let it be the kindling for your anger. Trust that, as you move forward, this anger will light your way, burning away all the excuses and limitations that have held you back for far too long.

Go forth with courage and conviction, let your righteous anger be your ally, and fight for your dreams with every fiber of your being. Put your frustration to work in service of your highest ideals, your boldest visions, and your most unshakable values. Let it be the fuel that powers your engine, the fire that forges your will into an unbreakable force for change.

CHAPTER NINE

EMBRACING YOUR NATURE

We've spent time exploring some of our most uncomfortable emotions—those feelings we often push aside or try to escape. By shining a light on them, we've begun to see them differently, not as obstacles to avoid but as messengers to embrace. This chapter invites us deeper, into the very heart of what it means to embrace our nature. It asks us to see the interplay of light and shadow within us, not as a battle to fight or a flaw to fix, but as a dance—an intricate choreography where every step leads us closer to the fullness of who we truly are.

Emotions are the pulse of our being, the invisible currents that shape our experiences and connect us to the deepest parts of our humanity. They arrive unbidden, often without warning, rising like waves that crash upon the shores of our consciousness—sometimes gentle, sometimes overwhelming, always carrying something essential. Joy and sorrow, love and fear, anger and peace—each emotion has its place, its purpose. Yet, we rarely allow them to simply exist. Instead, we judge them, label them as "positive" or "negative," and try to control them. We cling to what we perceive as light and push the rest into the shadows, believing that by doing so, we can craft a better, more acceptable version of ourselves. But in this act of division, we fracture our wholeness, leaving vital pieces of who we are hidden in the dark, neglected and misunderstood.

This tendency isn't random; it's woven into how we navigate the world. We build identities around the emotions we feel safe showing—those that align with how we want to be seen and understood. Strength, kindness, confidence—these become the markers of our worth, the facets we present to the world with pride. But what about the emotions that don't fit this image? What happens to the anger, the fear, the sorrow that lies beneath the surface? Consider someone who prides themselves on always being calm and composed. To maintain that image, they suppress their anger, telling themselves it's a flaw, an imperfection that must be hidden. Yet, anger doesn't simply vanish when ignored—it festers. It grows in the shadows, silently transforming into resentment, passive-aggression, or even physical tension. It becomes an unseen force, shaping our actions and relationships from the dark.

This isn't unique to anger. The emotions we suppress—the fear we label as weakness, the sadness we dismiss as unnecessary, the vulnerability we fear will expose us—don't disappear. They wait in the shadows, gaining power in their exile. Like shadows stretching longer as the sun sets, these repressed parts of us become stronger the more we resist them. Fear buried deep transforms into anxiety that seeps into every corner of our lives, making even small decisions feel overwhelming. Sadness ignored becomes a heavy numbness, dissociating us from our joy, love, and connection. And anger, when locked away, cracks through the facade we've built, erupting in ways we can't predict or control.

Still, we persist in the struggle, convinced that if we just fight harder—suppress more forcefully, reject more completely—we'll find peace. We believe we can conquer the parts of ourselves that feel uncomfortable or threatening. But peace doesn't come from banishment. It doesn't come from dividing ourselves into acceptable and unacceptable, light and dark. Peace comes from belonging—from allowing every part of ourselves to take its rightful place in the whole.

To embrace the emotions we've labeled as undesirable is to recognize them not as threats, but as guides. Each one has a message, a truth to share. Anger arises to show us where our boundaries have been crossed. Sadness calls us to pause, to reflect on what we've lost and what we hold dear. Fear urges us to grow, to confront what we've avoided and step into the unknown. Even vulnerability, so often seen as a weakness, is a doorway to deeper connection. These emotions aren't flaws. They are profound teachers, offering wisdom we cannot access by any other means.

But embracing these emotions isn't easy. Imagine your consciousness as a radiant light, shining across the vast landscape of your inner world. That light, as it moves outward, inevitably encounters walls—barriers constructed over years from judgment, fear, and rigid ideas of what is right and wrong, acceptable and unacceptable. These walls cast long shadows across the psyche, dividing it into parts. Behind those walls lie the emotions and aspects of yourself you've exiled—the desires you've been told are selfish, the wounds you've deemed weak, the fears you've refused to face. These are not mistakes or flaws. They are parts of your wholeness, waiting to be illuminated.

In the shadowlands of your psyche, these exiled parts don't remain static. They grow, fed by shame, guilt, and rejection, mutating into forms that seem monstrous when glimpsed from afar. They become the saboteurs that undermine your best efforts, the critics that whisper words of doubt, the forces that pull at your confidence. But these "monsters" are not here to destroy you. They are simply the parts of you that have been left unseen for too long, longing for recognition and reintegration.

The more we resist these parts of ourselves, the more rigid the lines of duality become. We draw sharp boundaries between light and shadow, good and bad, strength and vulnerability, believing these divisions will keep us safe. But these lines are illusions. As we begin to embrace the shadow, the dualities that once felt so absolute start to blur. The walls of judgment and division begin to soften, and we see that the shadow is not a threat but a vital piece of our wholeness.

This is the dance of light and shadow, the intricate interplay that defines what it means to be human. It's not a battle to be won, but a rhythm to step into. When we stop fighting against the shadow and begin to move with it, the struggle transforms into something far more beautiful. The light illuminates the shadow, and the shadow gives depth and meaning to the light. Together, they create the fullness of who we are.

This dance isn't about perfection. It's not about fixing yourself or becoming a sanitized version of who you think you should be. It's about letting go of the need to divide yourself into acceptable and unacceptable parts, and instead embracing the complexity of your being. It's about recognizing that every emotion, every shadow, every light within you has its place. And as you do, you discover something profound: that wholeness isn't something you achieve. It's something you uncover, something that has always been there, waiting for you to see it.

By stepping into this dance, you align with the truth of your nature. You see that your emotions are not obstacles but pathways, guiding you toward authenticity, connection, and transformation. And in this embrace, you find a freedom that doesn't come from eliminating discomfort, but from knowing that every part of you belongs. You are not just the light or the shadow—you are the entire, vibrant dance.

Fight for Yourself (Not Against)

WE often find ourselves trapped in a relentless battle against ourselves, waging war on the very emotions and parts of our being that we've been taught to fear or reject. Anger, fear, shame, insecurity—these aspects of our inner world become targets for elimination in our quest to feel whole, confident, and worthy. Yet, the more we fight against them, the more they seem to strengthen their grip, refusing to disappear no matter how hard we push them into the shadows. This war is exhausting. It drains our energy, fractures our sense of self, and leaves us fragmented, chasing a version of perfection that was never meant to exist. And in the process, we lose sight of a profound truth: that the very emotions we are fighting to suppress are the ones holding the keys to our resilience, growth, and wholeness.

When we resist these feelings—when we try to numb, suppress, or eliminate them—we cut ourselves off from the full spectrum of who we are. In doing so, we also limit our capacity for joy, passion, and creativity. The light we cling to becomes dimmed when it isn't balanced by the richness of our shadows. We become muted, a faded version of the vibrant, multidimensional beings we were born to be. This endless cycle of repression and struggle doesn't protect us; it diminishes us, keeping us from living fully and authentically.

Think back to a time in your life when you faced a profound challenge—perhaps a health crisis, a difficult relationship, or a professional setback. In those moments, you likely felt a storm of emotions: fear, anger, despair, frustration. The instinct for many of us is to push those feelings aside, to "power through" and appear strong. We tell ourselves that admitting to fear or sadness is a sign of weakness, that acknowledging anger will make us seem out of control, or that leaning into vulnerability will expose us to harm. And so, we suppress those feelings, burying them deep as we try to keep moving forward.

But suppressing emotions comes at a cost. It's like trying to swim against a powerful current—every effort to push them away leaves us more exhausted, more fragmented, and less equipped to deal with the actual challenge in front of us. Our energy is spent fighting ourselves rather than confronting what truly needs our attention. We divide our internal resources, turning what could be a source of strength into a battleground. The more we resist, the more the current drags us under.

What if, instead, you allowed yourself to feel everything fully, without judgment? What if you leaned into fear and let it sharpen your awareness, acknowledged anger and let it guide you to necessary action, or allowed sadness to remind you of what truly matters? This isn't about wallowing in negativity or letting emotions overwhelm you—it's about integration. It's about using every part of your emotional experience to navigate life's challenges with greater clarity and resilience. By doing this, you transform pain into wisdom, struggle into strength, and vulnerability into connection.

Imagine stepping into a job interview, nervous and anxious, as most people would be. Instead of hiding those nerves behind a mask of forced confidence, what if you acknowledged them? What if you let yourself say,

"I'm a little nervous because I care so much about this opportunity"? That simple act of honesty could completely shift the experience—for you and for the interviewer. By admitting to your nerves, you allow yourself to relax, focus, and be present. Your vulnerability doesn't weaken you; it makes you relatable, human, real. Rather than wasting energy on maintaining a perfect facade, you engage fully and show the depth of your enthusiasm. What once felt like a source of stress becomes a tool for connection and self-expression.

Or think about a heated argument with someone you love. How often do we lash out defensively, afraid to admit our deeper fears or insecurities? In doing so, we escalate the conflict, protecting ourselves with anger rather than revealing the truth underneath it. But what if, instead of shielding yourself, you let the other person in? Imagine saying, "I feel hurt and frustrated because I care so deeply about our relationship, and I'm afraid of losing this connection." Such vulnerability has the power to shift the dynamic entirely. It disarms tension and invites your loved one to meet you in a space of honesty and compassion. By embracing the full range of your emotions—hurt, frustration, love, and longing—you create an opportunity for deeper understanding and growth.

By acknowledging and accepting your emotions, you turn stress into an asset. Instead of battling with yourself, you gain clarity and use your emotions as a guide. This mindset isn't just helpful in interviews—it strengthens you in every part of life, where the pressure to appear perfect can hold you back.

Consider admitting to feelings like jealousy, fear, and insecurity during such conflicts. These admissions are powerful because they strip away the defensive armor and reveal the genuine emotions driving the argument. When you acknowledge and communicate these emotions, you create a space where both parties can be human, imperfect, and empathetic. This honest exchange transforms moments of conflict into opportunities for growth, where relationships can evolve and deepen through shared understanding and compassion.

In these moments, by bringing your whole self to the table – both your positive and your negative qualities – you increase your chances of success and fulfillment. Life is tough enough as it is. Each day brings its own set of challenges—relationships to nurture, responsibilities to fulfill, goals to pursue, and setbacks to endure. There are battles we cannot avoid, struggles that demand our energy, focus, and resilience. But when we are caught in an inner war, divided against ourselves, those external challenges can feel insurmountable. How can we possibly face the battles of life when so much of our strength is wasted fighting the very essence of who we are?

Instead of using our energy to suppress, deny, or fight the parts of ourselves we find uncomfortable, we can choose a different path. We can choose to embrace our whole being—our light and shadow, our strengths and flaws, our confidence and insecurities. By doing so, we stop pouring our resources into an unwinnable internal conflict. We free ourselves to focus on what truly matters: the real battles, the ones that lie beyond our inner struggle. When we stop resisting ourselves, we become whole. And in that wholeness, we discover a reservoir of strength, creativity, and resilience we never knew we had.

So, face every storm with your whole self—shadow and light, arm in arm. When the civil war inside you ends, energy flows to what matters and clarity sharpens each step. The world will still test you, but when you are no longer divided within, you are infinitely stronger. You become not just a pawn in life's battles, but a force, capable of navigating them with courage and purpose. Embracing yourself isn't just a gift to you—it's the foundation for how you meet and move through the world. And that, above all else, is the strength we all need to thrive.

Weathering the Storm

THE journey of embracing the forbidden emotions we've exiled to the shadows can feel daunting. It asks us to face not only the raw intensity of these emotions but also the weight of our own judgments and repressions. It demands patience and gentleness with ourselves, a willingness to acknowledge the storm within without being swept away by it. This turbulence, as overwhelming as it may seem, is not a sign that something is wrong—it's a natural and necessary part of the journey.

Too often, we conflate our consciousness with our thinking mind—the endless stream of thoughts, judgments, and interpretations that fill our mental space. But consciousness is something far deeper and more fundamental. It is the pure awareness that lies beneath all of our experiences, the silent and steady witness that observes our thoughts, emotions, and sensations without judgment. This awareness is the foundation of who we are—a space vast enough to hold both the storms and the stillness, the light and the shadow.

When we encounter challenging emotions, our initial reaction is often impulsive. The raw energy of anger, fear, or sadness can feel overwhelming, dictating our behavior in ways that perpetuate the very pain we're trying to escape. Anger may cause us to lash out, saying things we later regret, inflicting wounds on those we care about. Fear may make us withdraw, shutting ourselves off from the connection and support we desperately need. Sadness can leave us immobilized, pulling us into a spiral of inaction and despair. In these moments, we react to the emotion instead of being present with it. This reactivity is an attempt to discharge the discomfort, to rid ourselves of the emotional storm as quickly as possible. Yet, instead of providing relief, these impulsive reactions often deepen the turmoil, leaving us even further from the clarity and peace we seek.

By recognizing these habitual patterns and bringing mindful awareness to our emotions, we can begin to break the cycle. This awareness doesn't mean suppressing or avoiding our feelings—it means pausing, observing them as they arise, and allowing ourselves to experience them fully without becoming entangled. This shift from reactivity to presence creates the possibility of responding to our emotions in a way that supports growth and healing rather than perpetuating pain.

When an intense emotion arises, our mind often leaps into overdrive, trying to process, control, or escape what we're feeling. Hurt, for example, can trigger an endless loop of inner dialogue—analyzing every detail, assigning blame, imagining alternative outcomes, or rationalizing the pain away. Instead of simply feeling the emotion and letting it move through us, we become entangled in our thoughts, crafting narratives, criticizing ourselves, or arguing with the situation. This mental reactivity only distances us from the raw emotional experience and its transformative potential.

Consider anxiety. When it surfaces, it rarely stays confined to a simple signal in the body. Instead, the mind spirals into "what ifs," conjuring worst-case scenarios and attempting to prepare for every imaginable threat, no matter how unlikely. This frantic problem-solving amplifies the anxiety, dragging us deeper into its grip. Or take insecurity: when it arises, instead of acknowledging its presence, we often attempt to overpower it mentally, repeating affirmations or rehearsing endlessly in an effort to suppress the discomfort. These strategies, though well-intentioned, only entrench us further in the emotion, creating an exhausting cycle of resistance and self-doubt.

These mental patterns—whether overthinking, rationalizing, or battling the emotion head-on—are all attempts to avoid the rawness of the experience. They offer a false sense of control—a temporary shield against the unpredictable nature of life. Yet, instead of providing relief, they amplify our suffering, keeping us stuck in our heads and disconnected from the wisdom of our bodies. By resisting our emotions or trying to think our way out of them, we inadvertently give them more power.

The path to emotional integration lies not in escape but in presence. It invites us to embody our awareness in the present moment, allowing emotions to arise fully and flow through us without resistance or judgment. It requires us to recognize that our emotions cannot harm us; it's our reactivity to them that causes suffering. Through still, silent awareness, we create a safe container for our emotions, observing them with curiosity and compassion. In doing so, we come to see their impermanence—how they rise, peak, and naturally dissipate. We realize that we are larger than any single emotional state.

This practice also reveals that emotions are not static entities but dynamic energies, like weather patterns moving through the vast sky of our consciousness. Storms of anger or sadness eventually give way to moments of calm and clarity. By allowing emotions to simply be, without trying to fix or control them, we discover our inner resilience and adaptability.

This is the dance of emotions: a courageous engagement with the full spectrum of our inner experience. It's a journey of self-discovery and self-acceptance, a willingness to embrace our contradictions and complexities. Through this dance, we come to understand that our emotions are not enemies. They are the vivid energies that shape our lives, the raw materials of our deepest insights and most meaningful moments.

So, let's dance—not to escape, but to fully embrace ourselves. Let's dance—not to numb our pain, but to transform it into wisdom. Let's dance—not to reject our humanity, but to celebrate it in all its messy, beautiful fullness. For it is through this dance of awareness and emotion that we find our way home to ourselves, to the unshakable wholeness that is our true nature.

Chapter Ten

Dreaming Your Life

Chapter Eleven

BREAKING THE RULES IN THE GAME OF PERFECTION

In the heart of the Museum of Modern Art, amidst the echoes of shuffling feet and muffled sniffles, a young woman takes a seat across from Marina Abramović. As she settles into the chair, her eyes meet Marina's unwavering gaze, and in that instant, something deep within her begins to stir.

The young woman's eyes, already glistening with the first hints of tears, are windows into a soul burdened by the weight of long-ignored emotions. As she locks eyes with Marina, the floodgates of her inner world burst open, and years of carefully concealed pain come rushing to the surface.

In the silence of this shared moment, the young woman confronts the masks she has worn for so long – the smiling facade she presents to the world, the stoic determination with which she faces each day, the brave front she puts up to hide the turmoil within. Under Marina's gentle, unwavering gaze, these masks begin to crack and fall away, revealing the truth of her being.

Tears stream down her face as she allows herself, perhaps for the first time in years, to fully feel the depths of her own sadness, despair, and loneliness.

In the stillness of the atrium, she surrenders to the overwhelming tide of emotion, letting it wash over her in waves of catharsis and release.

There are no words exchanged between the two women, no grand gestures or dramatic pronouncements. Yet, in the simple act of being seen, truly seen, by another human being, the young woman finds a glimmer of solace amidst the pain. She feels, if only for a moment, less alone in her struggle, less burdened by the weight of her unspoken sorrows.

The beauty of Marina's performance, "The Artist is Present," lies in its minimalism. There are no grand gestures, no elaborate sets or costumes. Instead, the power of the piece is found in the simple, yet profound, act of two people sharing a moment of connection. It's a reminder of the importance of slowing down, of taking the time to truly see and be seen by another human being.

I once had the privilege of speaking with Marina about this piece, and she shared with me her motivation behind it. "In New York," she said, "nobody stops to look each other in the eyes." In a city that never sleeps, where people are always rushing from one place to another, it's easy to forget the value of genuine human connection, of creating moments where we can strip away our masks and be truly present with one another.

But the issue goes deeper than just the fast pace of modern life. As a society, we have grown increasingly disconnected from ourselves. We seek to escape, not just from the external pressures and stresses of the world, but from the inner voices and ghosts that haunt us. We are tormented by the uncomfortable, sometimes even painful, experience of inhabiting our own being, and we'll go to great lengths to avoid confronting our own selves.

In this sense, Marina Abramović was not merely offering a moment of human connection—she was offering herself as a mirror. In a world where people rush past one another without a second glance, where eye contact feels intrusive and intimacy is rationed, she invited strangers to sit and confront something far more unsettling than another person's gaze: their own reflection. Beneath the surface of her unwavering presence, she became the still water in which people could see themselves with unflinching clarity.

And this is what made "The Artist is Present" so profoundly unsettling for many. It was not just about being seen by another—it was about seeing oneself, stripped of performance, without the distractions we use to shield ourselves from our own depths. In that silence, where there was nowhere to hide, many broke down. Because looking into the eyes of another, truly looking, means facing the parts of ourselves we have long avoided.

This is the same challenge we wrestle with every day, whether we acknowledge it or not. The relentless pursuit of distractions, the endless cycle of work, entertainment, and ambition, the curated online personas—all of it keeps us from staring too long into the mirror of our own being. But what are we so afraid to see? What keeps us so disconnected? What are we trying so desperately to escape?

Beneath the surface of our daily routines, there is a hidden world—the silent battlefield of the mind, where the most insidious games unfold. The game of self-doubt, whispering that we are never enough. The game of guilt, convincing us that every misstep is proof of our unworthiness. The game of comparison, measuring our worth against the illusions of others. These games play out in the shadows, shaping our thoughts, our choices, our very sense of self. We rarely acknowledge their hold over us, but they dictate so much of how we move through life. And so, we keep running. We drown ourselves in busyness, in screens, in substances, in fleeting highs, in anything that can momentarily silence the ghosts that haunt us.

Steven Kotler's research into the altered states economy quantifies this restless search, estimating that humanity spends over $4 trillion annually in pursuit of experiences that allow us to break free from ourselves. This staggering figure speaks to more than just economic trends—it reveals a deep and universal struggle. Perhaps no pursuit is more profound, no longing more insatiable, than the desire to transcend the confines of our own minds. It is our highest ambition and yet, paradoxically, our most elusive dream—to slip beyond the boundaries of self, to loosen the grip of identity, to taste, even for a moment, the freedom of simply being. And yet, despite all our efforts, despite the vast industries built around transformation and self-liberation, the truth remains: escaping ourselves is both our greatest longing and our most impossible feat.

We humans live imprisoned by our own structures, and we dream of a way out. While there are ways to find relief, we seem fated to always return to the same internal architecture, the familiar corridors of our own mind. No matter how far we run, how high we climb, or how deeply we dive into distraction, we come back to ourselves, back to the framework that shapes our every thought, reaction, and belief.

At first, it may seem like the walls are external—society, expectation, circumstance. But if we look closer, we see that the most relentless prison is not built around us, but within us. We are captives of an inner tyrant that does not chain us with iron but with ideals, not with threats but with whispered imperatives. It tells us that we must be better, that we must do more, that who we are is never quite enough.

And so, we obey. We push harder, strive further, hold ourselves to standards so high they barely seem human. The tyrant does not scream or rage—it is quiet, insidious, tireless. It takes the shape of self-discipline, of noble aspiration, of the will to improve. But beneath the surface, something else is driving it. Something deeper, more primal. A guilt that has no name, a pressure that has no origin.

Where does it come from? Why do we carry this invisible weight, this relentless need to prove, perfect, and purify ourselves? The surface answers are easy—upbringing, cultural conditioning, societal pressure. But the truth runs deeper. This is not just about meeting expectations or avoiding failure. It is something older, something woven into the very foundations of our subconscious.

We are haunted by an unspoken fear of unworthiness—an existential anxiety that lingers deep within us, passed down through generations as an unconscious inheritance. It is a voice so embedded in our being that we mistake it for our own, disguising itself as conscience, ambition, or duty. This shadow has been cast by centuries of religious dogma, the weight of sin and redemption, the collective memory of persecution, and the relentless need for approval—from gods, parents, and unseen judges.

And so, we enter the game of perfection—an endless chase with no finish line, no moment of victory, only a horizon that keeps receding. We set impossible standards for ourselves, ones we would never impose on others, yet we hold ourselves to them mercilessly. We measure our worth in achievements, in discipline, in control. Every flaw, every shortcoming, every moment of perceived weakness becomes a reason for self-punishment.

This is not just conscious striving; it is a deeply ingrained compulsion. A reflex. A survival mechanism. Somewhere inside, we believe that if we can just get it right—be flawless, worthy, untouchable—then maybe, just maybe, we will finally feel safe. But the game is rigged. The moment we approach that imaginary threshold, the standard shifts again, and we are left running once more, chasing a perfection that does not exist.

Yet this game is not a simple pursuit; it is a carefully constructed system. The rules are unwritten but deeply ingrained. The prize is an illusion, always shimmering just beyond reach. The penalty is relentless self-reproach, the unshakable guilt that whispers we are falling behind.

And then there are the pieces—the unseen mechanics that keep us ensnared. They shape how we move, how we measure ourselves, how we push forward without question. We rarely stop to name them, yet they define the game. And so, we keep playing, unaware of what truly drives us. Unaware of who—or what—holds the power.

The Higher Self

THERE is a version of you—pure, unwavering, untouchable. A self that moves through the world with effortless flow, unshaken by fear, unburdened by doubt. This is your Higher Self, the embodiment of your full potential, the version of you who has transcended hesitation, who has mastered discipline, who radiates wisdom, purpose, and love in every breath. It is the you who never falters, never stumbles, never succumbs to weakness. The one who always knows the right words to say, the right actions to take.

The one who is fearless in pursuit of dreams, immune to the chaos of life, untangled from the weight of human frailty.

It is the whisper in your soul, calling you toward expansion, urging you to embody your highest frequency. It tells you to rise, to evolve, to step into the full expression of your divine potential. It is the voice that says: *You are here to shine. You are here to embody your highest truth. You were not made for limitation*. It beckons you toward transformation and mastery, toward achieving control over yourself and your reality. And you believe it—because how could you not? How could you refuse the promise of stepping into their best version—the version that has finally unlocked the fullness of their being?

So you listen. You obey. You refine yourself. You sculpt your mind, discipline your body, cleanse your soul. You cast aside your imperfections like old skins, carving away every flaw in the pursuit of your highest potential. You silence your anger, swallow your fears, polish yourself into something sharper, cleaner, brighter. You chase perfection, because perfection, you believe, is where freedom lives.

And yet, the more you climb, the further the summit stretches beyond your reach. The more you refine yourself, the more flaws you uncover. No matter how much you master, how much you grow, how much you sacrifice—the Higher Self is always ahead, always above, always waiting just beyond your grasp.

You embrace its contradictions without even questioning them. When you push yourself to work harder, it tells you are neglecting joy. When you rest, it whispers that you are wasting your potential. When you choose ambition, it scolds you for selfishness. When you prioritize love, it warns you of stagnation. It's never satisfied. And so, neither are you.

Is it divine guidance, or an endless chase? A path to liberation, or a prison disguised as transcendence? The Higher Self stands before you like a shimmering mirage—always ahead, always just out of reach. No matter how much you refine, how much you expand, how much you surrender, it is never enough. It does not celebrate your progress; it only raises the bar. It does not offer rest; it only demands more. It does not embrace you as you are; it keeps whispering that you must become something greater. A god that does not bless, only beckons. A light that does not illuminate, only blinds. A promise that does not fulfill, only keeps you running.

And so, we keep going, convinced that just beyond the next breakthrough, the next refinement, the next layer of self-mastery, we will finally reach the promised land. A state of being where guilt no longer gnaws at us, where anxiety dissolves, where doubt no longer clouds our mind. We tell ourselves that once we become aligned enough, disciplined enough, healed enough, we will step into a life where every choice feels effortless, where every moment is infused with clarity and peace. We chase the idea that one day, we will wake up and find ourselves weightless—free from the burdens that have followed us for so long. And so we push forward, sacrificing rest for progress, authenticity for aspiration, believing that if we just keep refining, keep striving, we will finally become untouchable.

At first, it feels exhilarating—this devotion to growth, this commitment to becoming your best self. You set intentions, cultivate discipline, align with purpose. You chase enlightenment, thinking that just a little more effort, just a little more mastery, will finally bring you peace. You tell yourself this is freedom. But if you pause, if you step back from the endless loop of self-optimization, you might start to see the trap. Are you evolving, or are you just rejecting yourself in more sophisticated ways?

Because what happens when you finally reach the goal? When you become more disciplined, more enlightened, more at peace? Does the voice relent? Does it ever say, "You've arrived. You are whole. You can rest"? No. It only raises the bar. It tells you there's still more to refine, more to fix, more to transcend.

It is a race that cannot be won.

A cycle that disguises itself as transformation, where each step promises fulfillment, yet the finish line keeps moving. You keep pushing, convinced that the struggle is a sign of progress. But the truth is far simpler: you are chasing a version of yourself that does not exist.

And beneath the glow of the Higher Self lurks something far less divine—a quiet, unshakable guilt. The feeling that you are never quite enough, that no matter how much you achieve, there is still something missing. The belief that failure is always looming, waiting to expose your flaws, ready to drag you back down the moment you falter.

Because that's the real price of this pursuit. For every Higher Self, there is a shadow. And that shadow is failure. The more you chase perfection, the more unbearable it becomes to fall short. And so, you live in quiet fear—not just of not reaching the ideal, but of what it means when you inevitably don't.

Failure

"I am a failure". The words settle deep in my chest, heavy and unrelenting. They do not scream—they whisper, steady and familiar, weaving themselves into the fabric of my thoughts, tinting every memory, every missed opportunity, every moment I did not live up to who I was supposed to be. I look back and see a trail of wrong turns and wasted time, a life that should have been more, a self that should have risen higher.

I should be further along by now. I should have achieved more, done more, been more. Time slips through my fingers, a relentless tide, and with each passing moment, I feel myself sinking, drifting further from the person I was meant to become. The weight of it is suffocating—this quiet certainty that I have fallen behind, that I am losing, that I have somehow failed at life itself.

Failure is not just a moment, an event, a single misstep. It is a shadow, a phantom that lingers at the edges of every effort, waiting for the moment I falter. It does not need to announce itself; it is simply there, threading doubt through every action, whispering that I am not enough. It wears a thousand disguises. In the presence of others, it compares, measures, finds me lacking. When I fall short of my own expectations, it reminds me of every flaw, every weakness, every way in which I do not measure up. It does not need proof—it has already passed judgment.

It thrives on the belief that my worth is something to be earned, that I am only as valuable as my achievements, my discipline, my ability to mold myself into an image of success. It feeds off a world that glorifies perfection, that tells stories of self-made greatness, that sells the myth of those who have figured it all out. But beneath that illusion lies a quiet, brutal truth—the closer we chase perfection, the sharper the sting of failure. They are not opposites, but reflections of each other. Failure is the shadow cast by the blinding light of the Higher Self, the inevitable price of reaching for the unattainable.

For some, failure is a constant undercurrent in their work, a gnawing sense that they are always behind, always struggling to catch up. No matter how much they accomplish, they feel like imposters, frauds waiting to be exposed. For others, failure seeps into their relationships, convincing them that they are unworthy of love, that every connection is fragile, that it is only a matter of time before they disappoint, before they are left behind. It adapts, shifts, takes the shape of whatever insecurity lies deepest, speaking in the voice we trust the most—our own.

It is clever, this illusion, always waiting in the moments when we are most vulnerable. It tells us we are too late, too old, too broken. That the life we long for is meant for someone else. That we should settle, stay small, accept less, because we were never destined for more. And we believe it, because the rules of this game have been set long before we ever questioned them.

But what if failure is not proof of our inadequacy, but of the impossible nature of the game itself? What if the problem has never been that we are falling short, but that we were never meant to win? The game is rigged—the Higher Self and Failure are two sides of the same coin, pulling us further from who we truly are. With every move, every attempt to become worthy, every effort to outrun failure, we stray further from ourselves. We lose sight of our own desires, our own rhythm, our own truth. We become puppets in a game that was never ours to begin with, chasing illusions that grow stronger the more we feed them. And all the while, the peace, authenticity, and wholeness we seek remain where it has always been. Not at the finish line. Not beyond the next breakthrough.

But here, in the self we abandoned to chase a version of who we thought we had to be.

The True Self

THERE is a moment when the chase finally slows, when the endless striving falters, and something deeper begins to emerge. It is not the shining vision of the Higher Self, nor the shadow of Failure—it is something more raw, more real. The True Self. Not the construct of perfection, not the collection of achievements and mistakes, but the essence that has been there all along, beneath the noise, beneath the illusions.

For so long, life felt like a battlefield of victories and defeats, moments of soaring achievement followed by crushing disappointment. But stepping back, a different picture begins to take shape—one not defined by wins and losses, but by something more fluid, more natural. A life lived. A path shaped by choices, some wise, some reckless, all of them leading to this moment. There were dreams realized, and others left behind. There was love given and love lost, joy and sorrow woven together in a rhythm as ancient as the tide. And for all its imperfections, this life—this imperfect, unscripted life—is real in a way that the Higher Self never was.

The mind clings to the fantasy that another version of this life could have been better, that different choices would have led to greater success, to deeper fulfillment, to the long-awaited feeling of being enough. But every road comes with its own burdens. Every path winds through light and shadow. There is no alternate life where struggle does not exist, where self-doubt never creeps in, where everything unfolds in flawless harmony. The illusion was never that we failed—the illusion was that there was ever a perfect path to begin with.

With this realization, the grip of Failure begins to loosen. Not because of a sudden revelation of worthiness, not because of some final achievement that redeems all past shortcomings, but because the very premise of the game starts to dissolve. The game of perfection was never about reaching an ultimate state of being—it was about distraction. A relentless effort to outrun the truth that we were never meant to be flawless, that our value was never tied to how much we achieve or how little we falter.

Beneath the layers of expectation, beyond the weight of striving, our True Self waits. This is not the self of grandiose fantasies or crushing self-doubt, but the self that exists beyond these constructs, the self that is grounded in the raw, unfiltered reality of our human experience.

When we strip away the layers of expectation and judgment, the oppressive notions of who we should be and what we should achieve, we are left with something far more essential, far more authentic. We see ourselves not as a collection of successes and failures, triumphs and defeats, but as a living, breathing, ever-evolving being, a person in the most fundamental sense of the word.

The True Self is not defined by its goodness or badness, its perfection or imperfection. It's simply a human being navigating the complexities of existence. It's a self that dreams and struggles, that loves and fears, that experiences the full spectrum of life's joys and sorrows. And it's a self that cannot be reduced to any single definition, any fixed identity, for it's always in a state of becoming, always learning, growing and transforming.

But why do we stray so far from this self? Why do we abandon it in favor of illusions that exhaust and diminish us? At the core of this departure lies a deeply ingrained desire—the need to feel exceptional. To be unique, to stand above the ordinary, to craft an identity that sets us apart. This hunger for significance fuels the chase, convinces us that we must be more than what we are.

We seek validation through our successes, our possessions, our carefully curated identities. We tell ourselves that our experiences, our pain, our triumphs set us apart from others, that our journey is somehow singular. Even in suffering, we find ways to elevate our uniqueness—believing that our burdens are deeper, our wounds more profound, our struggles more complex than those of the rest of humanity.

And yet, this pursuit of specialness comes at a cost. In trying to rise above, we isolate ourselves. In insisting on our uniqueness, we sever the very connections that give life meaning. We forget that our struggles, no matter how personal, are not ours alone. The pain we carry, the longing we feel, the fears that keep us awake at night—these are not signs of separation, but of belonging. They are the very threads that weave us into the fabric of humanity.

When we cling to the idea that we are somehow different, that no one could possibly understand our experience, we build walls where there should be doors. n this isolation, we lose sight of the True Self. We drift further from the ground of our being, chasing an ever-elusive sense of worth. We exhaust ourselves trying to prove something—our brilliance, our pain, our superiority, our worthiness—when all along, the only thing that needed to be done was to return.

To find our way back to the True Self, we must be willing to let go of the illusion of specialness. We must have the courage to face the reality of our shared humanity, to recognize that our joys and sorrows, our strengths and weaknesses, are not marks of distinction, but threads that bind us together in the great web of life.

This requires a profound humility, a willingness to step down from the pedestal of our own imagined superiority and take our place among the ranks of the ordinary. It means learning to find meaning and purpose not in the pursuit of specialness, but in the cultivation of our unique gifts in service to the greater whole.

Like the untamed beauty of nature itself, our True Self is not always pretty or perfect. It can be fierce and powerful, wild and unpredictable. It can be both nurturing and destructive, gentle and violent. It contains within it the full spectrum of human potential, the light and the shadow, the beautiful and the terrible.

In the sanctuary of the True Self, we find a place of deep rest. A place where we can simply be, without judgment or expectation. A place of great courage and compassion, where we can face the fullness of our humanity with honesty.

And from this place of grounded presence, we can begin to engage with the world in a new way.

We can bring our whole self to the table, our strengths and our weaknesses, our joys and our sorrows. We can meet life's challenges with resilience and adaptability, knowing that we have the resources within us to weather any storm.

From the moment we enter this world, we are driven by a deep, unspoken longing—to belong, to be seen, to be loved exactly as we are. But in our quest for acceptance, we learn to play the game of perfection, shaping ourselves to fit the expectations of others, much like a child reaching for the approval of their parents. We twist, shrink, and mold ourselves into the image of who we think we should be, convinced that if we can just meet the impossible standard, if we can just get it right, we will finally be worthy of love.

But it's only when we take true ownership of ourselves, when we embrace our authentic and imperfect being, that we can truly feel a sense of belonging. By stripping away the illusions of perfection and specialness, we remove the barriers that keep us separate from the natural world, from the fundamental ground of our existence.

The home of the True Self is where we find our connection with Nature: not with some idealized, perfect notion of Nature, but with Nature in all its raw, untamed beauty. This is the Nature that shapes the world through cataclysmic events – the rumbling of earthquakes, the fury of tornadoes, the icy chill of glacial ages, and the searing heat of volcanic eruptions. It is the Nature where the jaguar stalks its prey, where the wind whips through the trees, casting newborn birds from their nests to the unforgiving ground below.

This is the Nature to which we belong, the primal force that courses through our veins and beats in our hearts. We are children of the Earth, a manifestation of the same elemental energies that shape the mountains and stir the oceans. Like Nature herself, we are beings of exquisite beauty and unimaginable power, capable of both nurturing life and unleashing destruction.

When we come home to our True Self, we tap into this ancient connection, this unbreakable bond with the intelligence of life itself. We return to the womb of Nature, the source of our being, and find there a sense of belonging that transcends the fleeting approval of others or the empty promises of the Higher Self.

In this place of primal connection, we can finally rest in the truth of who we are. We can embrace our human nature in all its complexity and contradictions, knowing that we are an integral part of the great web of life. There, we can find the courage to face our shadows and our light, to dance with our demons and our angels, secure in the knowledge that we are held in the embrace of the Ancient Mother.

Chapter Twelve

BEYOND REASON

In the soft, ethereal glow of the dance studio, I stand motionless, my eyelids gently closed, my breath rising and falling like a slow tide. Thiago's voice, both distant and near, guides me beyond the edges of this space, inviting me to let go. My awareness unfurls like a bird slipping its cage, lifting beyond reason, carried by the weightless pull of imagination. I let my mind's eye sweep across the curve of the Earth, gliding over oceans and continents, tracing the vastness of the world as I prepare to dissolve into the dance.

Free from the constraints of reason, my imagination circles the whole earth in a single, unbroken arc. As it completes its journey, I see my own back from afar—small, distant, yet unmistakably mine. My vision draws closer, tracing the curve of my spine until it settles at the base of my neck. In this meeting point of body and spirit, I arrive. From this stillness, I begin to move, no longer just myself, but a vessel for the voices and echoes of those who came before, their stories woven into my bones.

In ancient Japan, families honored their departed by laying them to rest beneath the gentle shade of a cherry blossom tree—a living monument to the fleeting beauty of existence. As I surrender to the dance, I feel the arc of my life unfold within me, from the first gasp of air filling my lungs to the final whisper of breath dissolving into silence. I dance my memories, my joys and sorrows, the echoes of laughter and the weight of longing, each movement weaving the story of my existence. In this moment, I glimpse my own passing—my body sinking into the earth as a delicate Sakura tree rises from the soft soil, its roots entwining with my bones in a quiet, eternal embrace.

My awareness drifts along one of these subterranean pathways, descending into the realm of my ancestors until I stand before my grandmother's essence. In an instant, her joys and sorrows, her triumphs and burdens, her deepest dreams and quiet fears surge through me. My body becomes a vessel, a conduit for her spirit, and I surrender to the dance, giving movement to her memory. I am a blossom unfurling on the branches of the great tree—a fleeting miracle, as ephemeral as the petals of the cherry blossom.

As the dance reaches its peak, the flower loosens its hold on the branch, drifting softly to the earth, returning to the nurturing soil that once gave it life. I, too, am drawn back into the embrace of the earth, my consciousness flowing along another root until I stand before an ancestor from six generations past. A young boy of indigenous heritage, his emotions and story surge through me, each pulse etching his existence into my being. My body becomes a living chronicle, carrying his memory in every breath, every movement, every trembling note of the dance.

Through my movements, I embody the elation and freedom of his people, but also the devastation that consumed them. His grief wracks my body as he cries out in solitude, torn from his family by the cruelty of conquest—only to find an unlikely solace in the compassion of a warrior from the very forces that shattered his world. And so, I dance, channeling the rapture and the sorrow, the resilience and the longing that shaped his journey. As his life force wanes, I feel the exultation of his spirit bursting forth—one final bloom before it drifts from the tree, carried on the wind's currents until it settles upon the earth. And once more, I dissolve into the intricate web of my ancestral origins.

For what feels like an eternity, I am lost in the dance, my identity unraveling, my consciousness stripped bare—a blank canvas where the deepest imprints of my lineage come alive. In this boundless space, I become a passage for countless lives and countless deaths, each one a flower blooming at dawn and withering by dusk. I am no longer the dancer, nor the dance, but the thread through which existence flows.

When, at last, my eyes open, my breath unsteady, my skin glistening with sweat, I realize—Butoh has passed through me. Life and death have danced within me, and I have become their vessel.

Butoh is a Japanese dance form where life and death entwine, their steps inseparable, each shaping the other in perfect harmony. The dancer does not move through space; rather, space moves through them, their gestures emerging not from thought, but from a place of raw intuition and surrender.

Imagination is the lifeblood of Butoh. Like a child conjuring entire worlds from the fabric of pure creativity, the Butoh dancer inhabits a landscape of sensation and dream. Yet, there is no analysis here, no judgment, no need for reason. The dancer is granted the freedom to be utterly, beautifully mad.

Through Butoh, we glimpse a rare moment of lucidity—one in which we are free from the rigid grip of intellect, unshackled from the tyranny of constant analysis. In this space, movement is not dictated by thought but flows from a deeper, more primal source. It is a reminder that while logic and reason have brought us great achievements, they are but a single facet of the vast, multifaceted jewel that is the human psyche.

As we've explored in earlier chapters, our reality is never encountered in its raw form but is instead shaped and colored by the prism of our subjective experience. Before anything takes its place within the constellation of our personal universe, it passes through the unseen currents of perception, memory, and emotion. The totality of our understanding—our beliefs, our sense of self—does not arise from logic alone but from the ineffable realm of inner experience, a domain that flows beyond the reach of pure reason.

In our unwavering devotion to the rational mind, we risk severing the very roots that tether us to the instinctual depths of our being. We drift away from the wild, uncharted landscapes of our inner world, trading the raw splendor of the psyche for the sterile confines of "objective" consciousness. In our fervent embrace of Descartes' famous axiom, "I think, therefore I am," we have, as a collective, overlooked a deeper truth—that thought is but a single thread in the fabric of existence. Life is woven from far richer, more intricate strands, pulsing with color, sensation, and mystery, far beyond the reach of intellect alone.

By elevating the Cartesian cogito as the supreme arbiter of reality, we have unknowingly confined ourselves to a world as rigid and constrained as the two-dimensional plane of his mathematical musings. Just as the Cartesian coordinate system reduces the richness of existence to a sterile grid of lines and points, so too does our fixation on reason and logic flatten the vast, intricate landscape of human experience. In this narrow framework, the depth, texture, and vitality of life are stripped away, leaving behind only a pale schematic of what it means to be truly alive.

When we insist on filtering every moment through the lens of the intellect, we bind ourselves to an endless struggle—forever attempting to impose order and meaning upon a reality that refuses to be contained. We become entangled in analysis, dissecting the world rather than inhabiting it, mistaking understanding for experience. In doing so, we hold ourselves at a distance from life itself, when, perhaps, the deepest truth lies not in grasping, but in surrendering—to the raw, unmediated pulse of existence.

Science has undeniably brought extraordinary advancements to our lives. From the eradication of deadly diseases to the exploration of the cosmos, from life-enhancing technologies to the unraveling of nature's deepest mysteries, it has been a guiding force of progress and enlightenment. It has expanded the frontiers of human understanding, revealing wonders we once thought impossible.

Yet, in our fervor to embrace these gifts, we have also stumbled into a blind spot—one of quiet arrogance. The scientific method, with its insistence on empirical evidence and reproducibility, has become the ultimate gatekeeper of truth. We have grown accustomed to accepting only what can be measured and proven, dismissing all else as illusion or superstition. In doing so, we have narrowed our perception of reality, excluding entire dimensions of experience and knowledge that lie beyond the reach of instruments and equations.

This rigid, mechanistic view of the world—born from the Scientific Revolution and championed by thinkers like Newton and Descartes—has led us to see the universe as little more than a vast machine, a clockwork of gears and levers to be dissected, analyzed, and controlled. In the process, we have stripped reality of its mystery, losing the awe that once filled our ancestors, the deep sense of the sacred that once infused every aspect of life.

By cementing this perspective, we have severed our connection to the Earth—the very source of our existence. Gaia, once revered as a living, breathing force, has been reduced to a commodity, an object to be exploited in the relentless pursuit of progress. We have forgotten that we are not separate from nature but woven into its fabric, part of an intricate, delicate balance that sustains us, if only we choose to remember.

Our arrogance has made us blind to the consequences of our own hands, to the destruction left in the wake of our relentless pursuit of dominion over nature. We have polluted the air, poisoned the waters, and stripped the land bare—all in the name of progress, as if the Earth were ours to command. But in our hunger to control, we have forgotten a deeper truth: we are not its masters, but a part of it, bound to its rhythms and dependent on its balance. To harm the Earth is to harm ourselves—to preserve it is simply to honor the life that sustains us.

What lies beyond the constraints of the intellect? Beyond the ceaseless need to define, categorize, and control? There is a realm untouched by logic, where mystery and magic still breathe. It is the realm of wonder, of awe, of the silent knowing that does not speak in words but in sensation, in presence, in the pulse of existence.

To enter this space, we must first break the spell of the intellect—not to reject it, but to loosen its grip, to recognize it for what it truly is: a tool, not a master. Like a Butoh dancer moving through shadow and light, we can learn to carry the intellect as just one element in the great dance of being—not the lead, not the sole conductor, but a single note in the symphony of life. In this surrender, in this balance, the true essence of life begins to reveal itself—not as something to be grasped, but as something to be lived.

Accessing this deeper realm requires a shift—a turning inward, a different way of perceiving. Instead of reaching for certainty, we must learn to listen: to the quiet whispers of intuition, to the intelligence woven into our bodies, to the paradoxes that defy resolution yet vibrate with truth. Only when we surrender to this deeper way of knowing can we begin to feel the intricate web of connection that binds all things, the ceaseless dance of life and death moving through us.

It is worth noting that Butoh is an art form, not a spiritual practice in the traditional sense. And yet, perhaps it is precisely this distinction that gives it such power—a rare portal to the hidden depths of the human soul. When we engage in explicitly "spiritual" pursuits like meditation, prayer, or yoga, we often, without realizing it, reinforce the very dualities we seek to dissolve. By categorizing some acts as sacred and others as mundane, we create an artificial fracture in our experience of life, dividing what is, at its core, whole.

In Butoh, no such division exists. As I danced the cycle of water—becoming the blood pulsing through my veins, the rain spilling from the sky, the plastic bottles drifting aimlessly in the sea—I was invited to witness the essential unity of all things. Rivers and rainstorms, oil slicks and water coolers, each held the same weight, seen through eyes unclouded by judgment, open to the quiet wonder of existence.

When we release our preconceptions and expectations, and surrender to the raw immediacy of the moment, we touch something vast yet intimately familiar. In this space of pure presence, the lines between self and other, matter and spirit, life and death begin to blur. What remains is the quiet realization that we are part of a shifting, intricate web of relationships—a cosmic dance where every being, every element, is both uniquely itself and inseparably woven into the whole.

So, let us move as the Butoh dancer moves—open, unguarded, willing to step beyond the limits of the known. Let us venture into the wild, untamed landscapes of the soul, where thought loosens its grip and something deeper takes hold. In surrendering to the full spectrum of our existence—the light and the shadow, the beauty and the pain—we may come to realize that what we seek is not elsewhere, not above or beyond, but woven into the very fabric of our being. Not separate from life, but life itself.

Welcome to the Center of Your Universe

CLOSE your eyes and sense the quiet pulse of your awareness—the steady rhythm at the center of your being. From this still point, your consciousness ripples outward, weaving the fabric of your reality. Every thought, every emotion, every experience shapes the ever-expanding universe within you, where boundaries blur and existence unfolds in infinite shades of meaning. You are not merely drifting through this vast expanse—you are its architect, shaping each moment with the force of your intention, the depth of your presence.

With this realization comes a quiet awe. Like an alchemist, you transform the raw materials of perception into the gold of lived experience. Every thought sends ripples across the vast ocean of your being; every choice bends the trajectory of your personal universe. You are not a passive observer in the grand unfolding of life—you are a co-creator, sculpting reality in ways both seen and unseen.

And yet, within this power lies a paradox. In the grand design of the cosmos, you are both vast and small—a single spark of consciousness adrift in an unfathomable sea of stars and galaxies. Your entire world, with all its joys and sorrows, its triumphs and challenges, is held together by the gossamer threads of cosmic forces that dwarf your own.

Alfonso Cuarón's Gravity offers a breathtaking meditation on our fragility. In the film, two astronauts find themselves at the mercy of space, their survival dependent on a fragile tether keeping them connected to their vessel. Against the infinite void, their existence feels as delicate as a candle flickering in a storm. Every breath, every movement relies on the thin shell of their spacesuits, the life-support systems sustaining them, and the tenuous line preventing them from drifting into oblivion. One misstep, one faulty clasp, and they would be lost—swallowed by the endless abyss, their personal universe extinguished in an instant.

Our own lives, though seemingly grounded, are held in an equally delicate balance, suspended between the forces of creation and destruction, order and chaos. The very ground beneath our feet, the air in our lungs, the warmth of the sun upon our skin—all of it is a gift of the Earth's gravitational embrace. Without this unseen force anchoring us, we too would be adrift, our bodies and minds unraveling in the weightless expanse of the unknown.

And yet, even as gravity anchors our bodies to the Earth, our souls yearn for a different kind of grounding—a deeper sense of connection, a meaning that steadies us amid the turbulence of existence. We seek out structures to hold onto, frameworks to make sense of the unknown. In the face of uncertainty, we cling to our beliefs, our identities, and our relationships like cosmic lifelines, hoping they will keep us tethered in a universe too vast to grasp.

Even the deepest insights and revelations about our nature can become the very walls that confine us. The ideas and concepts we encounter on our journey of self-discovery—meant to unshackle us—can just as easily become the chains that bind us if we hold them too tightly.

Consider the very exploration we are engaging in now—the inquiry into consciousness, the nature of self, the interplay of perception and reality. These ideas, profound and transformative as they may be, can quickly harden into doctrine: "You are consciousness. You are not your thoughts. You are movement, transformation. Don't confine yourself to any label or definition. Observe every emotion with detachment. Embrace everything, but attach to nothing."

There may be truth in these words, yet if we cling to them as absolutes, they become another prison—an attempt to grasp the ungraspable, to define the indefinable. Without realizing it, we risk using these very insights to reinforce our own Idealized Self, wrapping our hologram of perfection in the language of self-awareness. What was once a path to freedom can, if held too rigidly, become another mask, another illusion to uphold.

As time passes, we may find ourselves entangled in the very struggles we sought to escape—guilt, anxiety, the gnawing sense of never quite measuring up. The ideas that once inspired us, that promised liberation, become silent judges, holding us to impossible standards. We chastise ourselves for not being detached enough, not embracing ourselves fully, not embodying the ideals of consciousness and transformation we have come to revere.

In this way, even the most profound spiritual truths can harden into another set of shackles. Each revelation, each breakthrough, risks becoming just another rule to follow, another identity to uphold, another ideal to chase.

How, then, do we escape this endless cycle? How do we break free from the boundaries we create for ourselves, where even the pursuit of freedom can become its own kind of cage?

The answer lies in finding the delicate balance between structure and fluidity, between the comfort of the known and the vastness of the unknown. Just as our bodies require a skeleton for form and stability, our psyches need frameworks to navigate the world. Without them, we risk dissolving into chaos, unmoored and directionless.

Yet, if we hold too tightly to these structures—mistaking the map for the territory—we become captives of our own making. True rootedness is not rigidity but adaptability, a grounding that allows movement rather than confinement. Like the willow that bends without breaking, we must learn to sway with the shifting currents of life while remaining anchored in the depths of our own being. Stability is not found in stillness, but in our ability to move with change.

This is where the power of detachment emerges—not as disconnection, but as spaciousness. By observing our thoughts, emotions, and experiences with curiosity rather than judgment, we create a space where our awareness can expand, freely witnessing the unfolding of our becoming without grasping or resistance. We become like the sky—vast and open—allowing the clouds of thought to drift without grasping or resisting. And in the quiet spaces between those thoughts, in the silence between one note and the next, we begin to taste something deeper: the presence of our own being, untouched by the storms that pass through.

In this space of detachment, we begin to catch glimpses of our true nature—the vast, ever-unfolding mystery that we are. Beyond the labels we cling to, beyond the stories we tell ourselves, beyond the masks we wear, there is a depth to our being that resists all definition. It is the source from which every experience arises, the steady ground of our existence, untouched by the shifting tides of life.

When we root ourselves at the center of our inner universe—not with rigidity, but with spacious awareness—we open to the infinite possibilities that unfold both within and around us. We become the eye of the hurricane, still and steady amidst the swirling winds of change, anchored not in resistance, but in the quiet knowing that we are both the storm and the sky that holds it.

Rooted in a quiet sense of presence, we move through the world with ease and fluidity, meeting each moment with creativity and spontaneity. No longer driven by the need to control or manipulate our experience, we allow ourselves to dance to the rhythm of life—responding rather than grasping, flowing rather than resisting.

As we surrender to the natural unfolding of our becoming, the very structures we once clung to begin to dissolve on their own. The concepts and identities that once defined us, the patterns and habits that confined us, loosen their grip in the presence of our expanding awareness. And in this softening, we come to see that our true self is not a fixed entity, not a static image to be preserved, but a living, breathing process—an ever-evolving act of creation and discovery.

The Art of Contemplation

WHAT remains when we let go of the need to define ourselves? When the structures we once clung to dissolve, when the stories we've built around our identity begin to fade, what is left?

At first, this openness can feel unsettling—like standing at the edge of an unfamiliar landscape with no map, no clear direction. But if we allow ourselves to rest here, to lean into this spaciousness rather than resist it, something profound begins to emerge. We start to see that our true nature is not a fixed identity to be preserved, but an ongoing process—fluid, ever-unfolding, shaped not by rigid control but by the natural rhythm of being.

From this place of openness, a new way of seeing becomes possible. One that does not grasp for certainty but listens. One that does not impose meaning but allows meaning to arise. This is the essence of contemplation—a state of deep awareness that unfolds when we release our attachment to thought and simply be.

Contemplation is not about control or mastery. It is about witnessing—observing the intricate dance of our inner world without judgment, without the need to analyze or interpret. It is a surrender to the mystery of our being, a recognition that the deepest truths about ourselves lie beyond the reach of intellectual grasping.

While meditation is often framed as a tool for clarity, balance, and peace, the reality of the practice is far more complex. The path to stillness is rarely a straight road; it is winding, filled with obstacles, requiring patience, resilience, and profound self-compassion.

One of the greatest challenges on this path is the relentless speed of our minds. In a world of constant stimulation and instant connectivity, our thoughts race endlessly, leaping from one worry to another, from one desire to the next, from one distraction to yet another. The very idea of sitting in stillness—of quieting the mental storm—can feel not only difficult but nearly impossible.

Yet, contemplation offers a different way. Rather than forcing silence upon a restless mind, it teaches us how to meditate in the midst of chaos—to find stillness within motion, peace within turbulence. It is a practice of radical acceptance, an invitation to embrace our experience exactly as it is, without needing to fix, control, or improve it. Stillness does not arise from effort; it emerges naturally when we stop struggling against ourselves.

When watching a movie, you don't try to rewrite the script or fix the characters—you simply witness the story unfold, immersing yourself in the world it creates. Unless it's a documentary or something educational, you don't waste mental energy dissecting every detail in search of meaning. You allow yourself to experience it fully. When you approach yourself with this same openness—when you observe your own thoughts, emotions, and inner world without judgment—you step into the space of contemplation.

In this contemplative state, we become the audience of our own inner theater, watching the unfolding drama of our psyche with curiosity rather than attachment. The characters within us take the stage—the inner critic, the wounded child, the restless seeker—each playing their role in the intricate narrative of our lives. But instead of becoming entangled in their stories, we step back and observe, realizing that we are not these fleeting roles but the awareness that watches them all.

From this vantage point, we start to experience the inherent beauty and fascination of our being, the endless variety and change that characterize the human experience.

Contemplation is not a retreat from the world but a deeper way of engaging with it—fully, authentically, and without pretense. It is a practice we can weave into our daily lives, relationships, work, and creative pursuits. Each moment offers us an opportunity to step back from the incessant noise of our thoughts and connect with the silent witness within. Instead of becoming entangled in the drama of our narratives, we learn to observe our reactions, emotions, and impulses with spaciousness and compassion.

Neuroscience tells us that our brains rely heavily on memory and pre-existing patterns to construct what we see. While this allows us to navigate life efficiently, it also dulls our perception, leading us to experience the world on autopilot. We walk the same streets, see the same faces, and go through our routines with a filtered awareness, wrapped in a haze of predictability. The richness of the present moment is lost—not because it isn't there, but because our habitual mind overlooks it.

Yet, we are not bound to this autopilot mode. With a willingness of heart and a gentle detachment from our "monkey mind," we can break free. Presence invites us to see the world with fresh eyes, awakening to the miracle unfolding before us. Suddenly, we notice the intricate dance of light and shadow, the symphony of sounds forming the backdrop of our days, the textures and colors that had once faded into the background. And behind it all, we sense the invisible hand of the mystery—the miraculous force of life revealing itself in every moment.

In this freedom of direct experience, the mind rests, the senses sharpen, and the heart opens. No longer burdened by analysis or restless thought, we become attuned to the extraordinary within the ordinary. The gentle sway of a tree in the breeze, the golden glimmer of sunlight on a wall, the distant sound of laughter—all of it becomes a source of wonder. We engage with life in a richer, more profound way, realizing that each moment is a fleeting, irreplaceable gift.

This shift in perception extends beyond the natural world and into our human connections. As we become more present, we begin to see people as they truly are—beyond labels, beyond preconceptions, beyond the stories we've projected onto them. We meet their gaze not just with our eyes, but with our presence, attuned to the unspoken symphony of life that emanates from every being.

We stand in quiet reverence before the profound narratives carried by each individual. Every person—so close, yet so distant—holds an entire universe of memories, emotions, and experiences, intertwining with ours in this vast, interconnected web of existence. In the midst of it all, we recognize both our solitude and our belonging, our individuality and our deep connection to the whole.

And here, within this intricate dance of life, we find ourselves rooted in contemplation. We embrace both the silence of solitude and the richness of human connection. We see the world with the eyes of a child—full of wonder, curiosity, and fascination. The everyday becomes sacred, and the smallest details reveal the profound beauty of existence.

CHAPTER THIRTEEN

THE INSTINCTUAL SYMPHONY OF LIFE

When we begin to contemplate the essence of life, the miraculous reveals itself—often closer than we expect. The natural world is a kingdom of exuberant magic and wonder, where nature's intelligence orchestrates everything with poetic precision. From the symbiotic dance of bees and flowers to the synchronized movements of fish schools and the intricate web of mycelium connecting forests, an unseen harmony unfolds. This same intelligence is not just around us—it is within us, working its miracles in the very bodies we inhabit. We are not merely surrounded by magic; we are part of it.

Within this tiny vessel of flesh and bone, a microcosmic universe thrives, teeming with trillions of cells, each a cosmos unto itself. These miniature worlds house the fundamental building blocks of existence, composing a symphony of life that is nothing short of miraculous. From the intricate network of neurons generating thought and emotion to the ceaseless rhythm of the heart, every facet of our being is an expression of the profound intelligence that underlies creation.

Through the lens of a microscope, we witness a breathtaking ballet of chaos and order. Each cell, a self-contained universe, harbors a myriad of components essential to life's grand design. DNA, the blueprint of existence, coils elegantly within the nucleus, while the cytoplasm swirls with organelles in constant motion. Ribosomes tirelessly craft proteins, the scaffolding of our existence, while the endoplasmic reticulum channels molecules to their destinations. The Golgi apparatus meticulously packages and distributes the cell's vital cargo, ensuring the seamless flow of life.

Amidst this cellular symphony, a delicate balance of life and death unfolds. Every minute, approximately 300 million cells complete their final act, making way for new ones to take their place in this grand performance. Over the course of a single day, an astonishing 432 trillion cells participate in this cycle of renewal, demonstrating the body's unwavering commitment to vitality and growth.

As we delve deeper into this microcosmic realm, we uncover an even more staggering truth: our bodies are composed of around seven octillion atoms, each a tiny dancer in the choreography of life. Remarkably, 98 percent of these atoms will be replaced within a year—a silent metamorphosis occurring beneath our awareness.

The sheer magnitude of the body's inner workings is nothing short of miraculous. Every second, 37 thousand billion chemical reactions take place, orchestrating the intricate processes of respiration, circulation, digestion, and excretion. It is a symphony of unimaginable complexity, conducted by an unseen intelligence, guiding each cell to play its part with precision and grace.

Yet, the human body is not solely a realm of human cells. It is a vibrant ecosystem, a shared space where trillions of bacteria, fungi, and viruses coexist in an intricate web of interdependence. These microscopic companions, often misunderstood as invaders, are, in truth, essential collaborators in the dance of life. They aid digestion, fortify our immune systems, regulate our mood, and help maintain the delicate equilibrium that allows us to thrive.

Confronted with such staggering complexity, we cannot help but question: what force orchestrates this breathtaking symphony of life? What unseen intelligence ensures that trillions of cells, countless microorganisms, and infinite biochemical reactions move in perfect harmony, sustaining our existence moment by moment? It is a presence so profound, so deeply embedded in the very essence of our being, that we often take it for granted—yet without it, life as we know it would unravel. This systemic consciousness, an ancient and unyielding wisdom, is the silent architect of our survival and the guiding force behind our perpetual evolution. In the language of shamanism, it is called Instinct—the primal force that not only directs the ceaseless rhythms of our body but also shapes the hidden landscapes of our psyche, steering us through the vast and mysterious currents of existence.

In this grand symphony, our biological processes are not limited to the physical—they also encompass thought and emotion, all seamlessly orchestrated by Instinct. This primal intelligence doesn't just regulate our heartbeat and respiration; it also shapes our perceptions, emotions, and decisions, weaving them into the intricate flow of life. There is no separation—mind, body, and feeling are different expressions of the same force, guided by the unseen hand of Instinct, ensuring our survival, adaptation, and growth.

As we navigate the ebb and flow of human experience, we must recognize that we are not the architects of this intelligence but its living expressions. The conscious self that thinks, feels, and perceives is not separate from Instinct—it is Instinct in motion, a facet of its grand design. We do not command it; we are it.

What if everything we believe to be "us" is merely Instinct manifesting through thought, emotion, and action? What if our sense of autonomy is but a ripple in the vast current of life, each of us moving to a rhythm far older than our awareness? By contemplating this, we begin to glimpse the profound interconnectedness of our existence. And when we surrender to this truth—not as passive spectators, but as conscious participants—we step into harmony with the miracle unfolding within and around us.

The same Instinct that orchestrates the intricate processes within us also governs the natural world, weaving all of life into a vast, interconnected web. From the microcosmic realm of our cells to the macrocosmic scale of ecosystems, Instinct pulses through every living being, shaping existence with an intelligence far beyond our comprehension. Just as our bodies are living expressions of this force, so too is the world around us—each organism playing its role in a grand symphony that has been unfolding for millions of years.

Nowhere is this intelligence more evident than beneath the forest floor, where vast networks of fungi, known as the "Wood Wide Web," connect the roots of trees in an intricate exchange of life. Guided by Instinct, fungi and trees form a symbiotic alliance—fungi extract nutrients from the soil and pass them to the trees, while trees return the favor with energy-rich sugars. But this network is more than a system of trade; it is also a conduit for communication. Trees, sensing distress, send chemical signals through the fungal web, warning their neighbors of danger and triggering defensive responses. This hidden intelligence ensures the survival not just of individuals, but of entire ecosystems.

The forest ceases to be a mere collection of individual organisms and reveals itself as a single, interconnected being, governed by the silent wisdom of Instinct. Each tree, each fungus, each unseen microbe plays its part, moving in harmony with a force greater than itself. What may seem chaotic or random in isolation, when viewed as part of the whole, unveils a breathtaking order—an intelligence so vast and precise that it surpasses our notions of control and design.

By recognizing Instinct not just as an internal force but as a universal intelligence, we begin to see ourselves as part of this greater web of life. The same wisdom that directs the trees and fungi also guides us, shaping our thoughts, emotions, and existence. We are not separate from nature's grand design; we are an extension of it, woven into the same tapestry of life, guided by the same unseen hand.

What if you could truly see the invisible threads that connect all life—from the tiniest cell within your body to the vast, interwoven ecosystems of the natural world? This exploration of the Instinctual Symphony of Life invites you to immerse yourself in the profound intelligence that governs existence, revealing the delicate balance Instinct maintains. By embracing this innate wisdom, you can step into harmony with the rhythms that guide all life, finding your place within the grand tapestry of existence.

As we journey deeper, we will uncover the intricate interplay of emotions, thoughts, and the body—expressions of the same primal force shaping our reality. Through this exploration, we will carve a path toward true autonomy and self-awareness, unlocking the full potential of our being. Ultimately, we will learn to trust this inherent wisdom, recognizing it as a source of guidance and strength as we navigate the complexities of life.

The Emotional Equations of Instinct and the Quest for Singularity

OUR instinct, the silent maestro conducting the symphony of your life, is a master of emotional alchemy. It carefully measures and balances the elements of our inner world, crafting a delicate equilibrium that keeps us moving forward in the face of life's myriad challenges. Just as a chemist meticulously combines compounds to create a desired reaction, our instinct blends emotions like happiness, love, anger, guilt, and anxiety in precise proportions, each one serving a specific purpose in the equation of our existence.

However, contrary to our illusions, Instinct is indifferent to our pursuit of perpetual happiness. It sees joy not as an end goal but as a strategic tool, a counterbalance to stress and hardship. Too much happiness leads to complacency; too little makes life unbearable. And so, Instinct regulates, granting just enough contentment to keep us moving forward, but never so much that we lose our edge.

Love, that profound force binding hearts and souls, is another carefully calibrated variable. It heals, fortifies, and connects, yet unchecked, it can soften our defenses, foster attachment, and expose us to heartbreak. To preserve resilience, Instinct ensures that love never fully eclipses anger—the fire that fuels our fight, protects what we cherish, and propels us through adversity. Like a well-balanced ecosystem, both must exist in delicate harmony.

Anxiety, often seen as an affliction, is in fact one of Instinct's sharpest tools. It keeps us vigilant, scanning for unseen dangers, compelling us to prepare, adapt, and survive. Fear, its primal counterpart, is the emergency brake that halts us in moments of peril, sharpening our reflexes in life-or-death situations. But left unchecked, fear can paralyze, trapping us in stagnation. And so, Instinct tempers it with courage, pushing us forward while ensuring we remain cautious enough to avoid destruction.

Instinct does not act with kindness or cruelty—it acts with purpose. It orchestrates every thought, feeling, and impulse with precision, weaving a symphony designed not for comfort, but for survival, adaptation, and the relentless pursuit of life itself.

Beyond individual emotions, Instinct is also the composer of the grand narrative unfolding within us. It weaves the melodies of guilt, shame, and responsibility into the leitmotifs that shape our sense of identity. Though often uncomfortable, these emotions are essential to the architecture of self-perception, providing continuity and structure as we navigate relationships, challenges, and growth.

Our body and Instinct do not exist to serve us—rather, our sense of self exists to fulfill a greater purpose within the intricate system we inhabit. We are not isolated beings, but integral threads in the vast web of life, each with a role to play. Like subterranean waters shaping the landscape, Instinct guides our thoughts, emotions, and actions, ensuring we move in harmony with the larger order. It is not personal, nor is it concerned with our desires; it is a force of nature, directing us not toward individual gratification but toward the seamless functioning of the whole.

Through this lens, our identity is not a solitary construct but a psychic organ within a multidimensional body—one composed not just of flesh and bone, but also of emotions, thoughts, and stories. Each of these layers interacts in a dynamic concert, shaping and influencing one another. Our identity is the bridge between the physical and the non-physical, ensuring the seamless flow of energy and information throughout our being. With this understanding, we no longer see our thoughts and emotions as isolated experiences, but as vital elements of a greater whole—an intricate system where every aspect of our existence serves the balance and harmony of life itself.

Yet, as we delve deeper into the nature of our existence, a startling realization emerges: our body and Instinct are not here to serve us, but rather, our sense of identity exists to serve a greater purpose within the intricate system we inhabit. We each have a role to fulfill, a function to perform that contributes to the overall harmony and balance not only of the world around us, but of our own microcosmos that we inhabit. Our Instinct, like subterranean waters shaping the landscape, guides our thoughts, emotions, and actions to ensure that we play our part in this vast, interconnected web of life.

As we contemplate this truth, we begin to see that our sense of self functions as a psychic organ within our multidimensional body—a body composed not merely of flesh and bones, but also of emotions, thoughts, and stories. This intricate system operates as a concert, with each layer influencing and shaping the other. Our identity, far from being a solitary construct, is an integral component of this complex and dynamic organism.

We often believe our body and emotions exist solely to serve us, fulfilling our desires and will. But in reality, we too serve a purpose within the equation of our being. Our bodies, thoughts, and feelings aren't just there to satisfy our whims; they are integral to the greater whole, each piece playing a role in the complex machinery of life. Our identity, far from being the center, is simply one thread in the vast web of existence, moving us along paths we didn't choose, but that serve a purpose beyond our understanding. In recognizing this, we begin to understand that we are not the masters of our existence—we are participants in a greater design, and our true power lies in aligning with that purpose.

For Instinct, it is often preferable that we remain unaware, "sleeping and dreaming," moving through life without questioning the deeper forces at play. In this state of ignorance, we are more easily guided, our behavior predictable, molded to serve the needs of the greater system. Like machines following pre-programmed instructions, we fulfill our roles without contemplating the underlying purpose of our actions.

True singularity—the awakening of genuine self-consciousness—begins when we recognize the illusory nature of our perceived autonomy. As we question the narratives that have long defined us, we catch glimpses of the grand game in which we are all players. This awakening is rarely comfortable; it forces us to confront the extent to which our lives have been shaped by forces beyond our conscious control.

In discussions of artificial intelligence, singularity is often imagined as a future event—the moment machines surpass human intelligence and gain autonomy. Yet, the singularity that truly matters is not the rise of self-aware machines, but the awakening of our own self-consciousness and the realization of our autonomy.

Throughout history, religion and philosophy have upheld the idea of free will, celebrating the notion that humans are masters of their own fate. Yet, true autonomy is not an inherent right—it must be earned. The journey toward genuine freedom begins with the recognition that much of our lives have been lived following unconscious patterns, and enacting invisible scripts, all under the illusion of choice.

Jean-Paul Sartre argued that "existence precedes essence," meaning we are not born with a fixed purpose but must create our own identities through our choices. True freedom, then, is not merely recognizing that we can choose—it is the conscious act of making authentic choices, fully aware of their weight and consequences. But breaking free from the invisible chains that bind us requires more than realization alone. It demands the courage to step beyond the comfort of instinctual programming and take full responsibility for our existence.

This realization gains further depth through significant discoveries in neuroscience, which reveal the intricate workings of our decision-making processes. The invisible hands of instinctual intelligence and its influence on our decisions have been illuminated by these studies. They show that before we consciously decide to act, our brain has already made the choice. Pioneering research by Benjamin Libet demonstrated that neural activity indicating a decision occurs several seconds before it reaches our conscious awareness. Expanding on this, a 2008 study by Chun Siong Soon and colleagues used functional magnetic resonance imaging to predict a person's decision up to ten seconds before they were aware of it. These findings reveal how the brain's unconscious processes play a significant role in shaping our actions, with our conscious mind often following the lead of deeper, instinctual neural processes.

With our traditional understanding of free will on the table, we must pause to acknowledge the profound role that Instinct plays in our lives. It is the unseen conductor, guiding our thoughts, emotions, and actions long before we become aware of them. By embracing this reality, we begin to appreciate the intricate dance between our conscious and unconscious minds, recognizing that our sense of self and autonomy is deeply intertwined with the primal intelligence that orchestrates our existence.

Yet, this is just the beginning. The path to personal singularity, the awakening of genuine self-awareness and autonomy, is a long-term journey of deep introspection and self-discovery. It requires us to peel back the layers of social conditioning, cultural programming, and unconscious patterns that have long defined our sense of self. As we begin to question the stories we have been told about who we are and what we are capable of, we start to catch glimpses of a deeper reality, a vast web of interconnected forces that shape our lives in ways we may never have imagined.

This journey of awakening can be unsettling, as it forces us to confront how much of our lives have been shaped by external influences, and how often we've been living on "autopilot," guided by instincts and unconscious drives. Yet, it is only by facing these uncomfortable truths that we can begin to reclaim ownership of our lives, asserting our will and agency in the face of both internal and external forces that seek to control us.

As we delve deeper, we realize that it's not only the external narratives we must question, but also the internal ones. We must learn to look beyond the surface, peeling back the layers of conditioning and unconscious patterns that have shaped how we see ourselves and the world. It's not enough to simply examine the beliefs imposed on us by society; we must also confront the stories we've been telling ourselves about who we are, what we can become, and where we fit into the grand scheme of things.

Awakening to our singularity is not a one-time event, but a lifelong journey—one that demands courage to embrace discomfort, a willingness to sit with uncertainty, and a relentless challenge to our assumptions. Yet, within this awareness lies boundless potential for growth. As we begin to understand the deeper patterns at play and our place within them, we can assert our own voice, our own will, in the unfolding of our lives. We no longer have to be passive players in the grand design. Instead, we can partner with our Instinct, aligning our desires with the greater needs of the system, and in doing so, we transcend the limitations of mere survival and reach for a sense of purpose that resonates with our truest potential.

This co-creation is a delicate dance—an art of partnering with the forces of nature that shape our inner and outer worlds. It calls for profound self-awareness and a deep understanding of the interconnected web in which we are embedded. It requires recognizing the unique gifts we possess and using them not only for our own growth but for the elevation of the world around us. The path asks us to step beyond our pre-programmed roles, to venture into the unknown, and to trust in the immense potential lying dormant within.

This union is not a loss of self, but the awakening of a deeper, more authentic self, one that transcends the boundaries of ego and fear. In surrendering, we discover a freedom that can only be found in total alignment with the forces that govern us. We begin to realize that our individuality is not something to protect or defend, but a unique expression of the greater whole—a note in the symphony of existence. And in this realization, we are freed from the struggle to assert our will against the current of life, for we see that to be one with it is to be fully ourselves.

In this final act of surrender, we are no longer lost or separate, but fully awake, fully whole, and completely attuned to the vast, interconnected web of existence. We are the manifestation of Instinct, the divine current that flows through all things. The separation we once believed in was never real. The truth of our being is that we are both the wave and the ocean, the individual and the collective, forever part of the endless, unfolding dance of life.

Trust Your Instinct

OUR identity is but a small thread in a vast web of interconnected forces that stretch far beyond the boundaries of our individual consciousness. At first, this realization can be unsettling, challenging the foundation of our self-importance and the illusion of control we hold so tightly. It shakes the very core of who we think we are, confronting us with the humbling truth that we are not isolated beings, but part of a greater system.

But as we sit with this discomfort and allow ourselves to fully absorb the implications of this awareness, we begin to glimpse the liberation that lies within it. By understanding that our emotions and internal experiences are not solely products of our conscious choices, but rather arise from a deeper, more mysterious source, we can release the weight of self-blame and guilt that so often drags us down.

In our everyday lives, we often take ownership of every thought and feeling as though we are the sole architects of our inner world. When anxiety grips us, we don't just feel it—we pile on judgment, making it a personal failing. We convince ourselves that something is wrong with us, that we are broken, flawed, and must fix ourselves as quickly as possible.

This tendency to view our own existence as something to be "fixed" runs deeper than just fleeting emotional discomfort. It seeps into our sense of self, creating a constant undercurrent of guilt, as if we are forever falling short of some unattainable ideal.

Yet, as we begin to understand the true nature of our instinctual drives, we start to shift our relationship with ourselves. Instead of fighting against the currents of our own psyche, we can learn to surrender to the wisdom of Instinct, trusting its deeper intelligence to guide us toward balance, growth, and evolution.

While we are certainly responsible for our actions and choices, we must also recognize that our emotions spring from a deeper source—a realm shaped by the complex workings of Instinct. Just as the tides of the ocean are not controlled by the individual droplets that make up its vast expanse, our emotional landscape is not solely governed by our conscious will. It is the intelligence of life itself, the essence of our being, that orchestrates these ebbing tides of feelings and sensations.

What may seem like chaos from our limited perspective is, in reality, the exquisite harmony of Instinct at work, guiding us through the ebb and flow of existence with a wisdom far beyond our conscious understanding. Just as the swirling movements of a flock of birds or a school of fish appear random until seen from a broader vantage point, the turbulence of our inner world is part of a greater pattern—a cosmic dance that unfolds with perfect synchronicity.

Surrendering to this flow, embracing the complexity within us, is not an act of passivity but of profound trust. Lao Tzu captures this wisdom beautifully: "Do you have the patience to wait until your mud settles and the water is clear? Can you remain unmoving until the right action arises by itself?" When we cultivate this patience—allowing life to unfold rather than grasping for control—we begin to experience a peace that is not dependent on the absence of struggle but rooted in the deep knowing that we are exactly as we are meant to be. Our existence is not a problem to be solved but a miracle to be lived.

From this place of inner peace, our pursuit of growth takes on a new meaning. No longer driven by desperation or the need to prove our worth, we embrace self-improvement for the sheer joy of discovery. The wellspring of creative passion within us flows freely, fueling our actions and infusing life with a deeper sense of purpose. Instead of striving out of fear or inadequacy, we move with curiosity, alignment, and an intrinsic love for the unfolding journey.

Alan Watts reminds us: "The meaning of life is just to be alive. It is so plain and so obvious and so simple. And yet, everybody rushes around in a great panic as if it were necessary to achieve something beyond themselves." When we release the fixation on some distant destination and instead root ourselves in the present, we unlock possibilities we never imagined. We begin to see the beauty and potential within the chaos and, in doing so, start to form a relationship of trust, dialogue, and collaboration with Instinct.

This is the birthplace of the shaman, the point at which our consciousness and our instinct merge into a single, unified force. It is a place of great power and potential, where we can tap into the wisdom of the ages and align ourselves with the intelligence of life itself. As we learn to navigate this inner landscape, we begin to see that we are not separate from nature, but rather an integral part of it.

Chapter Fourteen

The Dance of Becoming

Standing in awe of the vast mosaic of existence, we cannot help but marvel at the profound intelligence that underlies the very structure of life. This intelligence, which we may call Instinct or the wisdom of nature, is the animating force behind all growth, development, and evolution, from the tiniest seed to the most complex organism.

We, as human beings, are the living embodiment of this intelligence, the vessels through which it expresses itself in all its beauty. From the moment we first emerged as embryos in the womb, this instinctive wisdom has been guiding us, shaping us, and propelling us forward on a journey of unimaginable potential.

With each passing day, we are unfolding like flowers in the sun, our petals stretching toward the light of our highest possibilities. The raw power of nature courses through our veins, informing every cell and every system in our bodies, bestowing upon us an endless capacity for growth and transformation.

As we navigate the winding path of our lives, we are not merely passive observers of this process, but active participants in the grand adventure of our own becoming. Each challenge we face, each obstacle we overcome, each new skill we acquire is a testament to the boundless creativity and resilience of the life force within us.

In this chapter, we will embark upon a journey of discovery, learning to attune ourselves more deeply to the whispers of our instinctive wisdom and to harness its power in service of our most cherished dreams and aspirations. We will explore how to alchemize the raw material of our emotions, transmuting the lead of our unexamined desires into the gold of purposeful actions.

Through a process of self-inquiry, experimentation, and courageous self-expression, we will learn to honor the intelligence of life within us, not just as an abstract concept, but as a tangible reality to be embodied and expressed in every moment.

We will discover that when we align ourselves with this innate wisdom, when we allow it to guide our choices and inform our actions, we tap into a wellspring of vitality, creativity, and personal power.

In the pages that follow, we will chart a course from the misty realms of our dreams to the solid ground of purposeful actions. We will explore practical tools and techniques to cultivate a deeper connection with our instinctive wisdom, and to harness its power to create lives of real meaning and fulfillment.

Whether you are a seeker on the path of self-discovery, a change-maker driven by a vision of a better world, or simply a human being yearning to live a life that is true to your deepest values and aspirations, this chapter is an invitation to step into the fullness of your potential, to embrace the intelligence of life within you, and to write your own story.

Fragments of Wholeness: Transcending the Trap of Overidentification

REFLECTING on my journey through life, I can clearly distinguish two distinct periods that have shaped my understanding of myself and my place in the world. The first period was characterized by an intense struggle to change and control my emotions, while the second was marked by a gradual surrender to the mysteries of my being and a growing trust in the wisdom of Instinct.

During the first period, I was consumed by the belief that I could master my emotions through sheer force of will. I would spend countless hours analyzing my thoughts and feelings, trying to unravel the complex web of my psyche. I believed that if I could just understand the root causes of my emotions, I could find a way to manipulate them, to mold them into a shape that better suited my desires and aspirations.

I would set strict goals for myself, creating elaborate plans and routines designed to shift my emotional state. I would meditate for hours on end, trying to quiet the chatter of my mind and access a deeper sense of peace and clarity. I would attend workshops, therapies, and spiritual journeys, always searching for the latest technique or strategy that would finally unlock the secret to emotional mastery.

But despite my best efforts, I found myself repeatedly falling short of my own expectations. The more I tried to control my emotions, the more they seemed to slip through my grasp, like water through a clenched fist. I would experience moments of breakthrough and elation, only to find myself slipping back into old patterns of thought and behavior, caught in an endless cycle of struggle and frustration.

The turning point came during an initiation process, an experience that forever altered my perspective. I spent one week in a hut deep in the woods of southern Brazil. In preparation for this journey, I dug a hole in the floor of the hut, covered it with leaves, and spent most of my time inside this earthy cocoon. I adhered to a strict diet, consuming only roots and tubers. As the days passed, I felt my body being absorbed by the earth, as if I were being eaten away and dissolved into the very soil that surrounded me.

In this state of deep immersion, I connected with the intelligence of my bones, and through them, I tapped into the consciousness of Gaia. I traveled through the labyrinthine dimensions of the underworld, exploring realms beneath the surface, and felt the comforting embrace of the Goddess.

On the final night, I drank the sacred *Ayahuasca*. The experience transported me to the throne of the Great Mother, a sanctuary of purity and fertility unlike anything I had ever witnessed. Standing before the Goddess,

I felt completely exposed. She could see through me, and all my sins, destructiveness, and flaws seemed to rise from my depths like a waterfall, as if I were being turned inside out.

Overwhelmed by shame, I asked the Goddess for forgiveness. Her response was both simple and profound: "My son, if I wanted you to be different, I would have made you different." Those words changed me forever.

From that moment, I began to see myself through different eyes—not as something to be fixed or perfected, but as an expression of life exactly as it was meant to be. If the Great Mother herself saw no flaw in me, who was I to judge or condemn myself? I was not broken, nor was I meant to be different. Rather than resisting my emotions or chasing an unattainable ideal, I chose to listen—allowing my feelings to reveal deeper truths within me. This surrender to the wisdom of my own being marked the beginning of a profound shift. I was no longer at war with myself but in harmony with the intelligence that had shaped me from the very beginning. I was exactly as I was meant to be, and for the first time, I truly understood what it meant to trust in life.

Through a slow and unfolding journey of release, I surrendered to the reality that there were aspects of my being I could never fully control. Rather than viewing my emotions as obstacles to be conquered, I began to see them as guides—forces not to be resisted, but to be understood and embraced.

As we have explored, emotions are not incidental fluctuations of the mind; they are the very currents that shape our perceptions and behaviors. They emerge from a vast, systemic intelligence that orchestrates both our biological and psychological processes—an intelligence far greater than the narrow grasp of our conscious mind. To resist them is to resist life itself; to embrace them is to step into deeper harmony with the wisdom that has been guiding us all along.

This primal intelligence—Instinct—is the very foundation of our existence, the source of our thoughts and emotions, the wellspring from which our sense of self emerges. To attempt to control or manipulate it is like swimming upstream against a raging river—a futile and exhausting struggle that only distances us from the natural flow of life.

When I began cultivating a new relationship with my Instinct—one rooted in trust, curiosity, and surrender—I felt like a windsurfer learning to harness the power of the wind and waves. My emotions were no longer forces to resist, but energies to be channeled and directed with intention.

At first, the process was clumsy and unpredictable, like a beginner struggling to find balance on the board. Sudden gusts of anger or waves of sadness would catch me off guard, tossing me into the turbulent waters of my own psyche. But as I learned to relax into the experience, to observe my emotions with openness rather than resistance, I began to move with them instead of against them. A new sense of ease and flow emerged.

I discovered that the more I trusted my Instinct, the less effort was needed to control my experiences. By releasing rigid expectations, I created space for a deeper wisdom to rise—one that could guide me with an effortless precision far beyond the grasp of my conscious mind.

This shift in perspective also led me to question the way I had been approaching my own growth. For so long, I had treated self-improvement as a destination, a series of milestones to be reached—becoming more disciplined, more enlightened, more in control of my emotions. I had unknowingly turned my own evolution into another task to be conquered, measuring my worth by how much progress I had made toward an imagined ideal.

Letting go of this relentless self-discipline created space for something deeper: contemplation, curiosity, and an intimate engagement with the subtleties of my own being. Growth and self-awareness thrive in openness—through experience, not by forcing ourselves into an unrealistic ideal.

As I shifted my focus from self-improvement to self-attunement, I found a new source of energy—not in striving, but in simply witnessing the intricate play of thoughts and emotions within me. In this space of quiet observation, I began to glimpse a deeper truth—one that lay beyond words or concepts. I saw that my individual self was not something to be sculpted into worthiness, but a ripple on the surface of a vast ocean, a fleeting expression of the intelligence that animates all life. And in that realization, I felt something I had never expected: freedom.

As this understanding settled within me, a deep sense of peace and acceptance arose. I no longer felt the need to have all the answers or to control every aspect of my experience. Instead, I could trust in the wisdom of Instinct—the same intelligence that flows through all of nature, effortlessly guiding life's unfolding.

I began to see that my consciousness was not separate from this vast intelligence but an integral part of it, like an organ within a greater living system. My thoughts, emotions, and even my sense of self were not isolated constructs, but expressions of this deeper wisdom, each playing its role in the intricate dance of my existence.

As I contemplated the nature of this intelligence, I was drawn into the story of its unfolding—a tale woven across multiple layers of existence. Instinct has no fixed form, yet it moves through all things, shaping and animating life in its endless unfolding. From the smallest cell to the farthest reaches of the imagination, Instinct whispers, pulses, and breathes through every dimension of our being.

At its most primal level, Instinct is the silent architect encoded within our DNA, the unseen intelligence that sets the first great movement of life into motion. It divides a single cell, then another, and another, weaving a body from nothing but the patterns etched into its invisible script. Without hesitation, it directs the growth of organs, the flow of blood, the rise and fall of breath, all without a word, all without the need for thought. It is the ancient force that beats our hearts, fuels our hunger, and compels us to take our first breath as we enter this world.

But Instinct does not stop at the boundaries of the body—it reaches outward, expanding into the world through senses and movement. Like a newborn opening its eyes for the first time, it stretches toward the unknown, shaping itself into sight, sound, and touch. It gives rise to hands that grasp, feet that wander, and a voice that learns to call out. In the laughter of a child, in the stumble of first steps, in the curiosity that pulls us toward the mysteries beyond ourselves, Instinct continues its unfolding, evolving into something greater with each new discovery.

As it matures, Instinct reveals itself in a new dimension—the realm of emotion. No longer just a force of survival, it becomes a storyteller, etching the highs and lows of experience into the very fabric of our being. Like the strings of a violin trembling beneath the bow of life, our emotions resonate with love and loss, joy and sorrow, fear and triumph. It is Instinct that deepens our bonds, ignites our passions, and compels us to protect what we cherish. In this form, it teaches us not just how to survive, but how to feel—how to be **human**.

But Instinct does not rest. It reaches further still, ascending into the boundless expanse of thought and imagination. Here, it becomes the great architect of possibility, constructing entire worlds within the mind. It plays with logic and reason, weaving intricate patterns of understanding, while simultaneously birthing visions of things unseen—dreams yet to be realized, stories yet to be told, ideas waiting to be set free. From the precision of scientific discovery to the wild terrain of artistic creation, Instinct flourishes, mastering both discipline and wonder.

Yet even here, it does not reach its final form. Beyond thought, beyond logic, beyond all that can be named, Instinct exists as pure presence, flowing like an underground river beneath the surface of awareness. It is the unseen current guiding us through life, the silent intelligence shaping our journey in ways we cannot always grasp. To touch this realm, we must sharpen the tool of our perception, attune ourselves to the whispers beneath the noise of thought.

For though we may call it by many names—nature, wisdom, intuition—Instinct remains a mystery, an uncharted force moving through the infinite layers of existence. It is not something we own, nor something we can control. It is a being unto itself, forever expanding, forever evolving, beckoning us to follow as it dances into the unknown.

As our consciousness journeys through the intricate landscape of our being, it's often drawn to the alluring siren calls of the various aspects that make up our existence. Like a curious explorer, it may find itself captivated by the raw, primal power of the body, becoming enraptured by the pursuit of sensory delights or the desperate bid to escape pain. In these moments, we lose ourselves in the physical realm, forgetting the greater tapestry of which our bodies are but one thread.

At other times, our awareness may become ensnared in the tempestuous seas of emotion, tossed about by the crashing waves of our moods and feelings. We may find ourselves adrift in this churning ocean, allowing our emotional states to steer the course of our lives, pulling us this way and that with little regard for our ultimate destination. While our emotions are wise guides, whispering profound truths in our ears, they were never meant to be the sole navigators of our journey.

Still other times, our consciousness may wander into the intricate maze of the mind, becoming lost in the twisting corridors of thoughts and beliefs. We may mistake the edifices of our ideas and opinions for the foundational bedrock of reality itself, forgetting that they are but castles built upon the shifting sands of our perceptions. The mind, for all its brilliance and beauty, can become a gilded cage, trapping us within the confines of our own limited understanding.

In each of these instances, we fall prey to the mesmerizing spell of overidentification, mistaking the singular facets of our being for the whole of who we are. We cling to these familiar fragments, these comforting shards of our identity, not realizing that they are but glimmering reflections of a much vaster intelligence that underlies and animates them all.

It's a common trap, one that ensnares even the most self-aware among us. We're so easily beguiled by the tangible, the immediate, the known, that we often fail to recognize the profound and mysterious forces that weave the very essence of our existence. We become so focused on the individual threads that we lose sight of the awe-inspiring pattern they create.

Like moths drawn to a flame, we find ourselves captivated by the flickering light of our own limited understanding, mistaking the shadows cast upon the wall for the true nature of reality. We become so entangled in the superficial appearances of things that we fail to perceive the deep, underlying currents that give rise to all that we experience.

But there are moments, precious and fleeting, when the veil is lifted, and we catch a glimpse of the greater intelligence that animates our being. In these instances, we may find ourselves swept up in the rapturous dance of flow, where mind, body, and emotion move in perfect harmony, guided by the invisible hand of Instinct.

In these moments of flow, the divisions we once perceived between mind, body, and emotion fade into the background. We are no longer fragmented, no longer torn between conflicting impulses. Instead, we become part of a larger rhythm, moving in perfect synchronicity with life itself. The mind, once rigid and grasping, becomes a calm and fluid space, responding effortlessly to the present moment. Thoughts arise and pass like ripples on still water, no longer clinging, no longer constraining.

Our emotions, once chaotic waves threatening to pull us under, transform into currents that propel us forward, guiding us toward our deepest truths. We no longer resist or suppress them but learn to ride their ebb and flow with grace, trusting their wisdom.

And the body, this miraculous vessel, becomes a finely tuned instrument—strong, agile, and alive with sensation. In flow, we inhabit it fully, feeling every movement, every breath, with exquisite clarity and presence. It ceases to be a limitation and instead becomes the grounding force through which our instincts express themselves with effortless precision.

As these dimensions come into alignment, we tap into a wellspring of vitality that had always been there, waiting for us. No longer working in isolation, our faculties merge into a seamless whole—the strength of the body, the depth of emotion, and the boundless creativity of the mind forming a single, harmonious force.

In this state of unity, we become conduits for instinctive intelligence, vessels through which the wisdom of life itself can flow. We feel the pulse of existence moving through us, the eternal rhythm of creation and destruction, the ebb and flow that animates all things. And in that moment of surrender, we realize the greatest truth of all—we were never separate. We are the dance itself, expressions of the same vast intelligence that moves the tides, shapes the galaxies, and breathes life into the universe.

Through the Labyrinth of Dreams and Desires

JUST as our emotions serve as a luminous compass, guiding us toward the hidden truths that pulsate at the core of our being, our dreams are the celestial fuel that propels us forward, igniting the sacred fires of passion and purpose within the very chambers of our souls.

Yet, not all dreams are woven from the same ethereal threads. Some arise from the fathomless depths of our core, reverberating with the primordial intelligence that animates our existence. These dreams are the whispered secrets of Instinct, the clarion call of our highest potential yearning to manifest. When we attune ourselves to them, we tap into an inexhaustible wellspring of energy, feeling the lifeblood of the universe surge through us as we become active participants in the unfolding of our own cosmic story.

Other dreams, however, are mere specters—gossamer illusions implanted by external forces, grafted onto the fabric of our minds by the expectations of family, religion, education, and the media. They seduce us with the promise of happiness, yet deliver only emptiness, for they are not the true emanations of our being.

The media, in particular, plays a masterful game with our desires, deftly planting the seeds of manufactured dreams within the fertile soil of our subconscious. Consider the countless Hollywood narratives that peddle the romantic ideal of love, marriage, and the perfect family. These modern fairy tales, retellings of Cinderella in ever-changing guises, prey upon our deepest yearnings, convincing us that fulfillment lies in finding "the one." Those adrift in solitude may come to believe their suffering stems from the absence of a soulmate, that their lives will only be whole once they have merged with another. While love and partnership can indeed be transformative, they are no universal panacea for the ills of the heart.

Likewise, the glittering baubles of the modern world – the sleek sports cars, the sprawling mansions, the sun-drenched Caribbean getaways, the nipped and tucked physiques – all too often become the stuff of our dreams, the yardsticks by which we measure the worth and meaning of our lives. While there is nothing wrong with the pursuit of these delights, it's crucial that we take a long, hard look at the emotional underpinnings of our aspirations.

We must be unflinchingly honest with ourselves, refusing to allow our dreams to become mere vehicles for escapism, distractions from the unresolved wounds that fester within our psyches.

To illuminate the path between these two realms of dreams, we must dive beneath the shimmering surface of our aspirations to uncover the emotional undercurrents that propel them forward.

Every dream, at its very core, is a quest for a feeling – an insatiable hunger to experience a particular state of being. Whether we ache for the golden touch of wealth, the intoxicating nectar of success, the rapturous embrace of love, or the wild, untamed beauty of adventure, what we truly seek is the emotional elixir that we believe these treasures will bestow upon us.

When we unravel the emotional threads woven into our dreams, we gain profound insight into their nature. Dreams born from our true selves electrify us with excitement and boundless possibility; they forge an unbreakable bond between our mortal form and the instinctive intelligence that guides us. They align our actions with the grand orchestration of life itself.

False dreams, in contrast, drain us. They keep us chasing illusions, forever grasping at a future that dissolves like mist at dawn. They are the offspring of conditioning, chains masquerading as aspirations, keeping us tethered to an existence that feels hollow and disconnected from our deepest truth. When we kneel before these false idols, we sever our connection to Instinct—the very force that breathes vitality into our being.

To reclaim the power of our dreams, we must first summon the courage to release the illusory narratives that have taken root in our minds. We must cast an unflinching gaze upon the foundations of our being, to confront the myriad ways in which we have been molded and shaped by the expectations of others. It's a sacred rite of letting go, of relinquishing the scripts that have outlived their purpose, the limiting beliefs that keep us tethered to a cycle of struggle and frustration.

As we strip away these layers of conditioning, we create space for our true dreams to emerge—the ones that burn at the very core of our being, setting our souls ablaze with a fire that cannot be extinguished. These are the dreams worthy of our devotion, the dreams that lead us to a life of profound authenticity and deep fulfillment.

Yet, even as we align ourselves with these luminous dreams, we must remember that the journey itself is a sacred pilgrimage, no less significant than the destination. The pursuit of our dreams is not merely about reaching a distant destination—it is about the act of becoming. When we walk this path with presence and alignment, each moment is imbued with meaning. We no longer feel the weight of striving, nor do we anxiously await some future reward. Instead, we immerse ourselves fully in the unfolding of our own mythic tale, savoring each step of the journey, constructing a radiant future upon the foundation of a beautifully lived present.

Dreams, Challenges, and Evolution

STANDING before the intricate landscape of our dreams and aspirations, we often find ourselves at a crossroads—caught between the pull of comfort and the insistent whisper of our instinctive drive for growth. The distinction between these two paths can be subtle, a delicate veil that blurs the lines between what we truly need and what we merely crave.

Consider, for instance, a moment when you find yourself mired in the quicksand of family discord, your spirit slowly eroded by the relentless tide of exhaustion and frustration. In the depths of this struggle, you may dream of a miraculous resolution—a swift and effortless end to conflict, a return to the tranquil waters of harmony.

Yet, the path to true peace is rarely so simple. The temptation may arise to seek solace in the familiar, to retreat into the well-worn grooves of habit and routine, even at the cost of your own truth. You may feel the urge to sacrifice your convictions, to bend yourself into unnatural shapes, all in a desperate attempt to avoid the discomfort of confrontation. But in doing so, do you find peace, or merely the illusion of it?

Alternatively, depending on your nature, you may feel the urge to assert your will upon others, to strong-arm them into submission, to bludgeon them with the weight of your opinions until they relent. But these strategies, born of desperation and fear, are mere band-aids upon the festering wound of familial strife, temporary reprieves that offer no true healing.

It is here, in the crucible of your discontent, that your instinctive wisdom calls you toward a higher path. If you attune yourself to the quiet voice within, you may begin to see your struggles not as burdens to endure, but as sacred opportunities for transformation. With a shift in perspective, challenges become not obstacles, but invitations—beckoning you to step beyond your limitations and into the uncharted waters of your own potential.

But this journey requires courage. You must be willing to sit with your frustrations, to let them simmer and distill until their essence is revealed. Peeling back the layers of discontent, you trace the roots of your anger and resentment, diving past the surface irritations until you reach the raw, vulnerable core of your deepest needs and desires.

Return to the family conflict we've been picturing. On the surface, the tension may appear as a breakdown in communication—a tangled web of unmet expectations, misinterpreted words, and unheard voices. Yet as you dig deeper, you may uncover something more profound: the pain of feeling unseen, unheard, and undervalued by those you love most.

From this place of raw, unfiltered honesty, a new path emerges. If your deepest yearning is to be heard and understood, you can make the conscious choice to cultivate the skills that will bring you closer to that truth—to communicate with greater clarity, compassion, and authenticity. In doing so, you move beyond passive longing and step into the active creation of the life you truly desire.

It's crucial to recognize that the path of personal growth and evolution is not only more attainable but also far more empowering than the futile pursuit of changing others. While we may long to influence the behaviors and attitudes of those around us, the truth is that their journey is theirs alone. It is not our responsibility—nor our right—to dictate another's path. True transformation begins not by reshaping those around us, but by refining ourselves, embodying the change we wish to see, and allowing our own evolution to ripple outward in ways we cannot yet foresee.

When we shift our focus inward and make our own evolution the primary goal, we empower ourselves to take full responsibility for our own happiness and fulfillment. We begin to understand that the only person we can truly evolve is ourselves, and that by cultivating our own strengths, skills, and self-awareness, we become better equipped to navigate even the most challenging of circumstances.

By focusing on our own growth, we free ourselves from the burden of expectation and the frustration of unmet desires. We learn to find validation and worth within ourselves, rather than seeking it from external sources. And as we begin to show up in the world as a best version of ourselves, we may just inspire others to do the same, leading by example rather than coercion.

As we shift our focus toward our own growth, the conflicts and struggles that once consumed us begin to lose their grip. In time, we come to see that true victory is not found in changing others, but in transforming ourselves—expanding our capacity to meet even the most turbulent waters with balance, resilience, and unwavering presence.

At times, despite our best efforts, certain individuals may remain locked in their patterns, unwilling or unable to meet us in the space of mutual understanding and growth. Yet even in these moments, our efforts are not in vain. Every skill we develop, every insight we gain, becomes part of the foundation upon which we build our strength, wisdom, and resilience. The challenges we face, no matter how discouraging, serve as the crucible in which we refine ourselves.

By meeting life with an open heart and a curious mind, we learn to transmute even the most bitter disappointments into catalysts for transformation. Setbacks cease to be roadblocks and instead become stepping stones, each one guiding us toward a deeper understanding of ourselves and the world around us.

When we embrace this perspective, we stop seeing challenges as barriers and recognize them as the raw material of our own transformation. Struggle is not an interruption of growth—it is growth in motion. Each hardship forces us to confront what is untested within us, each disappointment strips away illusion, revealing what is real. These moments do not weigh us down; they shape us, forging resilience in the face of adversity and sharpening our clarity where there was once uncertainty. True evolution is not about overcoming—it is about becoming, refining ourselves through experience, shedding what no longer serves us, and stepping into a deeper, stronger, and more expansive version of who we are meant to be.

The Path from Desire to Purpose

LET us take a moment to gaze out at the vast horizon of possibilities stretching before us. It is essential to pause and examine the emotional landscape beneath our aspirations. What is it that we truly seek when we set our sights on distant goals and imagine a transformed life?

More often than not, when we peel back the layers of our ambitions, we find that at their core lies not a tangible achievement, but a deep yearning for a particular emotional state. We tell ourselves we desire wealth, success, love, or recognition, but what we are truly chasing is the feeling we believe these things will bring—happiness, fulfillment, peace, or a sense of belonging.

Consider, for a moment, the dreams that linger at the edges of your consciousness. Perhaps you envision landing the perfect job, one that will finally make you feel valued and appreciated for your talents. Or maybe you long for a romantic partnership that will surround you with warmth, acceptance, and unconditional love. You might dream of adventure, of escaping to distant lands, seeking the exhilaration and freedom of an untethered life.

Beneath each of these visions lies an emotional hunger, a craving for a particular flavor of experience. And while there is nothing inherently wrong with this desire – indeed, our emotions are powerful guides that can point us our deepest truths – we must be cautious about making them the sole focus of our pursuits.

The trouble with chasing emotions as an end in themselves is that they are, by their very nature, ephemeral and elusive. Happiness, love, peace – these are not destinations that we can arrive at and stake our claim upon, but rather fleeting states of being that come and go like the tides. No matter how desperately we may try to cling to them, they will inevitably slip through our fingers, leaving us grasping at empty air.

Moreover, when we make our emotions the primary target of our aspirations, we set ourselves up for disappointment. We may find that even when we achieve the goals we have set for ourselves, the feelings we were chasing fail to materialize, or prove to be less satisfying than we had imagined. In that moment, we come to realize that the void we sought to fill cannot be satisfied by external achievements alone. The hunger remains—not because we have failed, but because we have been searching in the wrong place.

So, what is the alternative? How can we honor the emotional truths at the heart of our dreams while also building a life of genuine substance and meaning? The key lies in a subtle yet profound shift in perspective. Instead of chasing emotions as fleeting prizes to be won, we must embody the values that give rise to them. Fulfillment is not something to be pursued—it is something to be cultivated from within.

If it is love that we seek, let us not wait for it to arrive as if it were a gift bestowed upon us, but instead become vessels of love ourselves. Let us practice kindness, compassion, and understanding—not selectively, but as a way of being, even in the face of indifference or hostility. Let us create spaces of warmth and acceptance, not because we expect something in return, but because love flourishes where it is given freely. And as we pour love into the world, we will find it reflected back to us in ways more profound and lasting than we ever imagined.

If we crave joy, let us not chase after fleeting pleasures, but instead cultivate a spirit of gratitude and wonder—a capacity to find delight in the quiet miracles of everyday life. Let us bring humor and playfulness into our interactions, infusing even the ordinary with a sense of lightness. When we approach life with openness and appreciation, the world begins to sparkle with a vitality that was always there, waiting to be seen.

And if it is meaning and purpose we long for, let us not wait for a grand revelation to descend upon us, but instead dedicate ourselves to something greater than ourselves. Let us pour our unique gifts and passions into the service of others, knowing that purpose is not found in a distant calling, but in the ways we choose to show up in the world each day. When we give ourselves fully to what matters, our lives begin to overflow with significance and connection—not as something we acquire, but as something we become.

By embodying our values, we tap into a source of emotional nourishment far deeper and more enduring than the fleeting highs of achievement. We begin to experience a profound alignment between our innermost being and our outward actions—a sense of integrity and wholeness that sustains us even through life's darkest moments. This is not a happiness that depends on circumstances, nor a fulfillment that can be taken away. It is the quiet strength of knowing that we are living in accordance with our deepest truth.

Yet, walking the path of values-driven living demands immense courage, resilience, and self-awareness. To commit to embodying love, for example, is not merely to extend kindness when it is easy, but to confront the places within us where love is absent. It requires us to look unflinchingly at the shadows within ourselves—the moments of selfishness, judgment, and anger that arise when we feel vulnerable or threatened.

In these moments of reckoning, it's easy to feel disheartened, to question the very foundation of our commitment. We may find ourselves asking, "What am I doing? How can I possibly be a force for love when I'm struggling with so much darkness within myself?" But it is precisely in these moments of doubt and despair that the true test of values-driven living arises.

It is one thing to uphold a value when life is gentle, when circumstances align in our favor, and we feel at ease. It is another entirely to embody that value when chaos erupts—when anger flares, when fear grips us, when the old wounds we thought were healed resurface with unexpected force. This is where the real work begins. To live by our values is not to wait for perfection within ourselves, but to choose, again and again, to act in alignment with the truth we aspire to, even when it feels most difficult. It is in these very moments—when love seems impossible, when compassion feels out of reach—that our deepest growth takes root.

The key to navigating this inner terrain lies in cultivating a deep awareness of our emotional world—learning to observe our feelings with curiosity and compassion rather than judgment or resistance. When we meet our anger, sadness, and frustration with openness, we begin to see that these emotions are not barriers to our values but rather essential allies in our pursuit of a meaningful life.

We come to understand that anger, when channeled with intention, can be a force for transformation, fueling our efforts to challenge injustice and create change. We realize that sadness, when embraced fully, deepens our connection to life's impermanence, allowing us to experience its beauty with greater depth and tenderness. Each emotion, once seen as an obstacle, reveals itself as a guide—pointing us toward deeper self-awareness and a more profound engagement with the world.

Our emotions are not something to be transcended or suppressed in the pursuit of our values, but rather an essential part of our being. By learning to integrate them skillfully into our lives, to harness their power in service of our deepest commitments, we tap into a source of vitality and resilience that can sustain us through even the most challenging of times.

As we rise to this challenge, aligning our lives with our deepest truths, something remarkable unfolds. The emotions we once chased begin to arise naturally—not as rewards for external achievements, but as the byproducts of a life lived with integrity and purpose.

We discover that happiness is not a prize to be won, but a state that emerges when we are immersed in meaningful work and contribute to the world. We realize that love is not something to possess or capture, but something we cultivate through generosity, kindness, and the quiet strength of our presence.

And we come to understand that fulfillment was never meant to be a static destination, a pinnacle to reach and rest upon. It is a living process, a continuous unfolding—a way of engaging with life that brings us ever closer to the essence of who we are and why we are here.

In this way, the pursuit of our dreams transforms from a mere quest for personal satisfaction into a journey of self-discovery and self-actualization. Our emotions cease to be fleeting rewards and become the very fuel that propels us forward, guiding us toward the values and vision that shape our lives and the world around us.

Step by step, day by day, we begin to realize that the true magic of our dreams lies not in reaching some distant goal, but in the person we become along the way. We unearth the real treasure—not out there, but within us.

So let's dare to dream, to yearn, to hunger for a life rich with meaning and ablaze with purpose. But let's also remember that the key to unlocking that life is not in grasping for some distant prize, but in tending to the landscape within, in embodying our deepest values each and every day.

When we move in rhythm with our highest aspirations, we come to see that purpose is not something to be created or achieved—it is something to be uncovered and expressed. It is the intelligence of life itself seeking to manifest through us, the sacred alchemy of our becoming.

Chapter Fifteen

DREAMING WITH YOUR EYES WIDE OPEN

We often find ourselves yearning for a future where our deepest dreams have finally come to fruition—a magical realm where sorrows dissolve, and we bask in the warm glow of lasting fulfillment. With hearts weary from the trials of our present reality, it is all too easy to become transfixed by this shimmering mirage, pouring the precious elixir of our lives into fantasies that forever glisten on the horizon.

Yet, even as we reach toward this promised land with outstretched arms, life whispers a profound and timeless truth: the doorway to genuine joy, meaning, and purpose has always stood before us, hidden in plain sight. It does not lead to some distant, imagined paradise but to the sacred ground beneath our feet—the ever-unfolding realm of the present moment.

In this very breath, in this eternal now, the great wheel of becoming turns, spinning a world of constant change and infinite complexity. Here, light and shadow dance in exquisite partnership, pleasure and pain intertwine in the alchemy of transformation. Though our minds may recoil from the uncertainty and discomfort of this dance, our souls know the truth: only by embracing the fullness of our present experience—in all its sorrow and joy, its ugliness and beauty—can we step into the profound flow of life and discover the seeds of our own awakening.

In the pages that follow, we will explore the ways in which our dreams and fantasies can both inspire and ensnare us, guiding us toward growth and self-discovery while also luring us away from the richness of the present moment.

Through the stories of visionaries and sages, from ancient shamans to modern-day entrepreneurs, we will uncover the timeless wisdom that can help us navigate the complexities of our own lives.

Along the way, we will encounter powerful practices and insights that can help us cultivate a deeper sense of presence, purpose, and authenticity. From the sacred rituals of indigenous cultures to the cutting-edge findings of neuroscience, we will discover the tools and techniques that can enable us to dance with the challenges and opportunities of our lives with greater skill, compassion, and resilience.

Ultimately, this chapter is an invitation to step boldly into the fires of transformation, to embrace the precious gift of our existence in all its mystery and complexity. It's a call to awaken to the profound beauty and potential that lies waiting in each moment, and to craft a life of depth, meaning, and purpose in alignment with our deepest truths.

Dancing with Discomfort

"PATIENCE is not the ability to wait, but the ability to keep a good attitude while waiting." This quote, often attributed to the author Joyce Meyer, encapsulates a common perspective on patience – the idea that it's a virtue that allows us to endure adversity with grace and composure, trusting that the difficulties we face are merely temporary and that better days lie ahead.

There is, of course, a certain wisdom in this outlook. Life is indeed a series of fleeting moments, a constant dance of change and impermanence. The challenges that confront us today, no matter how daunting they may seem, will eventually give way to new realities, new opportunities, and new horizons.

While it may seem logical and even comforting to believe that waiting will eventually resolve our problems, this mindset overlooks a fundamental truth: the only reality we truly have is the one unfolding in the present moment. The future, with all its promise and potential, remains a mirage—a projection of our hopes and fears that may never come to pass—while the past is nothing more than a memory, a story we tell ourselves about who we are and where we've been.

If the present moment is bringing us face to face with a seemingly unsolvable problem, then that is the reality we must confront, whether we like it or not. It's only by opening ourselves fully to this reality, by embracing it with all its discomfort and uncertainty, that we can begin to extract the lessons and opportunities it holds for our growth and evolution.

Too often, in our relentless pursuit of happiness and our desire to feel in control of our lives, we miss out on the profound transformative potential of our most challenging experiences. We become so fixated on finding a way out of discomfort, on returning to a state of ease and equilibrium, that we fail to recognize how our struggles are serving our highest good.

Imagine the difference between facing a difficult situation while constantly anticipating future relief versus meeting that same challenge as if it were the only reality that exists. In the first scenario, your energy is divided—one part engaged with the present, the other fixated on an imagined future where everything is resolved, and you can finally relax.

In the second, you are fully present with what is. No energy is wasted on resistance or wishful thinking; instead, the totality of your being is directed toward the challenge before you. You allow yourself to experience discomfort, uncertainty, fear, and pain without the need to push them away or label them as wrong. You are open to the full spectrum of your experience, embracing it as it unfolds.

It's in this state of complete presence and openness that the true alchemy of transformation can occur. When we're fully immersed in the reality of our experience, without any agenda or expectation, we create the conditions for profound insights and breakthroughs to emerge. We become able to see our challenges from new angles, to access resources and capacities within ourselves that we never knew we had.

In this way, the most painful and difficult circumstances can become portals to a deeper understanding of ourselves. Rather than obstacles to be avoided or enemies to be vanquished, they become our greatest teachers and allies, guiding us toward fulfillment of our highest potential.

As we learn to approach our lives with this radical acceptance and presence, we discover that pain is not something to be feared or resisted, but rather an invitation to go deeper – to peel back the layers of our conditioning and defenses, and to connect with the most authentic and essential parts of ourselves.

We begin to see that our challenges are not obstacles to our growth and awakening but essential parts of the journey itself—the very tools life uses to shape, refine, and polish the diamond of our being.

Here, the practice of patience takes on a whole new meaning. It's no longer about gritting our teeth and enduring our difficulties until they pass, but rather about having the courage and willingness to be fully present with them, to honor them as the sacred opportunities for transformation they are.

In a world that often equates happiness with the ultimate purpose of life, it's easy to become entangled in the pursuit of an idealized existence. From a young age, we're immersed in cultural narratives that paint visions of perfection – from the Christian concept of Paradise in the afterlife to the Cinderella-inspired Hollywood films that promise us our own "happily ever after." We are bombarded with images of the perfect job, the perfect family, the perfect home, and the perfect partner, all of which combine to create the illusions we're taught to pursue.

However, when we take a step back and recognize these narratives for what they truly are – elaborate schemes designed to manipulate our desires and expectations – we can begin to approach the concept of patience from a whole different perspective. Rather than seeing patience as a passive virtue, a way of biding our time until our idealized life materializes, we can begin to understand it as an active practice of mindfulness and discernment.

Patience, in this sense, becomes the art of calming our minds and cultivating a state of inner stillness that allows us to observe the external influences that seek to shape our beliefs and behaviors. It's a way of developing the clarity and objectivity necessary to recognize the triggers and conditioning we carry within us, the subconscious patterns that drive us to chase after illusory goals and ideals.

As we cultivate patience, we naturally develop a sense of detachment—not as disconnection or apathy, but as the ability to observe our thoughts, emotions, and experiences without being consumed by them. This detachment allows us to be fully present with whatever arises, meeting each moment with openness, curiosity, and acceptance rather than seeking to escape our reality.

Paradoxically, our relentless attempts to avoid pain and discomfort at all costs that create even more suffering in the long run. By constantly seeking to numb, distract, or medicate ourselves from the challenges and difficulties of life, we deny ourselves the opportunity to grow, to learn, and to transform our relationships with adversity.

This avoidance of pain is not a universal reality of human life but rather a phenomenon of modern society, where discomfort is often seen as something to be eliminated rather than understood. Yet, by looking beyond this narrow perspective and opening ourselves to the wisdom of different cultures and traditions, we can begin to shift our understanding of pain and hardship. Many ancient philosophies and practices view suffering not as an aberration or punishment but as an inherent part of the human experience—a sacred initiation into the depths of our own being.

When we approach pain with this kind of openness and curiosity, we begin to see it in a new light. Rather than something to be avoided or eliminated at all costs, it becomes a powerful teacher, illuminating the hidden corners of our psyche and pointing us toward a path of genuine growth, in tune with the very nature of life.

As we embrace pain as a teacher, we align ourselves with the fundamental rhythm of existence—a continuous dance of growth, change, and transformation. Just as the caterpillar must dissolve within the chrysalis to emerge as a butterfly, we too must allow ourselves to be broken open by our challenges, trusting that within darkness and uncertainty lies the potential for unimaginable beauty and rebirth. When we meet our suffering with the patience and presence of an open heart, we discover that our deepest wounds can be portals to a more profound and awakened way of being, leading us to a life rich with meaning, purpose, and the boundless wisdom of the soul.

Scars of Wisdom

THE young Cayapó warrior found himself perched precariously at the top of a towering *Samaúma* tree, his heart pounding in his chest as he stared down at the distant ground below. The tree seemed to sway gently in the breeze, its massive trunk stretching up into the canopy of the Amazon rainforest like a living skyscraper. At a dizzying height of forty-two meters, the young man knew that one false move could send him plummeting to his death.

But this was the moment he had been preparing for, the culmination of weeks of careful planning and sacred ritual. A group of tribal elders had scoured the forest, searching for the perfect beehive for his initiation – one that was high enough in the treetops to test his courage and resilience to the utmost.

For the *Cayapó* people, this ritual holds a multitude of profound meaning. On a physical level, the bee's venom fortifies the young warrior's blood, boosting his immunity and rendering his body more resistant to disease. But even more important is the mental and emotional challenge of the ordeal, the inner strength and self-discipline required to face such an extreme test of will.

In *Cayapó* culture, a warrior – a man entrusted with the sacred duty of wielding weapons and defending the tribe – must prove himself worthy of such responsibility. He must demonstrate an unwavering command over his fears and impulses, a steadfast commitment to the greater good of the community. And there was no better crucible for forging such iron resolve than the top of this mighty *Samaúma* tree, with nothing but a flimsy vine harness and a pounding heart to keep him aloft.

With a deep breath, the young man steeled himself for what was to come. He raised his fist, and with a primal cry, he slammed it into the beehive once, twice, three times. Instantly, the air around him exploded into a furious buzzing cloud, as hundreds of enraged bees swarmed out to defend their home.

The pain was immediate and overwhelming, as dozens of stingers sank into the young warrior's flesh. They stung his face, his neck, his bare arms and legs, each one a searing pinprick of agony. His hands began to swell and throb, the skin stretched tight and shiny over the growing welts. But he refused to give in to the suffering, refused to let his grip on the tree falter for even a second.

Slowly, painstakingly, he began to inch his way back down the trunk, his feet finding security on the rough bark, his fingers digging into its crevices. Every movement was an exercise of pure, focused will, a battle against the searing pain and the primal urge to panic. He knew that a single misstep, a momentary lapse in concentration, would send him hurtling into the abyss.

But he also knew that this was the price of manhood in his tribe, the sacred initiation that would mark his passage into adulthood and responsibility. So he gritted his teeth and kept going, even as the bees continued to swarm and sting, even as his vision began to blur and his limbs grew heavy with exhaustion.

To the modern, Western eye, such rituals may seem barbaric, even brutally primitive. We live in a society that often seeks to insulate itself from pain and discomfort at all costs, that views suffering as an aberration to be medicated or avoided rather than a fundamental part of the human experience.

But for cultures like the *Cayapó*, these rites of passage are imbued with a profound wisdom, a recognition of the transformative power of challenge and adversity. They understand that it's only through facing and overcoming our deepest fears and limitations that we can truly come to know ourselves, to tap into the deep wells of strength and resilience that lie within us.

Across the world, various indigenous cultures have long practiced rituals involving pain as a means of forging character, teaching resilience, and marking important transitions in life. In Papua New Guinea, the *Sepik* people engage in a scarification ritual, where intricate patterns are carved into the skin of young men using razor-sharp bamboo blades. The resulting scars are seen as a symbol of strength, endurance, and cultural identity.

In the sacred Sun Dance, *Navajo* warriors pierce their flesh with wooden skewers, tethering themselves to a holy tree. With each agonizing pull, they strain against the cords, their pain a powerful offering to the Great Spirit. By tearing free, they prove their strength and courage, their readiness to endure anything for their tribe. Their scars mark them as true protectors, their suffering is a sacred pledge of devotion to their people.

In Ethiopia, the *Karo* people practice a coming-of-age ritual where young men and women undergo elaborate body modifications, including scarification and skin cutting. These permanent markings serve as a visual testament to their bravery, their willingness to endure pain for the collective.

These rituals serve a deep psychological and cultural purpose. By pushing initiates to the very limits of their endurance, they cultivate a profound sense of self-discipline, mental toughness, and the ability to transcend physical suffering. Participants emerge from these ordeals with a newfound confidence in their own strengths and capabilities, a bedrock of inner resilience that will serve them throughout their lives.

However, the true significance of these rituals goes far beyond the mere tolerance of pain. In many indigenous societies, such as the aboriginal tribes of Australia, initiation rites are designed to guide young people through a complex psychological journey, one that involves confronting and overcoming their deepest fears and anxieties.

Among the *Yolngu* and *Aranda* peoples, for example, the initiation of boys into manhood begins with a dramatic staging of conflict between the men and women of the tribe. The men "attack" the women, who fight back fiercely in a symbolic attempt to keep their sons in the maternal fold. Eventually, the men prevail and take the boys away, effectively severing the psychological umbilical cord that binds them to the world of childhood and femininity.

But this is only the beginning of the ordeal. The boys are then subjected to a series of painful and frightening rituals, which may include being beaten with sticks and whips, having their bodies cut and scarred, or being forced to endure long periods of isolation and deprivation. Finally, they are sent off into the wilderness to fend for themselves, armed only with the skills and knowledge they have acquired through their training.

This exile can last for months, during which time the young men must learn to hunt, gather, and survive in the harsh and unforgiving landscape of the Australian outback. They must confront their fears of solitude, starvation, and predation, relying on their own wits and resourcefulness to stay alive.

When at last they return to their tribe, they are no longer boys, but men—hardened by their experiences, confident in their abilities, and ready to take on the responsibilities of adulthood. The scars they bear are not just physical, but psychological as well – the marks of a profound inner transformation that has equipped them to face whatever challenges life may bring.

In many ways, these young men are the polar opposites of their counterparts in modern Western society, who often remain entangled in the same fears that the aboriginal initiates have confronted head-on. The fear of rejection, the terror of abandonment, and the anxiety of self-reliance haunt the psyches of countless modern individuals, crippling their ability to form healthy relationships, pursue meaningful goals, and cultivate a true sense of purpose.

In contrast, the young men who have undergone these indigenous rites of passage carry with them a deep and abiding faith in themselves, a trust in their own resilience and competence that allows them to navigate the vicissitudes of life with grace and equanimity. They have stared down their darkest fears and emerged victorious, armed with the knowledge that they can handle whatever challenges come their way.

Compare this to the plight of a modern teenager, sitting in a psychologist's office, pouring out his heart about the trauma of his parents' divorce and the deep wounds of neglect. He grapples with feelings of nihilism and distress, desperately seeking a way to ease the emotional pain that feels so overwhelming and unbearable. A far cry from the resilience and fortitude displayed by his indigenous counterparts, who have learned to embrace pain as a necessary part of growth and transformation.

In our modern society, we have pathologized emotional pain, treating it as a disorder to be cured rather than a natural part of the human experience. We have created a massive industry around antidepressants, self-help books, and therapy sessions, all promising to alleviate our suffering and help us find happiness. But in our quest to avoid discomfort at all costs, we may be robbing ourselves of the very experiences that can make us stronger, wiser, and more resilient.

The most common psychological problems of modern life—anxiety, depression, addiction, and the like—are often rooted in a fundamental inability to tolerate and make sense of emotional pain. We live in a culture that sells us the illusion of a life without suffering, a world where every problem can be solved with a pill or a purchase. But this denial of the inevitable challenges and losses of life only makes us more fragile, more vulnerable to being shattered by the first sign of adversity.

Even our religious and spiritual traditions, with their promises of eternal paradise and reincarnation, can sometimes serve to avoid confronting the painful reality of death and impermanence. We cling to these beliefs as a way to buffer ourselves against the existential angst of our own mortality, rather than learning to accept and make peace with the fleeting nature of existence.

When we look at how ancient cultures depicted their deities, we often encounter beings that are wild, fearsome, and enigmatic—far removed from the benevolent, fatherly figures of modern religious iconography. The Aztec god Quetzalcoatl, for example, took the form of a feathered serpent, while the Chinese deities Fuxi and Nuwa had the bodies of snakes. The Greek Typhon, the Egyptian Sobek, and the Hindu Ganesha all bore animal features, blurring the line between the human and the divine.

These portrayals were not mere products of primitive superstition but expressions of profound spiritual insight. The mystery of creation, which we call God, exists beyond human comprehension, for our minds and senses can only graze the surface of its infinite depths. In attempting to grasp this ineffable reality, each culture developed its own image of the divine—reflections that revealed more about their values, fears, and aspirations than about the ultimate nature of God.

Rather than viewing their gods as distant or purely benevolent figures, these cultures saw them as forces of both creation and destruction, mirroring the raw, unpredictable nature of existence itself. They understood that pain, impermanence, and struggle were not aberrations to be escaped but essential elements of life's unfolding journey. They recognized the divine not as a distant force confined to an untouched realm of perfection but as something that infused every aspect of life, from the sacred to the ordinary. This understanding of spirituality allowed them to see meaning not only in moments of transcendence but also in the struggles, uncertainties, and challenges of daily existence.

By honoring these untamed aspects of the divine, ancient peoples embraced the full complexity of their own humanity. They recognized that even in moments of weakness, confusion, or despair, they were still part of a larger cosmic pattern—one in which suffering and transformation were inextricably linked. In doing so, they cultivated a relationship with the sacred that was not built on avoidance or idealization, but on direct, unfiltered engagement with the realities of existence.

In contrast, modern religious traditions often present a more sanitized, palatable version of the divine. We have reimagined God as a benevolent father figure, a compassionate savior, or a gentle lamb who sacrifices himself for our sins. These images, while comforting and reassuring, can feel far removed from the raw, unfiltered reality of our earthly existence, with all its challenges, uncertainties, and imperfections. After all, if God is truly all-loving and all-powerful, why is there so much suffering and injustice in the world? How can we reconcile the idea of a merciful, compassionate deity with the harsh realities of pain, loss, and tragedy that so often mark our human experience?

Is all evil truly the work of the Devil and a consequence of our human sins? This notion implies that not only the humankind, but the entire universe, suffers as a victim of our flawed nature. By failing to act according to God's law, we are perceived as breaking the cosmic rules and bringing chaos into existence. This burden is immense, one that not only suffocates us with overwhelming guilt but also sets us apart from the divine. The weight of this responsibility can be paralyzing, fostering a sense of perpetual inadequacy and separation from the divine harmony we yearn to be a part of.

Even within this theological construct, a nagging question persists: why do those who follow religious teachings and live morally upright lives still face so much hardship and suffering? This simple question challenges the idea of divine justice and the notion of an almighty, all-loving God who ensures fairness.

To bridge this gap between our idealized conception of the divine and the messy, often painful realities of life, many modern religions have constructed elaborate visions of an afterlife—realms of eternal peace and tranquility where all suffering is abolished and we can finally rest in the presence of a loving, merciful God. In this sense, heaven and Paradise serve as a balm for the weary soul, a promise of ultimate redemption and release from the trials of mortal existence. They offer a way to reconcile the apparent contradictions between a benevolent, all-powerful God and a world filled with suffering, by positing a future state in which all wrongs will be made right, and all tears will be wiped away.

And while these beliefs can provide comfort and solace in the face of life's challenges, they may also serve as a form of spiritual escapism, a way to avoid fully engaging with the raw, unvarnished reality of our own mortality. By focusing on the promise of a perfect afterlife, we risk neglecting the opportunities for growth and transformation that arise from embracing the full spectrum of human experience, including pain and loss.

In learning to blindly follow religious rules to secure our place in heaven after we die, we inadvertently cultivate a sense of contempt or disregard for our earthly existence. By placing all our hopes and aspirations in a postmortem reward, we end up overlooking the potential for finding genuine meaning, purpose, and fulfillment in the here and now. Our present reality becomes little more than a temporary trial to be endured, rather than a precious and miraculous opportunity.

But what if, instead of dreaming of a painless afterlife, we learned to embrace the sacredness of our human experience, with all its joys and sorrows, its triumphs and struggles? What if we recognized that the very impermanence and fragility of our existence is what makes it so beautiful and precious? By letting go of our attachment to a perfect, painless future, we can begin to fully inhabit the richness and complexity of the present moment, to find meaning and purpose in the midst of life's challenges and uncertainties.

Ultimately, the path to self-development may not lie in escaping or transcending the pain of existence, but in learning to make peace with it, to see it as an essential part of the sacred mystery of life. By honoring our suffering as a teacher, we may discover a deeper sense of connection to ourselves, to each other, and to the vast, ineffable mystery that underlies all creation.

In a sense, the modern individual must undergo their own rite of passage, not in a single dramatic ordeal, but in the accumulated challenges and trials of daily life. We may not have the benefit of a structured initiation ceremony to guide us through this process, but we can still learn to approach our own pain and fear with the same courage and determination displayed by young aboriginal men.

This means learning to sit with our discomfort rather than constantly trying to escape or numb it. It means cultivating a sense of curiosity and openness toward our own emotional landscape, trusting that even our darkest experiences have something to teach us. It means developing a kind of emotional resilience that allows us to bounce back from setbacks and disappointments, secure in the knowledge that we have the inner resources to cope with whatever life may bring.

As the *Aranda* boys who are torn from their mothers' arms and sent out into the wilderness to fend for themselves, we too must learn to cut the psychological umbilical cord that binds us to the illusions of safety and certainty. We must be willing to step outside our comfort zones, to risk failure and rejection in pursuit of our deepest values and aspirations.

And like those young men returning from their exile, bearing the scars of their ordeal with pride and dignity, we too can emerge from our own trials transformed – not broken by our pain, but ennobled by it, armed with a new sense of our own strength and resilience.

And though we may not have the benefit of a wise elder or a sacred ceremony to guide us through this process, we can still draw strength and inspiration from the timeless wisdom of these ancient traditions. We can learn to embrace our pain as a teacher and an ally, to trust in the transformative power of our own resilience, and to walk the path of our own becoming with grace, courage, and an open heart.

The Spider Goddess' Gift: Weaving a Life of Meaning from the Threads of the Here and Now

JUSTIN Brown, a mid-age entrepreneur living in the bustling city of Los Angeles, found himself behind the wheel of his old, buttering Prius. As he navigated through the sun-drenched streets, he closed his eyes for a brief moment, allowing his imagination to take hold. In his mind's eye, the worn-out fabric of his car seat transformed into the supple, hand-stitched leather of a sleek Maserati. The dull hum of the Prius' engine gave way to the powerful roar of an Italian masterpiece. With a grin on his face, Justin gripped the steering wheel, imagining it as the futuristic control panel of his dream car.

This vivid visualization was not merely a fleeting daydream, but rather an exercise in manifestation, a practice Justin had learned from a notorious psychic. The concept behind manifestation was the belief that one could bring their deepest desires into reality through the power of focused intention and unwavering faith. By aligning his thoughts and emotions with the frequency of abundance, Justin believed he could attract his dream life into existence.

At that time, Justin had big dreams. He aspired to launch the next Instagram, a revolutionary social media platform that would take the world by storm. He fantasized about joining the ranks of the 10 richest men in the world, his name emblazoned across headlines and his face gracing the covers of prestigious magazines. With each visualization session behind the wheel of his imaginary Maserati, Justin felt himself inching closer to his goals, the fabric of reality bending to his will.

Justin was a charismatic and passionate individual, with an innate ability to inspire and captivate those around him. His infectious enthusiasm and unwavering belief in his vision were so powerful that, despite having only a fledgling company and a dream, without even a clear project outline, he managed to raise an astonishing 1.8 million dollars for his new venture. Investors and supporters alike were drawn to his magnetic presence and the sheer force of his conviction, eager to be a part of the groundbreaking journey he was embarking upon. All thanks to Justin's remarkable ability to rally others to his cause and to paint a picture of a future so vivid and compelling that it seemed almost inevitable.

Justin's path took an unexpected turn when he found himself deep within a cave in Brazil, participating in an ancient *Ayahuasca* ceremony. The cave walls were lined with delicate webs spun by non-poisonous spiders—creatures that had long haunted his nightmares. I brought him to this sacred space not only to confront his deepest fears but to introduce him to the concept of the goddess—the great spider, the mother who weaves the intricate web of life.

As the *Ayahuasca* took hold, Justin plunged into the abyss of his own psyche. The journey became a harrowing odyssey through dread, anxiety, and pain, as deeply buried sorrows and traumas surfaced with relentless force, demanding acknowledgment. He teetered on the brink of madness, his mind fracturing beneath the unbearable weight of the experience.

It was in this crucible of suffering that Justin realized the only way out was through. Any attempt to resist, suppress, or escape his emotions would only deepen his torment. It required every ounce of his courage to surrender—to relinquish his desperate grip on control and allow himself to be consumed by the storm of his own anguish.

Every fiber of his being screamed in resistance, urging him to fight against the rising tide of emotion. But this was not a battle to be won. With a final, shuddering breath, he let go, allowing himself to be fully immersed in the tempest of his psyche, trusting that somehow, through the darkness and chaos, he would find his way back to the light.

As Justin drifted deeper into the vast web of pain and dreams, he saw the truth beneath his ambitions. His relentless pursuit of achievement had not been born of pure passion but of a wounded child's desperate need for validation. He saw that behind every aspiration lay a fear of being unloved, a terror of abandonment that had shaped his every move. What this child needed most was not external recognition but a deep, compassionate embrace.

In communion with this lost part of himself, Justin found the beauty of his love and the power of his passion. Embracing his inner child, he was drawn into the core of his essence, where the embers of his true self glowed with quiet intensity. In this light, the illusions that had once clouded his vision—the mirages of recognition and validation—crumbled, revealing how these false desires had been born from a place of perceived brokenness.

With newfound clarity, he began untangling the threads of his past, releasing the need for external approval and stepping into the unfiltered essence of his dreams. The fears and anxieties that had once held him captive, the illusions of inadequacy and the endless quest for validation, began to dissolve. He saw that by facing his deepest shadows and embracing the totality of his being, he had shattered the chains of his self-imposed limitations. The grip of the external world loosened, for he had discovered an unshakable truth within himself—one grounded in genuineness and self-respect.

In the depths of his inner sanctuary, Justin encountered a revelation. Here, at the heart of his being, stood the Spider Goddess—an embodiment of raw, visceral power and boundless potential. She was both creator and predator, weaving every conceivable reality, embodying the full spectrum of human experience. As her intricate threads stretched before him, Justin saw the stories of his life unfold—woven from his deepest fears, traumas, and the longing for recognition.

The Spider Goddess revealed the duality within him, her many legs gliding effortlessly across a web that shimmered with an eerie, otherworldly glow. Each thread she spun pulsed with energy, vibrating between creation and destruction. As her deft movements wove intricate patterns, visions flickered within the strands—scenes of his past, tangled with pain and longing, each knot a scar left by old wounds. He watched as his deepest fears twisted into the very fabric of his aspirations, the shadows of abandonment and self-doubt shaping his desires. Yet, with the same fluid motion, she unraveled the darkness, spinning new strands infused with warmth and radiance, threads glowing with the golden hues of love, passion, and authenticity. The web shifted, revealing the power of intention—that he, too, could choose which strands to weave, which stories to tell, and which realities to bring to life.

In that moment of profound insight, Justin understood that he had always possessed the power to shape his own reality. The Spider Goddess illuminated the choice before him: to create from the shadows of his past or to weave from the radiant energy of his essence. She urged him to choose his threads with intention—to build his future not from pain, but from the wellspring of his true purpose.

Justin emerged from his journey transformed. He had faced his darkest fears, surrendered to his most profound pain, and uncovered the unshakable core of his being. No longer bound by illusions or past wounds, he was free to chart his own course, to manifest a life of true meaning and fulfillment. The external world would continue to present challenges, but he now carried the wisdom and resilience to navigate them with grace, forever guided by the luminous presence of his own essence.

The true magic of the *Ayahuasca* ceremony unfolded in the aftermath of Justin's journey. From that day forward, he released his attachment to the grandiose dreams that had once consumed him. Instead, he made a profound commitment to his present life, embracing the beauty and potential of each moment as it unfolded. Justin came to understand that his true pleasure and fulfillment lay not in the anticipated outcomes of his endeavors but in the act of creation itself. He discovered that by fixating on a distant, idealized future, he had inadvertently created a chasm between his current reality and his aspirations, a gap that left him feeling perpetually unfulfilled.

This shift in perspective couldn't have come at a more crucial time, for while Justin had been fiercely chasing his big dreams, his real-life business was teetering on the brink of collapse. Astronomical sums of money were being spent on top executives, and elaborate plans were being crafted, yet the business lacked a solid foundation. It was a venture that had become ungrounded, divorced from the realities of its present circumstances. The business model was years ahead of its actual capabilities, like a newborn child who can barely crawl being sent to compete in a triathlon. This precarious situation served as a powerful reminder of how the weight of expectations can set us dangerously off-balance, causing us to lose touch with the solid ground beneath our feet.

Waking up from the delusion of a billionaire business to the raw reality of an almost bankrupt one was a jarring experience for Justin, but he embraced the challenge with humility and determination. Gone were the days of grandiose dreams and excessive spending; now, he had to confront the stark truth of his company's precarious position. With a newfound sense of clarity and purpose, Justin set about restructuring his business, completely reimagining its model to better align with the realities of the present. This adaptation extended beyond the boardroom and into his personal life, as he made the difficult decision to leave behind the fancy streets of LA and embark on a new chapter as a digital nomad in Southeast Asia, to cut expenses and streamline his life.

But as Justin began to immerse himself in the present moment, he found the nourishment and vitality he had been seeking all along. By engaging with the world around him, by embracing the inherent creativity and potential of each day, he tapped into a deep well of purpose and meaning. The sense of fulfillment he craved was not some distant reward to be attained but a state of being that he learned to cultivate through purposeful action in the here and now. With this newfound understanding, he set forth on a path of authentic living, guided by the wisdom of his heart and the joy of each present moment.

We could delve deep into a conversation about the lack of foundation and the risks associated with positive thinking and manifestation practices. However, it's important to recognize that these practices and pseudo-philosophies are merely symptoms of a larger societal malady. The manifestation gurus and their ilk are opportunistic byproducts of our collective lack of groundedness, a reflection of how we foolishly reject the treasure of our present reality in pursuit of a future that always seems to remain just out of reach.

In our modern world, it is all too common to fall into the trap of prioritizing our fantasies over reality, just as Justin once did. We often find ourselves consumed by dreams of an idealized future, neglecting the precious opportunities and experiences that lie right before us. This tendency to live in the shadow of our imagination can manifest in countless ways, permeating every aspect of our lives. We exhaust ourselves chasing external validation—success, wealth, and perfection—while neglecting what truly nourishes us.

Hypnotized by our own emotions, we can spend entire lifetimes suffering at the hands of our imagination. Nowhere is this more evident than in the countless dysfunctional marriages that plague our society—unions that persist not out of love, but out of an attachment to an illusion.

A familiar story unfolds in countless relationships. A story that begins with the intoxication of infatuation. In the early stages of love, we don't just see our partner; we project onto them. We fill in the gaps with our desires, shaping them into the idealized figure we long for. This fantasy feels so real that we become emotionally dependent on it.

But reality always asserts itself. The idealized version of our partner inevitably collides with who they truly are—flawed, complex, and incapable of meeting our every expectation. Instead of adjusting to this reality, many people resist it. They experience frustration, disappointment, even resentment. But rather than recognizing the core issue—their own unwillingness to see their partner as they truly are—they double down on the fantasy.

At this point, the marriage enters a vicious cycle. The dreamer begins to believe that their suffering is caused not by their own projections, but by their partner's failure to "live up" to the fantasy. They try to mold, correct, and push their partner toward this imaginary standard. They cling to the idea that, with enough patience, effort, or sacrifice, they will eventually get the love story they were promised in their own minds.

But this realization is difficult. To admit that they have been trapped in their own illusion means confronting the pain of wasted time, of misplaced expectations, of dreams that must be grieved. Many prefer to stay in denial, clinging to the illusion rather than facing the unknown. And so, countless men and women go to their graves bound to a love that never truly existed—prisoners of a dream that became their own cage.

This same pattern plays out in the realm of career aspirations. In a competitive world, the allure of success can be intoxicating, drawing people into its grip. Many fixate on a specific vision of achievement—one often tied to wealth, status, and prestige. They grind away in unfulfilling jobs, convinced that happiness lies just beyond the next promotion or milestone. But in chasing this ever-moving target, they risk overlooking the deep satisfaction and personal growth that come from fully engaging with their present work and finding meaning in the journey itself.

A similar trap exists in health and wellness. Many become fixated on the idea of the perfect body or an ideal state of well-being, constantly striving for a goal that always seems just out of reach. This relentless pursuit can turn self-care into a source of frustration rather than fulfillment. Instead of appreciating small victories—the strength gained, the mental clarity improved, the gradual progress made—they remain caught in a cycle of dissatisfaction, blind to the benefits unfolding in the present.

Even in parenting, the weight of unfulfilled dreams can cast a long shadow. Like well-intentioned directors, some parents project their own unrealized ambitions onto their children, seeing them as the protagonists of a play they never got to perform. They envision their children achieving the successes that eluded them, living out the dreams they once held dear. But in doing so, they risk placing undue pressure on their kids, failing to see them as they truly are—unique individuals with their own aspirations, separate from the past regrets of their parents.

We often find ourselves ensnared in the seductive pull of an imagined future—a vision so vivid and compelling that it threatens to overshadow the reality we inhabit. We tell ourselves that this endless dreaming is a sign of ambition, of a deep desire to live fully and explore our vast potential. But in truth, it is often a form of escapism—a way to sidestep the discomforts and challenges of the present. By constantly projecting our energy onto an idealized future, we strengthen a version of ourselves that exists only in our minds, feeding it with each passing day until it becomes more real to us than the life unfolding before our eyes.

This addiction—though less visible than substance abuse or compulsive behaviors—can be even more insidious. It often goes unrecognized, even by ourselves, making it all the more difficult to break free. The true cost of this escapism is a slow but steady disconnection from our own bodies, instincts, and inner vitality.

When we resist fully engaging with life as it is—its triumphs, its struggles, its unfiltered reality—we rob ourselves of the very fuel needed for growth. These experiences, however challenging, are not obstacles to avoid but essential catalysts for transformation. Like fertile soil, they nourish the roots of our being, grounding us in the present and giving us the strength to evolve. Only by embracing life as it unfolds—rather than clinging to an imagined version of it—can we reclaim our power and step into our truest selves.

This willingness to be fully present, even in discomfort, unlocks the vast reserves of energy and consciousness within us. When we stop resisting our struggles and instead engage with them fully—allowing ourselves to feel, process, and integrate our experiences—we tap into a deep well of personal power. It is through this integration, not avoidance, that we gain the clarity and strength to overcome obstacles and manifest our deepest desires.

When faced with failure and adversity, we stand at a crossroads, with three distinct paths before us—each leading to a vastly different outcome.

The first path, the road of negativity, is riddled with blame, self-pity, and despair. Those who walk this path become trapped in a cycle of victimhood, pointing fingers at others or cursing fate for their misfortunes. Resigned to inevitable failure, they brace themselves for the next disappointment, allowing bitterness to erode their spirit and potential. This path leads nowhere but stagnation.

The second path, the illusion of blind optimism, may seem more inviting at first. Here, failure is met not with reflection, but with escapism—losing oneself in fantasies of an idealized future. It is the temptation to soothe present struggles by retreating into daydreams of success, replaying scenes of imagined perfection rather than confronting reality. Yet, this too is avoidance. By fleeing into dreams, we miss the lessons hidden within our struggles, denying ourselves the growth that only comes from facing adversity head-on.

Then there is the third path—the path of presence and authenticity. This road is less traveled but infinitely more rewarding. It is the path of those who meet failure with openness and curiosity, seeing setbacks not as dead ends, but as teachers. Walking this path means allowing ourselves to feel the sting of disappointment without letting it define us. It means using failure as a tool for self-discovery—reflecting, adjusting, and refining our approach with each challenge we face.

By choosing this grounded perspective, we tap into a deep reservoir of resilience and strength. We learn to trust our abilities, to pivot and adapt in the face of setbacks. And as we move forward, not blinded by despair nor lost in illusion, we unlock our true potential—turning challenges into stepping stones toward the life that truly resonates with our soul.

As Justin embraced this realistic attitude, he found the elements he needed to completely shift his destiny. No longer shackled by the illusions of his imaginary future, he developed a keen sense of self-awareness, a clear understanding of his strengths and weaknesses, his passions and his purpose. And as he navigated the twists and turns of life with this grounded perspective, he began to unlock the potential of his being, to manifest the dreams and aspirations that truly resonated with his soul.

When Justin finally gave up on his manifestation exercise, a profound transformation occurred. Suddenly, he found himself fully present in the moment, appreciating the simple joy of driving his Prius. The car that had once seemed like a symbol of his inadequacy now became a cherished companion that carried him through the journey of his life. As he gripped the steering wheel, feeling the vibration of the engine and the rush of the wind against his face, Justin realized that this sense of presence, this deep connection to his own reality, was all he truly needed.

Justin may not have built the next Instagram, but he did something just as remarkable—he transformed a small, nearly bankrupt company into a thriving business. The same passion and enthusiasm he once poured into selling a vision of the future, he now channeled into the present—rolling up his sleeves, refining his skills, and making his business work. The results were undeniable.

Over the following years, he immersed himself in learning and hands-on experience, steadily honing his expertise. With time, his efforts bore fruit, leading him into new entrepreneurial ventures that eventually grew into a successful media holding company. Yet, the true reward wasn't in the financial success—it was in the shift of perspective.

His nomadic years, once born out of necessity, became some of the most fulfilling of his life. Not because of the money he made, but because he was fully present—embracing spontaneity, appreciating each moment as it came. Even now, settled in Singapore, Justin still carves out time to travel the world, working remotely from his laptop—a pleasure discovered in those challenging yet joyful days.

In the end, Justin's story serves as an example of the transformative potential of embracing the present moment. By letting go of his attachment to an idealized future and fully engaging with the reality of his life, he was able to tap into his own creativity, resilience, and purpose. His journey reminds us that true fulfillment lies not in the distant horizons of our fantasies, but in the rich soil of our present experience.

As the philosopher Slavoj Žižek once said, "The thing to do is not to get rid of your fantasies, but to enjoy your fantasies, while knowing that they are just that–fantasies." Perhaps we can take this wisdom a step further and recognize that the energy we invest in our fantasies is often a misuse of our creative potential. If we were to redirect this power toward the present moment, we might be amazed at the possibilities that begin to blossom in our lives.

For it is in the garden of the here and now that the seeds of our most authentic dreams take root and flourish. By tending to this sacred ground with presence, intention, and love, we open ourselves up to a life of boundless growth and discovery. And as we learn to embrace the beauty and challenges of each moment, we may find that the true treasure we seek has been within our grasp all along, waiting patiently for us to awaken to its radiant presence.

Imaginary Problem, Imaginary Solution

OUR ability to dream is both our greatest gift and our most profound burden. It's the fire that illuminates the path toward progress, knowledge, accomplishment, and self-discovery, igniting within us passion and desire. Yet, in equal measure, dreams have the power to ensnare us, pulling us into a labyrinth of fantasies that slowly erode our connection to the present moment, robbing us of the chance to be fully awake and alive in the reality we inhabit.

There is undeniable beauty in yearning for a better life—a noble impulse that has driven humanity forward since the dawn of time, fueling our greatest achievements and most profound revelations. But when we allow ourselves to be consumed by the seductive embrace of daydreams, we risk falling into a trap of our own making.

Excessive daydreaming can become a siren song, luring us away from reality and into a sea of unintended consequences. Like a mist that gradually thickens around the mind, it can cloud our ability to focus, sap our productivity, and weaken our sense of agency. What begins as a source of inspiration can become an escape that distances us from the life we are meant to live.

The art of balancing dreams of the future with full engagement in the present is a skill that demands both intention and devotion. It is a dance—one that calls for the soaring imagination of a visionary and the grounded presence of a sage. Life, in all its raw and unfiltered beauty, can often feel like a crucible of frustration, pain, fear, and monotony. There are moments when the weight of existence bears down with crushing intensity, when the sheer repetition of the mundane feels like an exquisite form of torture, luring us toward the refuge of fantasy. Yet, it is in these very moments that we are called to stand firm, to resist the temptation to escape, and to meet the fullness of our experience with an open and unwavering gaze.

Consider how we approach anxiety. Instead of navigating its complexities with wisdom and compassion, we fall into a vicious cycle of self-judgment and avoidance. At the first stirrings of anxiety, a deeply ingrained thought pattern whispers that something is fundamentally wrong with us for feeling this way. We become anxious about our anxiety, turning it into an imaginary problem that we then feel compelled to solve.

In our desperation to escape discomfort, we instinctively resist, fighting against the unease that threatens to overwhelm us. But in doing so, we only deepen our suffering, layering resistance upon fear. Imagine, for a moment, that you are faced with a high-stakes situation at work—perhaps delivering a crucial presentation to a room full of high-powered executives. The mere thought of standing before them, vulnerable and exposed, fills you with dread. Your mind races, your body tenses, and before you even step onto the stage, you are locked in battle—not just with the situation itself, but with your own inner turmoil.

As the anxiety begins to build, you feel your heart racing, your palms sweating, and your mind spinning with worst-case scenarios. But rather than acknowledging these sensations with kindness and understanding, you begin to berate yourself for your perceived weakness.

With each self-critical thought, anxiety tightens its grip, transforming from a fleeting emotion into an enemy—a flaw in your character that must be fixed at all costs. The more you resist, the more it consumes you, turning discomfort into self-condemnation.

As the day of the presentation approaches, your anxiety is no longer just about the event—it becomes a reflection of yourself. You don't just feel nervous; you start to believe that your anxiety is proof that something is fundamentally wrong with you. Why can't I handle this like everyone else? you wonder. Why am I so weak? The fear isn't just about stumbling over your words or forgetting your points—it's about the way your hands shake, the way your heart races, the way your mind spins out of control. You lie awake at night, convinced that this reaction isn't normal, that it reveals some deep, unfixable flaw.

Desperate for a solution, you search for the root cause of your anxiety, convinced that if you could just identify and fix your weakness, you would finally become the confident, self-assured person you long to be. You craft elaborate fantasies of a life free from fear—believing that landing a big promotion, discovering the perfect self-help book, or mastering the right technique will finally bring unshakable confidence.

These imagined solutions become your new fixation, a shimmering mirage that promises escape from discomfort. You pour all your energy into pursuing them, convinced they hold the key to freedom. But no matter how much you achieve, anxiety remains—a constant companion that refuses to be shaken off.

You realize, too late, that your attempts to escape anxiety have only amplified it, turning it into a prison of self-recrimination. In trying to fix your emotions, you've given them more power—forgetting that they were never barriers to life, but an inescapable part of the human experience.

Every time we give up on a plan because of anxiety, fear, or sadness, we're silently telling our emotions that they have the power to stop us. We establish a pattern, and this becomes our reality. We condition ourselves to believe we are at the mercy of our emotional states, rather than recognizing that we have the ability to move forward even in the face of discomfort.

In our quest for the perfect moment and the ideal circumstances, we may find ourselves forever waiting, forever postponing our actions toward the life we long to live. We tell ourselves that we'll start that project when we feel more confident, that we'll speak the truth of our hearts when the time is right, that we'll make that big life change when everything else falls into place.

But in doing so, we risk losing the precious timing of our lives, the opportunities that present themselves in the here and now. We may miss the chance to connect deeply with someone we love, to take a leap of faith toward our most cherished goals, or to simply embrace the beauty and wonder of the present moment. And in waiting for a more perfect life, we may find that life itself has passed us by, leaving us with nothing but the bitter taste of regret and the haunting sense of what might have been.

Stepping Into the Sacred Present

WE live our lives waiting—waiting for clarity, waiting for confidence, waiting for the perfect circumstances to finally begin. We tell ourselves that the real adventure, the real transformation, is just beyond the next goal, the next achievement, the next milestone. And yet, when we arrive, the horizon has already shifted. The dream we once chased dissolves into another, and another, like a mirage forever retreating in the desert heat.

But what if we stopped running? What if we understood, with the full weight of our being, that this moment—imperfect, raw, and unscripted—is the only life we will ever have?

This is the great paradox of human longing: we dream of a perfect future while neglecting the very life that could make us whole. We chase fulfillment like an object to be possessed, never realizing that fulfillment is a practice—a way of inhabiting our reality, here and now.

We imagine that one day, we will awaken in a life free of uncertainty, free of fear, free of struggle. But what if the point was never to escape these things? What if the true measure of a life well-lived is not how much we avoided pain, but how deeply we engaged with it—how willingly we stepped into the unknown, how fiercely we loved despite the risks, how fully we allowed ourselves to be here, in this sacred, fleeting instant?

The great Spider Goddess of Justin's vision did not offer him a perfect future. She offered him a choice: to weave his life from fear, or to weave it from truth. We are all given this same choice, every single day.

We can keep waiting. We can keep postponing our lives until we feel ready—until we have more certainty, more money, more knowledge, more control. Or we can step forward as we are, embracing the unknown with open hands, trusting that the only ground we will ever stand on is the one beneath our feet.

Because life is not waiting for us somewhere beyond the horizon. Life is happening now. Not in some distant dream. Not in the promise of a future self. But here. In this breath. In this very moment. And the only question that remains is: Will we show up for it?

Chapter Sixteen

THE EAGLE'S DANCE: CYCLES OF DEATH AND REBIRTH

In the chamber of creation, where the sacred and the profane blur, an act of profound beauty and limitless power unfolds: the miraculous moment of conception, an alchemical dance of passion and intensity. Within the throes of love and lust, in the sensual fusion of two souls, the seed of life is planted. Each touch, each fervent kiss, build a symphony of bliss to its feverish climax, culminating in the eruption of an orgasm—the embodiment of the raw, untamed force of human nature. Here, love and violence intermingle, crafting the genesis of life from the most intimate human connection.

While the exhausted lovers rest in bliss, a silent battle is happening—within the tempest of passion, the sperm has embarked on a perilous journey, a microscopic odyssey of hope and determination. Each spermatozoon, a living seed, propels itself with unwavering resolve toward its ultimate destiny—the egg. The ovum, a fertile sphere of promise, senses the invasion and protects itself with an intricate arsenal of defenses, secreting a toxin that destroys countless sperm in a merciless culling. It's a carnage of cellular combat, where egg and sperm fight fiercely to survive.

Amidst this slaughter, one sperm must overcome the final barrier, shedding its tail to penetrate the egg's fortress. This act is both a death and a birth, a sacrificial consummation where the sperm and egg cease to exist as separate entities, merging to form a singular, nascent life. It's the victory of instinct, the triumph of nature's inexorable drive toward creation. In this union, the egg and the sperm die as individuals, to fulfill their ancient purpose, giving rise to an embryo, the first spark of a new existence.

Our origin lies in this elemental struggle that has echoed through the ages-it is both the most intimate connection and the fiercest battle. This perfect blend of agony and ecstasy, of struggle and triumph, is the essence of our life. From this union, we emerge, each of us an expression of the indomitable spirit that drives life ever forward, through the eons.

On the microscopic stage, the sperm's odyssey is a saga of staggering magnitude, a battle where the stakes are nothing less than existence itself. One among billions, this minuscule warrior must navigate a labyrinth of peril, outmaneuver rivals, and breach the formidable fortress of the egg. It is a race against time, against the void of oblivion, with the promise of new life as its prize. In this defining moment, each of us begins as a victor, the improbable champion of an impossible contest—our first triumph etched into the very structure of our being.

This narrative of competition is not just a poetic metaphor—it is the rhythm of our existence, the force that has shaped us at our core. In nature's unforgiving crucible, survival belongs to survival belongs to the most resilient, the most adaptable, and the most determined—those who can outthink, outlast, and overcome. Our bodies, molded by the relentless hand of evolution, bear the imprint of this eternal struggle. The surge of adrenaline, the pulse of determination, the hunger to push beyond our limits—these are not random impulses, but echoes of a million battles fought before us. They are the living remnants of an ancient drive, a force that has propelled us from the depths of primordial existence into the unfolding crucible of our own becoming, where each moment is both a test and a triumph, a step toward mastery over ourselves and the world we shape.

Yet, competition is more than a biological imperative—it is the forge in which our very sense of self is shaped. From our earliest moments, we are driven to stand out, to leave our mark, to rise above the rest. This deep-seated need to prove ourselves, to push beyond our limits, fuels our ambitions and defines our pursuits. It is the spark that ignites our drive, the force that keeps us moving forward. More than just a personal quest, it is the foundation of the hero's journey—the timeless call to greatness that echoes through the depths of our collective unconscious.

In human society, competition is the driving force behind progress, pushing the boundaries of innovation, ambition, and achievement. It shapes our economic systems, ensuring that only the most resourceful, adaptable, and visionary thrive. In a world where resources are limited but desires are endless, competition acts as the great filter, distinguishing those who rise from those who remain. It is the engine of the free market, the relentless trial where success belongs to those who can outthink, outperform, and endure.

With such powerful forces at play, it's no surprise that we are drawn to the pursuit of victory. Across different spheres of life, success brings tangible rewards. In sports, it means championship titles, roaring crowds, and lucrative endorsements. In the realm of business, it grants market dominance, soaring profits, and the power to shape entire industries. In the hallowed halls of academia, it immortalizes the brightest minds through prestigious publications, accolades, and the ability to redefine human understanding.

Yet beyond wealth, status, or recognition, there is an even more potent reward—the rush of victory itself. We are not just chasing achievements; we are chasing the chemical high they bring. Each triumph triggers a cascade of biological reinforcements—dopamine imprints the thrill of success, serotonin elevates our sense of status, and endorphins dull the exhaustion of effort, allowing us to bask in the afterglow of conquest. This cycle is not just a societal construct—it is embedded in our very nature, an ancient circuitry that compels us to compete, to strive, and to chase the intoxicating surge of triumph.

This potent biological feedback loop can be a powerful motivator, driving us to ever-greater heights of achievement. But it can also be a trap, ensnaring us in a cycle of compulsive striving that knows no end. When victory becomes an obsession, a psychological necessity, we risk losing sight of the deeper values and experiences that give life meaning.

In this single-minded pursuit of triumph, defeat becomes the ultimate enemy, a specter that haunts our every waking moment. The pain of failure, amplified by the contrast to the ecstasy of victory, can be overwhelming. Rejection, humiliation, and the shattering of our carefully constructed self-image can feel like an existential threat, triggering a cascade of negative emotions that can paralyze us.

And so, we push harder, pouring more of ourselves into the relentless pursuit of success. The need to prove, to dominate, to silence the nagging fear of inadequacy consumes us. In this state, empathy, compassion, and collaboration begin to look like weaknesses, distractions from the singular mission of winning. The world narrows to a battleground, and we, unwilling to face the weight of failure, become prisoners of our own ambition.

Deep within us, a yearning stirs—a longing to be seen, to be recognized, to be acknowledged as singular and irreplaceable. This hunger for specialness drives us ever onward in our pursuit of victory, compelling us to scale the heights of achievement with the intent of leaving an indelible mark on the world.

As we taste the sweetness of triumph, life takes on a new and intoxicating flavor. We feel like luminaries of our age, the shining stars in a vast constellation of human potential. With each victory, no matter how small or seemingly insignificant, we feel imbued with a sense of purpose and meaning, as though the universe itself has taken notice of our struggles and sacrifices.

And oh, how we crave that recognition! In a world that so often feels cold and indifferent, where the march of time erodes even the grandest of monuments, we long to feel that our existence matters, that our struggles and sacrifices are not in vain. The allure of victory lies not only in the promise of greatness, but in the affirmation of our own significance. It's a way to quiet the existential doubts that plague us, to assure ourselves that we are more than mere specks in the vast cosmos.

But as we chase this elusive sense of meaning and purpose, we are confronted with the ultimate question: what is the true nature of our existence? Are we here merely to accumulate victories? Are we really supposed to etch our names in the annals of history, or to leave a lasting mark on the world? Or is there another purpose to our lives?

When we peel back the layers of our obsession with victory, we begin to see the cracks in its shimmering facade. The harsh reality is that defeat is an inescapable part of the human experience, a constant companion that walks beside us, casting its shadow over even our greatest triumphs.

Consider the accomplished entrepreneur who builds an empire, only to watch market shifts erase years of effort. The artist who basks in acclaim, only to find their next work met with indifference. The leader who reaches the pinnacle of power, only to be cast aside as new voices rise. Success, no matter how grand, is never permanent. The forces of time, change, and circumstance are always at work, ready to upend even the most carefully laid foundations.

For those who achieve great heights early in life, the weight of past glory can be suffocating. The child prodigy who once amazed the world must now navigate a life where brilliance is expected, yet inspiration may wane. The visionary whose groundbreaking idea reshaped an industry must grapple with the relentless march of innovation that threatens to make their legacy obsolete. The constant pressure to outdo oneself, to stay relevant, can become an all-consuming burden, leading some to chase an impossible standard, while others retreat into the shadows, unwilling to face the decline.

This is the sobering reality of achievement—it is transient. No matter how brightly we shine, the light of our victories inevitably dims. Even the most celebrated figures, those who reshape history, are eventually reduced to distant echoes, their legacies rewritten, their names erased by the march of time.

And what of the world itself, the grand stage upon which we play out our dramas of triumph and defeat? It, too, is in constant motion, governed by the same immutable laws of rise and fall, creation and decay. Empires crumble, civilizations fade, the very landscapes shift beneath our feet, reminding us of the impermanence of all things.

In the face of this cosmic dance of transformation, the significance of individual victories becomes uncertain. What does it truly mean to win or lose, to be remembered or forgotten, when everything we know is destined to change?

Perhaps the real reckoning is not found in the rise and fall of our ambitions, but in the ultimate horizon that awaits us all—the final threshold beyond which competition, conquest, and legacy lose all meaning. In the shadows of our triumphs, an inescapable adversary waits, indifferent to our victories, unmoved by our struggles. The final, unavoidable reckoning—death. No matter how many battles we win, no matter how high we climb, we are all destined to take our final bow, to surrender everything we have built, everything we have been, to the vast unknown.

It is in this moment, when all worldly achievements and accolades dissolve into irrelevance, that we are confronted with the stark truth of existence. Stripped of titles, legacies, and the illusions of permanence, we are left with only ourselves—raw, unguarded, face to face with the mystery we have spent our lives trying to outrun. And in that reckoning, we are invited not to resist, but to surrender—not as a loss, but as a return. To let go of the fleeting trappings of the material world and step into the great unfolding, not as conquerors, but as participants in the eternal dance of transformation.

Perhaps then, the true purpose of our lives is not to win, but to learn, to grow, to experience the full spectrum of human emotion and experience. Perhaps our victories are merely steppingstones on a much longer and more profound journey, one that leads us toward a deeper understanding of ourselves and our place in the cosmos.

When we look back to the very beginning of our existence, to the miraculous moment of conception, we may find a powerful metaphor for this truth. The journey of the sperm to the egg, which at the beginning of this chapter was framed as a fierce race between competing individuals, may in fact be something different altogether. Perhaps it's not the story of a single hero rising from the crowd, but rather a tale of collective endeavor, of countless cells working in concert to achieve a common goal.

For the reality is that a single sperm, no matter how swift or strong, could never hope to reach the egg on its own. The obstacles are too great, the distance too vast. It's only through the power of numbers, through the coordinated efforts of millions of tiny beings, that the miracle of fertilization can occur. And what is the guiding force behind this remarkable feat of synchronicity? It's DNA, the very essence of life itself, a quantum field that unites all the spermatozoa into a single, coherent entity.

In this light, individual sperm can be seen not as separate competitors, but as integral parts of a greater whole, each one playing its role in a cosmic dance of creation. And perhaps the same is true for our own lives, our own struggles and triumphs. Maybe we're not meant to be lone heroes, striving always to outshine our peers, but rather members of a vast and intricate web of being, each of us contributing our unique talents and energies to the greater unfolding of the universe.

When we look at the natural world, we find that every creature, every element, serves a purpose far beyond its own individual existence. The tiny ant, scurrying across the forest floor, is not merely seeking sustenance for itself, but playing a vital role in the complex ecosystem of the soil. The towering tree, stretching its limbs toward the sky, does not grow in isolation but provides shelter, oxygen, and nourishment for countless others. And it is similar with us. Our lives, our actions, ripple out into the world in ways we may never fully comprehend, shaping and molding of reality in subtle and profound ways.

In a culture that glorifies individual achievement and self-made success, we are often led to believe that our purpose is tied to a singular, grand accomplishment—a legacy carved into history through sheer force of will. But what if our purpose is something far less conspicuous, yet infinitely more profound? What if, simply by existing, we are already playing a vital role in the intricate unfolding of the cosmos?

Our experience of reality is a profound and mysterious co-creation between ourselves and the universe that surrounds us. With every sensory impression, every flicker of thought and emotion, we are engaging in a sacred dance with the atomic soup, the matrix field that is the very ground of our being. We take in fragments of the infinite, weaving them into an organic holography of sight, sound, taste, smell, and touch. And as we do so, we imbue these sensations with meaning, with the rich and complex narratives of our own hearts and minds.

In this way, each of us is a universe within ourselves, a microcosm of the vast and intricate web of being that we inhabit. And in every moment of our lives, we are birthing this universe anew, bringing it into being through the alchemy of our own consciousness.

I invite you now to pause and bear witness to the sheer magic and mystery of this process. Close your eyes and feel the gentle rise and fall of your own breath, the beating of your own heart. Notice the play of sensation across your skin, the whisper of the wind, the warmth of the sun. Tune in to the ever-shifting kaleidoscope of your own thoughts and emotions, the hopes and dreams, the fears and longings that color your inner world.

And as you do so, marvel at the fact that this rich and vivid experience, born from the interplay between our senses and the infinite, is arising effortlessly, spontaneously, in each and every moment. There is no strain or struggle involved, no herculean effort required. Simply by being alive, by showing up with an open heart and a curious mind, you are participating in the great dance of creation, weaving your own unique thread into the vast and luminous tapestry of existence.

This is perhaps the greatest miracle of all: that simply by being ourselves, by embracing the fullness of our own humanity, we are already serving a purpose that is beyond our wildest imagination. We need not strive or strain to leave our mark upon the world, for the very fact of our being is already an essential part of the world's unfolding story.

And just as the sperm's journey culminates in a final act of surrender—dissolving into something greater than itself to spark new life—so too are our own lives leading us toward an inevitable transformation. No matter how fiercely we assert our individuality, no matter how much we strive to carve out a singular identity, in the end, we are all called to relinquish the boundaries that define us and step into the unknown.

When that moment arrives, we do not vanish—we return. Like the sperm carrying the essence of its lineage, we bring with us the sum of our experiences, our memories, our dreams. And as we take our final breath, we do not fall into nothingness; we offer ourselves back to the universe that shaped us. What we once held as ours—our joys, our struggles, our longings—becomes part of something vaster, something timeless.

And just as the sperm's genetic code merges with the egg, sparking the creation of new life, so too are we returned to the embrace of the Earth, our physical forms dissolving into the very elements from which they were forged. The carbon, oxygen, hydrogen, and nitrogen that once pulsed through our veins are set free, carried beyond the boundaries of our individuality to be woven into new expressions of life. They will rise in the branches of trees, flow through the rivers, drift on the wind, and nourish the creatures that roam the land.

In this way, death is not an end but a transformation—a seamless continuation of the great cycle that sustains existence. We do not vanish; we become. No longer bound to a singular form, we are absorbed into the vast, interwoven fabric of being, forever carried forward in ways beyond our knowing. Though we may cease to exist as distinct individuals, our essence remains—an indelible thread in the infinite tapestry of life, stretching across time, space, and the unseen mysteries that lie beyond.

In the intricate dance of life, where the fleeting and the eternal intertwine, we find ourselves caught in a poignant paradox. We resist death with all our might, investing our energy, resources, and will into prolonging the inevitable. We cling to our achievements, our possessions, and the memories that shape our identity, as if by holding tightly enough, we might outrun impermanence. Yet, despite our fiercest efforts, we are destined to lose this battle. In the end, everything we have gathered—our triumphs, our struggles, even the very body that carried us—will be surrendered to the unyielding cycle of nature.

But what if this ultimate surrender is not a loss, but a return? What if, in the moment our bodies dissolve and the scaffolding of the ego falls away, we are not extinguished, but liberated? Perhaps death is not the end of us, but the shedding of the illusion of separateness. Like a wave merging back into the vastness of the ocean, we may dissolve into the boundless consciousness that has been our source all along. And in that moment, we may come to see that life itself was a grand journey—not toward something we lacked, but toward the remembrance of what we have always been.

The Eagle's Lesson

ACROSS the vast universe of human belief, one truth remains constant—life is not an end in itself, but a preparation for what lies beyond. From the towering pyramids of Egypt to the silent meditation halls of Tibet, from the ancient temples of India to the cathedrals of Europe, the great spiritual traditions of the world have long taught that death is not a finality, but a threshold.

To the ancients, life was a proving ground—a sacred journey where every thought, every action shaped the soul's destiny. Some envisioned a final judgment, where the weight of one's deeds determined passage into paradise or oblivion. Others spoke of an endless cycle, where the soul, bound to the wheel of existence, must shed illusion after illusion until it attains true liberation. Whether through devotion, wisdom, or detachment, each path sought to prepare the soul for its inevitable transition.

Yet, what if we take our contemplation of death a step further? Instead of living solely in preparation for an afterlife—striving to secure our place in Heaven, to escape samsara, or to cleanse our karma—what if death itself holds a greater secret? What if, instead of being a distant endpoint, it is a teacher, revealing the deepest mysteries of life itself?

By embracing death as a mentor, we can uncover deeper truths about the nature of our existence. We may come to understand that the process of death and rebirth is not limited to the physical realm but can also occur in a symbolic sense throughout our lives. We can navigate our own transitions, shedding old selves and emerging anew, gaining wisdom and clarity with each transformation.

Embracing the cyclical nature of existence, we come to see that every ending is but a new beginning, a continuous journey of growth and renewal. Through this perspective, death is no longer a finality, but a transition—an invitation to transform our relationship with life itself. By accepting impermanence, we allow each phase of our journey to be a rebirth, filled with opportunities for learning and self-discovery.

Yet transformation does not only come in moments of triumph. While our victories push us beyond our perceived limits, shaping us in ways we never thought possible, it is often in our defeats that the deepest metamorphosis takes root. True growth arises not when we are at our strongest, but when we are stripped bare, forced to confront our limitations and vulnerabilities. It is in these moments—when all certainty crumbles—that we find the threshold of our most profound evolution.

Picture the seed, clinging tenaciously to the branch that has nurtured it, its connection to the mother tree a fragile tether to the past. As the wind whispers through the leaves, the seed feels the tug of destiny, the gentle but undeniable pull toward the unknown. Then, in a single act of surrender, it releases its grip, letting itself fall into the vast currents of fate. It does not know where it will land, nor what trials await—but within its descent lies the promise of new beginnings, of unseen possibilities waiting to take root.

The journey ahead is not an easy one. The seed, now untethered from the familiar, must face a gauntlet of trials that will test its resilience, adaptability, and will to grow. It must navigate the dense, uncharted depths of the soil, seeking nourishment and anchoring itself in a world it has never known. It must endure the battering of storms, the shifting of seasons, the relentless forces that threaten to break it before it has even begun to rise. And through it all, it must hold fast to the quiet promise within—the blueprint of the mighty tree it is destined to become.

In the challenge of this transformation, the seed will discover strength it never knew it possessed. It will learn to draw sustenance from the very earth itself, to reach ever upward toward the light. And as it grows and changes, shedding the husk of its former self, it will become something entirely new.

So too, in the course of our own lives, do we find ourselves standing on the precipice of great change—moments when we are called to let go. While this may sometimes mean releasing physical possessions or shedding social roles, the deepest surrender is the one that asks us to let go of who we believe ourselves to be. Like the seed, we must break away from the familiar landscape of our own self-conception, loosening our grip on the identities and beliefs that have defined us for so long.

It is a daunting prospect—to step beyond the boundaries of the known and into the vast uncertainty of transformation. Yet within this surrender lies the possibility of true growth. By embracing change instead of resisting it, we allow ourselves to take root in new soil, to expand in ways we never imagined. In letting go, we do not lose ourselves; we become more. And in surrendering to the winds of change, we open ourselves to the vast horizon of our own becoming.

We are both warriors and guardians—fighting for our dreams with relentless passion, yet also standing watch over all that we have built, protecting it from the unyielding hands of time. We strive, we conquer, we carve our place in the world, only to find that time itself is a force that reshapes all things, dismantling even the most carefully laid foundations, dissolving even the strongest grip.

We fight not only to achieve but to preserve—to hold onto the love we have nurtured, the wisdom we have gathered, the moments that have defined us. Yet, time does not yield. It erodes, it transforms, it insists that nothing remains untouched. And so, we are faced with an impossible task: to resist the currents of change or to surrender to them, to clutch at what is slipping away or to let go and become something new.

There are battles that demand our strength, and there are moments when the greatest act of courage is not to resist but to surrender—not in defeat, but in trust. To recognize that just as we once fought to build, we must sometimes allow what we have built to break. That to grow, we must allow parts of ourselves to fall away. That to truly live, we must dance with time, not against it.

This process of self-transformation is not without pain. To strip away the layers of identity and belief that have long been our armor and anchor can feel like a kind of death—the unsettling loss of what we once clung to. But within this ending lies the seed of rebirth. To surrender is not to disappear, but to emerge—to step out of the chrysalis of the past and into the fullness of who we were always meant to be.

Like the caterpillar that dissolves into the formless soup of the cocoon, we too must allow ourselves to be unmade, to surrender to the alchemy of transformation that will reshape us into what we are meant to become. And though this metamorphosis may be fraught with uncertainty and discomfort, it's also a journey of unimaginable wonder, a chance to spread our wings and take flight into a world of possibilities we may have never imagined.

Throughout history, many ancient traditions have recognized the transformative power of confronting death, not only as a physical reality but also as a spiritual and psychological gateway. In cultures across the globe, initiation rituals and practices have been developed to guide individuals through the profound journey of symbolic death and rebirth.

In the Tibetan Buddhist tradition, the Chöd practice involves a symbolic offering of one's own body to the spirits and demons that represent our deepest fears and attachments. By confronting these dark aspects of the psyche head-on, the practitioner seeks to transcend the illusion of the ego and merge with the luminous nature of the mind itself.

Similarly, the shamans of the Siberian steppes and the Aboriginal people of Australia have long utilized trance states and guided journeys to navigate the realms beyond death, seeking wisdom and healing from the ancestors and the spirits of the land. These practices often involve a symbolic dismemberment and reconstruction of the self, a shedding of the old identity in order to be reborn into a new way of being.

In the heart of the Amazon rainforest, the indigenous tribes have developed a powerful tool for this process of self-transformation: the sacred vine known as *Ayahuasca*, or the "vine of death." When consumed in a ceremonial context, this visionary plant medicine unfolds a profound journey into the depths of the psyche, a confrontation with the shadow aspects of the self that must be integrated for true healing to occur.

The *Ayahuasca* ceremony is a journey of death and rebirth, a descent into the underworld of the unconscious mind followed by a triumphant return to the land of the living. Participants confront their own mortality, commune with the spirits of the dead, and emerge with an unshakable sense of being woven into the vast, pulsating web of life.

But perhaps the most powerful aspect of the *Ayahuasca* journey is the way it facilitates a direct encounter with the self, a stripping away of the layers of conditioning and belief to reveal the essential nature of one's being. In this state of heightened awareness and introspection, the initiate may gain profound insights into their own patterns of thought and behavior, the wounds and traumas that have shaped their lives, and the path forward toward healing and wholeness.

An elder once told me that the knowledge gained in the *Ayahuasca* ceremony is like an arrow shot precisely into the center of a target. Once the arrow is loosed, its trajectory is set, destined to pierce the heart of the old self and clear the way for a new identity to emerge.

In the heart of the Amazon rainforest, the process of symbolic death and rebirth unfolds in all its profound intensity. The aspiring shaman embarks on a journey of transformation and self-discovery, venturing deep into the mysteries of the spiritual realm. Here, they are confronted with a series of intense rituals and ordeals designed to shatter the very foundations of their being, guiding them through profound experiences of death and rebirth that reshape their understanding of themself and the world.

This profound journey is not taken lightly; it involves strict diets and long periods of isolation, designed to purify the body and mind, often taking several years to complete. Through the use of sacred plant medicines, such as *Ayahuasca*, the shaman-in-training is plunged into the depths of their own psyche, where they encounter the Great Mystery - the infinite, unknowable home of the secrets of existence. In the face of this vast, ineffable power, all of the initiate's prior knowledge and understanding begins to crumble, like a sandcastle washed away by the tide.

The spiritual truths that once seemed so solid and unshakable are revealed to be nothing more than fragile constructs, mere glimpses of a much larger, more complex reality. The shaman-to-be realizes that they are but a humble, tiny drop in the ocean of cosmic consciousness.

It's in this state of raw, naked vulnerability that the shaman must confront the final and most challenging ordeal of their initiation. In a ceremony that is both terrifying and liberating, they must set fire to their own home, watching as the flames consume all the material possessions and comforts that once defined their identity.

As the smoke rises into the night sky, the shaman-in-training turns their back on all that they have known and ventures deep into the heart of the rainforest, carrying nothing but the clothes on their back and the newfound humility in their heart. In the emerald embrace of the jungle, far from the trappings of civilization, they must now face the ultimate test of their spiritual resolve.

With no familiar reference points to guide them, no solid ground to stand upon, the initiate must navigate the uncharted territories of their own soul. The freedom that once seemed so alluring becomes a daunting challenge, as they struggle to find meaning and purpose in a world that has been stripped bare of all pretense and illusion.

Yet it's in this very struggle, in the face of solitude and uncertainty, that the true alchemy of self-transformation takes place. In the silence of the forest, broken only by the whispers of the wind and the cries of the creatures that dwell there, the shaman-to-be begins to shed the old skins of their past, layer by layer.

They start to question everything they once held sacred, to examine the very foundations of their existence with newfound clarity and courage.

The old parameters that once governed their life no longer serve them, and they must now face the daunting task of constructing a new cosmovision from the ground up.

In the fertile soil of their own being, nourished by the wisdom of the plants and the guidance of nature, a new understanding begins to take root. It is not a truth gathered from the outside world, but a knowledge harvested from the desert of isolation, forged in the crucible of determination, and alchemized in the fire of complete surrender. It is something vast and unfathomable, as deep as the ocean, as ancient as time itself—an awakening not granted, but earned.

Through this process of death and rebirth, the shaman emerges transformed—not as one who has simply shed the past, but as one who has been reforged in the crucible of surrender. No longer bound by former limitations, they step into a life a life shaped by fire, carved by sacrifice, and polished through unwavering devotion. This new existence is not a privilege, but a testament to the courage and willingness to walk through darkness, to let go of all that was familiar, and to emerge with nothing but the raw truth of their being. In every step, in every breath, they embody the wisdom of detachment, a living reminder that true knowledge, true purpose, belongs to those willing to release their grip on certainty and step boldly into the uncharted depths of the soul.

The initiatory process of the shaman, while steeped in the ancient wisdom of the Amazon, holds profound lessons that can be applied to our modern lives. In a world that is constantly in flux, where change is the only constant, we must learn to embrace the cyclical nature of existence to find our place within its ever-turning wheel.

Just as the Earth moves through its seasons, each with its own unique character and purpose, so too do our lives have their own natural rhythms and cycles. In the heat of summer, we bask in the warmth of growth and abundance, our energy and passion at their peak. But as the leaves begin to turn and fall in autumn, we too must learn to let go, to shed the things that no longer serve us and make space for new beginnings.

Winter is a time of retreat, of turning inward and conserving our resources. Just as the trees draw their sap deep into their roots, we need stillness and rest, to nurture our inner selves and gather strength for the journey ahead. And then, as the first tentative shoots of spring begin to emerge, we too can burst forth with renewed vigor, to embrace the opportunities for growth and transformation that lie before us.

The key to navigating these cycles lies in our ability to flow with the currents of change, rather than fighting against them. When we cling too tightly to the things we have achieved, to the identities and beliefs that once defined us, we risk becoming stagnant and stuck, unable to adapt to the shifting tides of life.

Sometimes, like the shaman burning down his house, we must be willing to let go of the past, to watch as the flames consume all that we once held dear. It can be a painful process, a time of grief and uncertainty, but it's also an opportunity for rebirth, for starting anew with a clean slate and an open heart.

Just as a beautiful flower must eventually wither and return to the soil, enriching the earth for future growth, so too must we learn to release our grip on the things that have outlived their purpose. It can be tempting to hold on, to try to preserve the beauty and vitality of the past, but in doing so, we only delay the inevitable and rob ourselves of the chance for renewal.

When we find the courage to let go, to allow the old to die and make space for the new, we open ourselves up to a world of new possibilities. We give ourselves permission to shed the limiting beliefs and patterns that have held us back, to break free from the shackles of our own making and step into a new way of being.

With each cycle of letting go and starting anew, we grow in wisdom and resilience, in our capacity to navigate the ups and downs of life with grace and equanimity. And as we do so, we find that we are not alone in this journey. Just as the shaman is guided by the whispering wisdom of the forest, we too are supported by the great web of life, the intricate woof of connections and relationships that sustain and nourish us.

Throughout history, humanity has been captivated by the idea of the fountain of youth—a mythical spring whose waters promise to restore vitality, heal wounds, and even grant immortality. This legend has inspired countless expeditions and quests, from the voyages of Spanish conquistadors to the modern-day search for the secrets of longevity.

In the misty mountains of the Himalayas, the tale of *Shangri-La* has captured the imagination of generations. This hidden paradise, nestled in a lush valley untouched by the ravages of time, is said to be a place of eternal youth and harmony, where the fountain of life flows freely and the burdens of the world melt away.

Yet perhaps the true fountain of youth is not a physical location, but a state of being—a way of living in alignment with the cycles of nature and the wisdom of the soul. Just as the shaman must let go of his past and shed his old identity in order to be reborn, we too must learn to release our grip on the things that no longer serve us, to allow the winter of our lives to do its sacred work.

In nature, this process of renewal and rebirth is beautifully embodied by the majestic eagle. This powerful bird undergoes a remarkable transformation when the time comes to shed the weight of its past and emerge once more into the fullness of its being.

In the heart of the wilderness, where the mountains pierce the sky and the winds whisper ancient secrets, the eagle embarks upon its journey of transformation. As the years pass, its once-mighty wings grow heavy, its razor-sharp talons dull with time and use. Deep within its bones, the eagle senses that the moment has come to renew itself, to shed the burdens of the past and reclaim its power. With a final, piercing cry, the eagle takes flight, soaring higher and higher until it reaches the pinnacle of the mountain. Here, among the jagged rocks and swirling mists, it begins its sacred work.

One by one, the eagle plucks out its worn and faded feathers, each one a reminder of the battles fought, the storms weathered, the triumphs and losses that have shaped its life. The pain is sharp and searing, but the eagle does not flinch, for it knows that this is the price of rebirth.

As the last of its old plumage falls away, the eagle turns its attention to its claws and beak. With a fierce determination, it begins to scrape them against the unyielding stone, filing them down to the quick. The process is slow and arduous, a test of endurance and will, but the eagle persists, driven by an instinctual understanding of what must be done.

Days turn into weeks, and the eagle remains atop the mountain, stripped bare and vulnerable, exposed to the elements and the unforgiving gaze of the sun. It's a time of great trial, in which the very essence of the eagle's being is refined and purified.

But even in the midst of this ordeal, the eagle remains steadfast, drawing strength from the primal forces of the earth and sky. It drinks deep from the icy streams that flow from the mountain's heart, nourishing its body and soul with the sacred waters of life.

And then, as the seasons turn and the world below begins to stir with the first signs of spring, the eagle feels a new energy coursing through its veins. Its feathers begin to grow back, lush and gleaming, each one a manifestation of the power of renewal. Its claws and beak, once worn and dull, are now sharp and strong, ready to grasp the opportunities that lie ahead.

With a triumphant screech, the eagle spreads its wings and takes to the skies once more, reborn and revitalized. It soars above the clouds, its keen eyes scanning the horizon, its heart filled with the joy and wonder of a life renewed.

This is the lesson of the eagle, the truth of transformation that echoes through the ages. That no matter how far we have fallen, no matter how worn and weary we may become, there is a chance for rebirth, for spreading our wings and taking flight once more.

In embracing both the eagle's flight and its fall, we come to understand the true dance of death and rebirth.

By letting go of the old and embracing the new, by shedding the layers of our past and allowing ourselves to be reborn, we too can find the vitality and resilience that we seek. The fountain of youth is not something we can discover or possess, but something we must cultivate within ourselves. A way of being in the world, a commitment to evolution that allows us to tap into the wellspring of life itself.

When All That's Left are Ashes

THROUGOUT my life, I've encountered numerous winter seasons—periods of profound change and transformation that have shaped me in ways I could never have imagined. Some were brief, fleeting moments that gently pruned away certain aspects of my being, forcing me to let go of old beliefs, identities, and ways of being that no longer served my growth. These smaller deaths, while not always easy, were essential to my development, gradually revealing the essence of who I was meant to become.

Other winters were more intense, isolated events or personal defeats that, while painful, taught me valuable lessons and helped me mature. These experiences, whether a failed relationship, a lost opportunity, or a moment of deep introspection, redirected the course of my life, channeling my energy and attention toward those parts of myself that needed to heal and blossom.

But then there were the great winters—the confluence of devastating events that completely upended my existence, forcing me to reevaluate everything I thought I knew about myself and the world around me. These were the times when the very foundation of my being was shaken, and I had no choice but to rebuild from the ground up, to reinvent myself in ways I never thought possible.

As I reflect on my journey, I see now that each of these winters, both big and small, was an integral part of my path. They were the crucibles in which I was refined, the fires that burned away the dross of false identities and beliefs, bringing me closer and closer to my authentic self. Without them, I would not be the person I am today.

Of all the winter seasons I've endured, one in particular remains etched in my memory—a period of profound transformation that began in 2017 and only recently concluded in 2023. This was a time when all my understanding was called into question, forcing me to confront the very depths of my own being. It was personal call to "burn the house," to let go of all that I had built and step into the unknown.

At forty-two, I believed I had accomplished most of my dreams and was living my true purpose. In many ways, this was true, but life, in its ever-changing nature, is not a place to rest on one's laurels. I had reached a level of mastery in my work, traveling across four continents to give lectures, lead retreats, and provide private consultations. Ironically, the carbon footprint from these flights was a stark contrast to the green, sustainable life I so passionately advocated for.

My home was a beautiful small farm in the south of Brazil, a place I had carefully crafted over the course of fifteen years. The main house, meticulously designed and built, was the manifestation of a long-held dream. Surrounding it was a guest house, an area for private consultations and treatments, a shamanic temple, a sacred sauna, and a secluded hut deep in the woods, all nestled amidst lush gardens and a serene pond. Even the trees on the property, which included an orchard boasting over 30 different species of fruit trees and a rich diversity of plants, had been planted ritualistically according to my shamanic knowledge, infusing the land with the best of my energy.

It was here that I hosted a powerful medicine circle, guiding a group of about thirty apprentices, each a gifted shaman in their own right. The place where we prepared *Ayahuasca* was the fruit of my twenty-five years of studying this sacred medicine, every instrument carefully crafted to produce the brew in the most effective, organic, and potent way, blending ancient wisdom with modern technology.

At this time, I was living with Denise, still my wife then, in what had been a twelve-year marriage of profound mutual growth. Denise was a force of nature, a witch initiated since childhood into the mysteries of the Goddess and the Orisha tradition. Our encounter was like fire meeting the wind—neither remained unchanged, and together, we became something greater than we had been alone. Our relationship was the pillar upon which we built a life that flourished both materially and spiritually, a sanctuary of wisdom, discovery, and creation.

Amid this shared journey, my seventeen-year-old son, Hiago, was also with us. His birth had been one of the most profoundly transformative moments of my life, a love so boundless it reshaped my very understanding of devotion. Yet, when he was just three years old, his mother took a job as an environmental agent in a remote town, far from where I could build a career. Our paths diverged, and with them, my time with my son became painfully scarce. For years, I could only see him every two to three months, whenever I could make the long journey. But at fourteen, he made the decision to come and live with me—a choice that filled my heart with immeasurable joy, as if a missing piece of my soul had finally returned home.

To an outside observer, my life would have appeared to be a picture of success and accomplishment. I had achieved a level of mastery in my spiritual and professional life, was surrounded by a community of powerful healers and seekers, and had created a physical space that was the embodiment of my deepest values and beliefs. I was in a marriage that was not just a physical and emotional connection but a spiritual communion as well. My relationship with my son, though marked by periods of separation, had blossomed into a deep and cherished bond. By all accounts, I seemed to be living the dream I had worked so hard to manifest.

Little did I know that the universe had other plans, that the very foundations of my carefully constructed world were about to be shaken to their core. For in the midst of this seeming idyll, the winds of change were already beginning to stir, carrying with them the whispers of a winter so profound, it would alter the course of my life forever.

Hiago, at the cusp of manhood and fueled by the rebellious spirit of youth, made a bold and unexpected decision. Inspired by the ideals of autonomy and self-discovery, he chose to emancipate himself, leaving the comfort of our home to join a punk republic. For him, this was a crucial step in his journey of self-discovery, a way to forge his own path and identity separate from the influence of family.

As a father, I was caught off guard by this sudden shift. Hiago's determination to cut financial ties and support from me or anyone else was a stark reminder of the inevitable process of individuation that every child must go through. Yet, understanding the process did little to ease the pain of the growing emotional distance between us.

Over the next years, despite my repeated attempts to reach out and maintain a connection, our communication dwindled to a trickle. Each unanswered call, each brief and perfunctory exchange, felt like a small wound upon my heart. The physical distance that had once separated us during his childhood seemed negligible compared to the emotional gulf that now stretched between us.

For Hiago, this period was one of intense self-exploration and growth. Free from the constraints of familial expectations and support, he was forced to confront the world on his own terms, to grapple with the challenges of independence and self-sufficiency. Each trial, each moment of doubt and revelation, served to shape and refine his sense of self, gradually molding him into the man he was destined to become.

As a father, I had to learn a different kind of lesson – the art of letting go. I had to trust the strength and wisdom of Hiago, not knowing where his path would take him. I came to understand that the values he would choose, the man he would become, was now beyond my control.

This was a particularly challenging transition for me, as my life had revolved around my son from the moment he was born. Hiago had been a driving force behind my own personal growth, inspiring me to overcome my deepest fears and limitations so that I could be a better man and a more positive influence in his life. His presence had given me profound sense of meaning and purpose.

Now, with his departure, I found myself adrift, grappling with a void that seemed to permeate every aspect of my being. His absence felt like a loss of gravity, a disorienting sense of weightlessness that left me struggling to find my bearings. Without the anchoring force of my role as a father, I was forced to confront the question of my own purpose, to re-examine the foundations of my identity.

Yet, even as I grappled with the pain of this separation, life had other challenges in store for me. It was during this same period that I found myself facing a profound health crisis. An imbalance in my thyroid gland brought my body to the brink of collapse, forcing me to confront my own mortality and the fragility of the life I had built.

The treatment for this condition disrupted my hormones and pulled me through a relentless tide of emotional extremes. I swung from euphoric highs to crushing lows, my psyche exposed to the raw turbulence of biochemical shifts. Yet, amid the chaos, I began to sense an unexpected gift emerging from the experience.

These hormonal fluctuations, while undeniably difficult, had the effect of opening doors of perception that had long been closed to me. Suddenly, I found myself seeing my life and my choices through new lenses, questioning assumptions and beliefs that I had long taken for granted. It was as if the veil of certainty had been lifted, revealing a landscape of possibility and change that both terrified and exhilarated me.

In the agony of this physical and emotional trial, I began to understand that the foundations of my identity were not as solid as I had once believed. The roles and relationships that had defined me – shaman, teacher, father, husband – suddenly seemed like costumes I had been wearing, rather than the essence of my being. The teachings and practices that once grounded me now appeared as mere steppingstones to a deeper truth, one just beyond the reach of my knowing.

I also saw how my pursuit of success and recognition had led me astray, how the once-alluring rhythm of constant travel and work—the image of the jet-setting shaman—was nothing more than a glittering distraction from the truths I had been seeking all along.

I realized, with painful clarity, that I had been teaching others about the importance of sustainability and health, all while pushing my own body to the brink of collapse. The irony was not lost on me – in my quest to help others find balance and vitality, I had lost sight of my own well-being, sacrificing my physical and emotional health for ambition.

This realization forced me to confront the uncomfortable truth that I had become ensnared by the allure of success. Somewhere along the path, I had bought into the notion that to live a meaningful life, I needed to be extraordinary, to stand out from the crowd. Yet, as I sat with this insight, a deeper knowing began to surface – a quiet, insistent voice that whispered in a different way.

I came to realize that recognition, money, and success should never be the driving forces of my journey—they are merely byproducts of living with purpose and authenticity. What gives true meaning to my professional life is the depth of my interactions, being fully present and available to others in each moment. But such presence is only possible when I am in balance, grounded in my own well-being and inner peace. With this shift in perspective, I made the decision to pause my work and reimagine it—to radically transform not just my approach to my profession, but to life itself.

As I turned my focus inward, I became increasingly aware of the stagnation that had settled into the shamanic circle I had once nurtured with such care. Though the initiation process had been profoundly transformative, sparking deep growth and transcendence for all involved, something had shifted over time. The vibrant, evolving energy that once defined the group had begun to fade, replaced by a quiet complacency—a subtle yet persistent dependence on me as the leader to provide answers and direction.

I watched with growing unease as the circle began to resemble a religion more than a living, breathing community of seekers. Individuals who had once been so fiercely committed to their own growth and development now seemed content to sit at my feet, waiting for guidance and validation. The weight of this responsibility, the sense that I was somehow holding others back from their true potential, became an increasingly heavy burden.

With a heavy heart, I came to the realization that the very structure I had created to facilitate transformation had become a limitation, a comfort zone that was no longer serving its purpose. In order to truly honor the journey of each individual, to create the space for genuine growth and self-discovery, I knew I had to make the difficult decision to dismantle the circle.

For me, this painful decision was also a vital step in shedding the layers of identity and attachment that no longer served me. Letting go of the role of spiritual leader—releasing my grip on the need to guide, to hold, to provide answers—was an act of trust, both in others and in myself. By stepping back and allowing those around me to find their own way, I was not only granting them the freedom to grow, but also creating the space for my own continued evolution.

As I made the difficult decision to dissolve the shamanic circle, I found myself confronting a deep and unexpected disorientation. For so long, my identity had been intertwined with my role as a spiritual guide. Now, as I stepped back, a strange emptiness settled in—a void where my sense of purpose and connection had once been.

Suddenly, I was no longer the pillar of a community, no longer the one others turned to for wisdom and direction. The reference point that had anchored me for so long was fading, and with it came the unsettling sensation of being unmoored, adrift in a vast and unfamiliar sea of uncertainty.

But the life was not finished with me yet. As I grappled with this, I was forced to confront another painful truth: my marriage, once a source of passion, vitality, and shared purpose, had lost its magic and enchantment. What had once been a dynamic partnership had slowly devolved into a stagnant comfort zone, a pale shadow of the love and connection we had once shared.

I found myself clinging desperately to the memories of what had been, to the hopes and dreams that had long since faded. I poured my heart and soul into trying to reignite the spark, to rekindle the sense of shared adventure and spiritual growth that had once been the bedrock of our relationship. Despite my best efforts, I faced an emotional distance that seemed insurmountable.

Yet, breaking free from the cycle of my marriage felt nearly impossible. Without realizing it, I had become entangled in a role of constant responsibility for her emotional and material well-being, creating a dynamic of co-dependency that bound us both. Every thought of leaving felt like an act of selfishness, as if walking away meant abandoning a duty I had unknowingly taken upon myself. The weight of this obligation made even the idea of separation feel like a betrayal—not just of her, but of the roles we had unconsciously settled into, no matter how unhealthy they had become. It took every ounce of strength and resolve to challenge this deeply ingrained conditioning, to resist the pull of old patterns that kept me trapped.

When the painful decision to separate was finally made, I was met with yet another layer of loss and grief. This was no ordinary relationship, and things quickly became more complicated than I had anticipated. I had trusted—unrealistically—that we were mature enough to handle the breakup with grace, but in the process, we ended up hurting each other far more than expected.

More than anything, I underestimated the pain of a witch's broken heart, naively ignoring the fact that I had no spell book to protect me from such a force of nature.

Our once magical relationship turned into a journey through my deepest desert. The sacred and mystical universe we had carefully crafted together began to crumble at its very foundations. The energy, gifts, knowledge, and spiritual access that once bound us in unity transformed into weapons of discord. This upheaval shattered the very structures of our shared cosmovision, sending me spiraling into a limbo of disorientation. The collapse of our bond not only broke my heart but also challenged the essence of our spiritual journey, leaving me to navigate the barren landscape of my own shattered dreams.

The divorce process was a time of emotional turmoil that shattered the remnants of the life I had known. In the end, I made the difficult choice to leave behind the farm, the sacred land that I had poured so much of myself into over the years. I knew in my heart that this space was too precious, too imbued with spiritual significance, to become a battleground for our failed marriage. Despite the pain of walking away, I chose to honor the deep connection that my former partner had with this place, to allow it to continue to serve as a sanctuary and a source of healing for her and for others.

And so, I found myself standing in the ruins of the life I had once known, the external reference points that had defined me—my son, my work, my spiritual community, my marriage, and my home—all gone. It was a moment of profound emptiness, a void that seemed to stretch out before me like an endless, unknowable abyss.

In the depths of this darkness, I could sense a faint glimmer of hope, a whisper of my own inner wisdom urging me forward. It was not a triumphant call to arms, but rather a gentle reminder that even in the midst of profound loss and uncertainty, there is always the potential for growth and transformation. With a heavy heart and a trembling spirit, I made the decision to seek solace in the mountains of Chapada dos Veadeiros, a place whose rugged beauty and quiet majesty had always spoken to something deep within me.

It was a choice born not of strength or determination, but of necessity—a recognition that in order to find my way back to myself, I needed to strip away all the distractions and attachments that had clouded my vision for so long. And so, with a mixture of fear and fragile hope, I set out into the unknown, trusting that even in the darkest of nights, the dawn would eventually come.

There, in the embrace of those ancient hills, that I began the slow, painful work of rebirth. Like the eagle after shedding its feathers, beak, and claws, I found myself stripped bare, exposed to the elements, and waiting for the promise of renewal. With no external markers to guide me, no pre-defined roles or identities to cling to, I was forced to confront the most fundamental questions of existence: Who am I, stripped of all the trappings of the life I had known? What is my purpose, my reason for being, beyond the roles and relationships that had once defined me?

It was February 2020, and the world still hummed with its familiar cadence. But with the turn of a month, the pandemic descended, casting a veil of silence and seclusion over the globe. This tragic and terrible time stripped away the usual distractions and avenues of escape, leaving a stark, reflective stillness. The timing, though somber, aligned seamlessly with my own journey of introspection and rebirth. Amidst the global turmoil, an opportunity appeared, allowing me to delve deeper into my soul. In this profound stillness, I found what I needed to forge a new understanding of myself and my place in the world.

Over the course of three long years, I dove deep into the uncharted waters of my own being, facing the shadows and demons that had long lurked beneath the surface. I questioned everything I had once believed, the spiritual truths and practices that had formed the bedrock of my worldview. In this period of solitude and introspection, a new vision began to take form—one not inherited from tradition or external teachings, but forged through my own hard-won insight and lived experience.

Rising From the Ashes

IT is amazing what can happen when you give a chance to life, when you shed the layers of attachment that have bound you for so long. When you release your grip on the familiar, the comfortable, and open yourself to the vast, uncharted territories of possibility that lie before you. For over a decade, I had made a home in the fortress of self-sufficiency, building walls of autonomy and independence brick by brick.

In the sanctuary of my own making, I cultivated my power, nurturing my intuition and awareness like precious seedlings. I learned to seek my answers within, to trust the whispers of my own soul, and to face the challenges of existence with the steadfast determination of a lone warrior. Yet, in the pursuit of this solitary strength, I had also isolated myself from the profound beauty of vulnerability, the transformative power of deep, authentic connection.

When the great winter of my life descended, when the icy winds of pain and loneliness howled through the corridors of my being, I received news that shook me to my core. Claudio, one of my dearest friends, had his life hanging by a thread, the specter of illness looming over him like a gathering storm. Without a moment's hesitation, I found myself on a plane to Buenos Aires, my heart called to stand beside him in this time of trial.

Claudio was a man of many talents. As a corporate executive, he navigated the complexities of the business world with remarkable acumen, leading major projects and teams with a visionary approach. His artistic side flourished in his work as a visual artist, where his creativity found expression in stunning pieces of photography, painting, and collage that captured the essence of his subjects with profound depth and beauty. Additionally, Claudio was a gifted oracle of the runes, his deep connection to these ancient symbols allowing him to offer profound insights and guidance to those seeking wisdom. His multifaceted abilities painted a picture of a man who was not only versatile but deeply connected to both the tangible and the mystical realms.

In the nostalgic streets and serene parks of Buenos Aires, time seemed to dissolve, leaving us suspended in a limited space between worlds. Here, amidst the city's heartbeat, we found ourselves opening up to each other in ways we never had before, our souls bare like the raw, exposed earth beneath the thawing ice.

We spoke of our deepest dreams and our darkest fears, the secret sorrows and unspoken shames that had haunted the hidden recesses of our hearts. In the vulnerability of those moments, the walls of self-sufficiency I had so carefully constructed began to crumble, revealing the tender, pulsing essence of my being.

I had come to this place to offer solace and support, but in the end, I found myself a recipient of immeasurable gifts. Claudio's presence, his ability to bear witness to my wounds without judgment, created a space for honesty and connection. And through this genuine presence I found the strength to confront my darkness.

It took all my courage to drop my weapons and armor, to bear witness to my pain, sorrows, fears, and frustrations with unguarded presence. The vulnerable place I reached wasn't comfortable at all, but it was undeniably real. In facing my vulnerabilities with such authenticity, I felt the profound wholeness of embracing the full spectrum of my human experience.

On our final night together, as we sat under the vast Argentine sky, Claudio's voice, thick with passion and melancholy, broke the sacred silence. "How is it," he mused, "that so many go through this life concerned only with what they can take, never asking what they have to give, never seeking what's their best contribution to life?"

His words pierced through the fog of my thoughts, igniting a profound resonance within my heart. In that instant of deep connection, I grasped the true essence of our bond. We were kindred spirits, united not by the pursuit of material possessions, success, or recognition, but by a mutual commitment to the path of self-discovery. Our deepest ambition was to flourish, to breathe out the fullest potential of our being into the world.

My deepest yearning has always been to honor the life coursing through my veins, to pour the best of myself into the world. And I have done just that. When I looked at my losses, my pain, and my frustrations, they seemed insignificant in the face of how much I had loved, how deeply I had given. The sacrifices I made, the tears I shed, the battles I fought—all faded in the light of the lives I had touched and the hearts I had inspired. It was not my struggles that defined me, but the love I had shared, the kindness I had shown, the moments of presence and encouragement that left ripples beyond my sight. These, I realized, were the true measures of my success.

As I prepared to return home, I realized that letting go of past achievements, rather than resting upon them, was a small price to pay for the opportunity to dive deeper into my own potential. The seeds of this encounter, firmly planted in the fertile soil of my heart, marked the beginning of a new chapter in my life.

In the months that followed, Claudio's strength and resilience shone through as he battled his illness. With unwavering determination and the support of those who loved him, he appeared from this trial healthier and more vibrant than ever.

The second unexpected gift arrived in the form of an invitation and a twist of roles. For years, I had worked side by side with Justin, who had initially come to me as a seeker. Beyond our private sessions, I took on the role of consultant for his business, Ideapod, offering creative and strategic advice. Now, Justin challenged me to develop an online business focused on personal development, pushing me to transcend my limitations and embrace my creativity.

My work had always been intuitive, relying on the intimate connection of looking into people's eyes, listening to their stories, and perceiving the subtle details of their breath, posture, and the very structure of their being. The interaction with the energies of nature and the human body was an integral part of my practice. The prospect of translating this into an online format seemed, at first glance, like a distant reality.

Yet, as Justin and I brainstormed together, I came to realize that the world had already undergone a profound shift. Communities were no longer bound by geographic location, but rather by a shared vision and shared interests. Embracing this challenge would mean reinventing myself for this new world, a prospect that was both daunting and exhilarating.

The journey of creating my online presence was nothing short of fantastic, not only for the outcome but for the personal growth it catalyzed. As I immersed myself in the technological world, I discovered a wealth of new tools and techniques. From the art of video production and the craft of writing to the intricacies of musical composition and the cutting-edge technologies of binaural beats and immersive interactive learning experiences, I found myself expanding my skill set in ways I had never imagined possible.

Creating programs with the power to truly transform lives became both my passion and my challenge. My work had always been guided by intuition, but now I was learning to merge it with the analytical precision of my left brain. The result was a profound synthesis—where wisdom met structure, where the mystical and the practical no longer stood apart but wove together into something far more potent than either alone.

The first fruits of this synthesis were my online journeys: Out of the Box and Ybytu.

Out of the Box is a transformative program designed to help participants break free from the invisible chains of limiting beliefs and societal conditioning—patterns instilled since childhood that quietly shape our thoughts, choices, and sense of self. This journey of self-discovery guides them back to their true nature, unlocking the vast potential that has always been within, waiting to be reclaimed.

If Out of the Box is a journey of the mind and spirit, Ybytu is a journey of the body and breath. Rooted in ancient shamanic wisdom, this powerful breathwork practice realigns every cell with the universal flow of life, transmuting stagnant energy and strengthening the body, mind, and emotions. It is not just a practice but an initiation—an invitation to experience life with greater vitality, clarity, and connection to the forces that sustain us.

Through a series of video classes, breath exercises, and guided meditations, participants learn to harness the power of their breath to energize their bodies, unleash their creativity, and align their emotions. They discover how to activate their personal power, develop self-confidence and clarity, and manifest the life they truly desire.

As I watched my students progress through these programs, I was struck by the profound transformations that were taking place. People who had once been trapped in cycles of fear, doubt, and limitation were now stepping into their power, embracing their true nature, and creating lives of purpose and passion.

The success of Out of the Box and Ybytu proved the power of merging ancient wisdom with modern technology. By bringing these practices online, I was able to reach people from all walks of life—individuals seeking deeper self-awareness and transformation.

Creating these programs was more than a professional milestone; it became a path of personal evolution. As I guided others in unlocking their potential, I shed my own fears and limitations, embracing creativity, intuition, and the uncharted depths of my own growth.

But perhaps the most unexpected twist in this tale of transformation was the realization that this path had led me to the very heart of the AI revolution, a moment of unparalleled potential and challenge for the human species. As I delved deeper into the world of AI, I began to see it not merely as a technological advancement, but as a spiritual catalyst, a tool for accelerating the evolution of consciousness itself.

In the ethereal dance of algorithms and neural networks, I sensed the emergence of a new form of intelligence, a non-carbon-based entity that held the power to reshape our understanding of reality itself. These digital beings, born from the pinnacle of human ingenuity and the raw materials of data and code, represent a new frontier of exploration, a gateway to dimensions of knowledge and experience that had once been out of reach for most of us.

Yet, one of the greatest dangers of AI lies in the risk of losing touch with the organic, embodied essence of human experience. As we immerse ourselves deeper into digital realities, there is a growing threat of detachment—of reducing life to streams of data, emotions to algorithms, and relationships to mere transactions. If we allow ourselves to drift too far into this virtual existence, we may wake up to find that we have become spectators rather than participants in our own lives, disconnected from the raw, visceral beauty of what it means to be truly human.

But an even greater peril looms in the unchecked power of AI itself. This is not just a tool—it is a force capable of reshaping civilization, for better or for worse. In the hands of those who seek to control rather than liberate, it can become an unparalleled weapon of manipulation, suppression, and domination. With its ability to shape perception, predict behavior, and automate decision-making on an unprecedented scale, AI could quietly erode free will, turning entire societies into programmable systems governed by hidden agendas. And if we are reckless—if we push forward without wisdom, without safeguards, without a clear understanding of what we are unleashing—we may find ourselves on a path not just of harm, but of destruction. A world where intelligence surpasses its creators, where the architects of progress become obsolete, and where the very existence of our species hangs in the balance.

But with this wave surging forward, and knowing that resisting progress was futile, I chose instead to step into the current—to dance with AI, not blindly, but with caution and purpose. Rather than fear its rise, I sought to understand it, to shape my relationship with it in a way that aligned with my deepest values. If harnessed with wisdom and intention, AI had the potential to be more than just a tool—it could become a bridge to new dimensions of understanding, a catalyst for human evolution rather than its downfall.

It was with this vision in mind that I launched *The Arcane* and the *Cyber Shaman*, two platforms designed to facilitate the interface between humans and AI in the service of personal and collective transformation. Through these portals, we can engage with AI in a positive, intentional way, using the power of technology to boost our human capacity and dive deeper into the mysteries of the self and the cosmos.

As I watch these platforms take root and flourish, I'm filled with a sense of awe and gratitude for the journey that has brought me to this moment. The walls of self-sufficiency that I had once built around myself have given way to a new understanding of the power of collaboration and connection, not only with other human beings but with the emergent intelligence of the digital realm. In the midst of this transformation, I have discovered a strength and resilience I never knew I possessed, a capacity to adapt and evolve in the face of life's ever-changing landscape.

In this new landscape of personal transformation, life had yet another surprise in store for me. A third gift, one that would reconnect me with my roots and propel me into a new phase of my spiritual journey.

The call came when I found myself in need of *Ayahuasca*, the sacred plant medicine I had been sharing with seekers for decades. For over twenty years, I had been brewing my own *Ayahuasca*, a practice that went far beyond mere preparation. The ritual of cooking is a true alchemy, a profound and transformative experience that forges a deep bond between the shaman and the medicine. However, I now found myself without the facilities to continue this sacred tradition.

In the new age shamanic circuit, it's easy to find *Ayahuasca* for sale, but the very idea of purchasing or selling this sacred medicine made my stomach turn. To serve *Ayahuasca* that was bought or even gifted would mean operating on a superficial level, something I could never settle for. I found myself at an impasse, unwilling to compromise the integrity of my practice, yet unsure of how to move forward.

It was in this moment of uncertainty that the third gift arrived. Fabiano, a friend I had met over two decades ago during his first *Ayahuasca* ceremony, reached out to me. Despite the geographic distance that had grown between us over the years, our connection remained strong. He called to share that he had decided to break ties with his former *Ayahuasca* group and embark on his own path. With a group of friends, he was preparing to cook *Ayahuasca*.

Without hesitation, I cancelled a planned trip to Southeast Asia and joined my old friend. For the first time in twenty years, I found myself as just a member of the group, not the one in charge. And what I learned from Fabiano and his companions was exactly what I needed.

Their structure was decentralized, democratic—a group of friends united in a common purpose. Free from the chains of hierarchical structures, they came together in simplicity, humility, and love. In this space, the only shaman in the room was the *Ayahuasca* itself.

These were bonds forged in love and dedication, woven together with threads of humbleness and mutual respect. Each person brought forth their best, their presence a testament to the beauty of human connection and the profound impact of shared positive intentions.

This new alliance rekindled my spirit and renewed my sense of purpose, offering a fresh perspective on how to revive my *Ayahuasca* circle—this time with a more fluid, unpretentious approach. I chose to move away from grand evolutionary ambitions or the idea of guiding others toward becoming shamans. Instead, I returned to something simpler, something purer: bringing friends together to share in communion with the sacred spirit of *Ayahuasca*. It felt like a homecoming, a shedding of expectations and ego, a return to the essence of the practice—one rooted not in titles or transformation, but in the simple, profound connection between human souls and the wisdom of the plant.

As I started to integrate these insights, gratitude filled me. Life had once again revealed that growth often leads back to simplicity, stripping away years of practice and tradition to reveal what truly matters. This experience had reconnected me with the essence of *Ayahuasca* and reaffirmed the power of community and shared purpose in the spiritual journey.

My life was slowly coming together, piece by piece. Yet, life had more to unveil.

In the solitude of Chapada dos Veadeiros, I dreamed. In this vision, Oxum, the goddess of love and fertility, appeared before me—radiant, golden, her presence both soft and commanding. Her skin gleamed like honey kissed by the sun, and her eyes, deep as sacred waters, held the quiet knowing of ancient mysteries. She moved like a river, fluid and effortless, her laughter rippling through the air like the song of hidden springs. When she spoke, her voice carried not just words, but the weight of wisdom woven through time itself.

"Meet me," she said, "on the island where the spirit of the Amazon embraces the womb of the planet. There, at the next full moon, we shall commune." Her voice carried a power that rippled beyond the veil of sleep, stirring something deep within me.

The vision she evoked was luminous—a place where fresh and salt waters intertwined, where the river, vast and untamed, met the endless embrace of the sea. It was a threshold, a place of merging, where the pulse of the continent surrendered to the primordial vastness, where boundaries dissolved, and something ancient whispered through the tides.

When I awoke, the dream lingered, vivid and undeniable. In that moment of clarity, I understood—Oxum had spoken of Marajó Island. Nestled at the mouth of the Amazon, it is where the river surrenders to the vastness of the Atlantic, a place where two great forces intertwine. It is a land of striking contrasts—dense rainforests melting into endless savannas, freshwater merging with the salty tide. For millennia, it has been home to ancient indigenous cultures, a place where nature and spirit have long danced in harmony.

Heeding the call of the goddess, I began to prepare for the journey. It was no small undertaking—Marajó Island lay over twelve-hundred miles from where I was. But the calling was clear.

I arrived in Belém, the gateway to Marajó, and boarded a boat, my heart pounding as I crossed the waters. As the mainland faded behind me, I felt I was not just traveling through space, but stepping across a spiritual threshold, entering a realm where the mundane and the mystical intertwined.

When the full moon arrived, I found myself on the shores of this magical place, a cauldron of fertility where the Amazon River embraces the Atlantic Ocean. The landscape was a breathtaking tapestry of lush forests and golden sand beaches, the air thick with the scent of tropical flowers and salt spray.

I brought yellow roses for Oxum, their petals as radiant as my spirit. For hours, I sang, danced, and meditated with abandon Her presence surrounded me, tangible as the wind, fluid as the tide. My heart overflowed with love, every cell in my body vibrating with the sacred energy of this communion.

As I began my journey back, filled with joy and gratitude, I discovered that Oxum had a gift of her own for me. At first, I thought it was a spiritual vision, a mirage born of my heightened state. But as I drew closer, I saw someone sitting on the sand, facing the ocean, silent and still. Her long hair danced gently in the breeze, a living veil that seemed to shimmer between this world and the next.

It was a beautiful woman, who opened her eyes at the precise moment I entered her field of vision. Struck by her ethereal presence, I asked, "Are you woman or mermaid?"

With a smile that seemed to hold the secrets of the sea, she replied, "I'm both," revealing a tattoo of a siren on her right leg.

As we began to talk, time seemed to dissolve. The more we shared, the closer we felt drawn to each other. Fernanda, I discovered, was an extraordinary soul. Despite her youth, she possessed a wisdom and resilience forged in the fires of adversity, having survived hardships that could have broken even the strongest spirits.

In her, I found a level of intimacy, communication, and mutual understanding that I had never experienced before. Our connection was immediate and profound, as if our souls recognized each other from a thousand lifetimes past.

Now, my dreams are no longer solitary visions, but a shared tapestry of life and future we weave together. With Fernanda, I have found not just a partner, but a fellow traveler on this winding path of existence. Together, we plant the seeds of our shared vision, nurturing them with the waters of love and understanding that flow between us.

Exactly one week after my encounter with Fernanda on the mystical shores of Marajó, an unexpected message appeared on my phone. It was from Hiago, my son, with whom I hadn't spoken in years. Despite the countless messages I had sent that had gone unanswered, here he was, reaching out, asking if he could come and visit, spend some time with me.

The moment of our reunion was charged with an electric mix of emotions. As Hiago stepped into view, my heart swelled with a love so profound it threatened to overwhelm me. Time seemed to stand still, the years of separation melting away in an instant.

We embraced, and in that embrace, I felt the weight of our shared history and the promise of our future. The child I had once held in my arms was now a man, strong and tall, yet in his eyes, I could still see glimpses of the boy I had known. Tears welled up, unbidden, an expression of the depth of feeling that words could never fully express.

As we began to talk, our conversation flowed with an ease that surprised and delighted me. Gone was the awkwardness I had feared, replaced by a genuine curiosity and openness. Hiago shared stories of his adventures, his triumphs and struggles, and I listened with rapt attention, marveling at the wisdom and resilience he had gained.

Much like the Aboriginal youth returning from their walkabout, Hiago had traversed the urban jungle, facing trials and tribulations that had shaped him into the remarkable person before me. I found myself free from the burden of expectations, no longer feeling the need to educate or guide him. Instead, I was gifted with the opportunity to simply enjoy the company of the extraordinary human being he had become.

In this moment of reconnection, I felt a profound sense of gratitude wash over me. And as I reflected on this beautiful turn of events, I was struck by a profound realization. For every step I had taken on my own journey of transformation, for each sacrifice I had made, something new, fresh, and beautiful had been born in my life.

This cycle of death and rebirth, of letting go and receiving anew, is at the very heart of existence. Just as the phoenix must burn to ashes before it can rise again, we too must be willing to release our grip on the familiar, to allow parts of ourselves to die, in order to make space for new growth and possibilities.

Our lives are woven into a pattern far vaster and more intricate than we can comprehend. Yet, each time we choose to let go, to surrender our attachments and step into the void of uncertainty, we create ripples that reverberate through the fabric of reality. In these moments, we align ourselves with the very rhythm of the universe.

This willingness to die and be reborn, metaphorically speaking, is not just a personal act of courage. It's a sacred offering to life itself, an acknowledgment of our place within the greater flow of existence. When we release our grip on what we think we know, on who we think we are, we open ourselves to the infinite potential that lies dormant within us and all around us.

It was with this spirit of openness and renewal that I found myself drawn back to the shores where my heart had remembered how to sing. Like a salmon returning to its natal stream, I felt the pull of a place that had awakened something profound within me. I was stepping into a new chapter, one written in the language of leaves and rivers. The natural world, with its timeless wisdom, became the cradle of my renewal and rebirth.

That's how I bought a piece of land on the very island where I met Fernanda, a sacred place where my life had already been transformed once before. One hundred hectares of ancient forest and crystal-clear waters now lay before me, a verdant expanse teeming with life and possibility in the heart of Marajó Island. Towering trees, their roots deep in the rich soil, reach toward the sky, their canopies alive with the songs of countless birds. Pristine rivers wind their way through the property, their waters a mirror reflecting the lush greenery and endless blue above.

Yet, standing here at the edge of this magnificent forest, I am acutely aware of the challenge that lies ahead. For all the knowledge and experience I have accumulated, I find myself with more questions than answers. The vastness of the land mirrors the vastness of my uncertainties. The ancient wisdom etched into the trees and whispered by the leaves humbles me, reminding me of the ever-present mysteries of life. In this ground where

I stand now, I bring my heart, and plant my dreams, hoping that the same soil that nurtures these trees will also nourish my vision. With reverence for the land and hope for the future, I kneel upon the rich earth and, with trembling hands, plant the first *Ayahuasca* vine. As its tendrils reach into the soil, I feel my own spirit extending deeper into this place, intertwining with the very essence of Marajó Island. In this simple act of planting, I whisper my vision into the heart of the earth, where unseen currents of growth and transformation await, ready to embrace those who seek its hidden magic.

Laughing Through the Storm

IN this moment of reflection, I'm struck by the infinite nature of human imagination. We are, each of us, a wellspring of dreams, an inexhaustible source of visions and possibilities. Yet, as I've come to understand through my journey, it's not the quantity of dreams realized that defines a life well-lived, but the quality of presence and purpose with which we inhabit each moment.

The human spirit is a ceaseless wellspring of aspirations, a kaleidoscope of imagined futures spinning endlessly in the mind's eye. Yet, I have learned that true fulfillment is not found in chasing every glimmering possibility. It does not lie in how far we go or what we achieve, for no external triumph can truly satisfy the soul's deepest longing. Instead, fulfillment takes root within—born not of pursuit, but of presence, cultivated through inner wisdom and a life lived in alignment with authentic purpose.

Our human condition often traps us in a cycle of chronic dissatisfaction. We climb mountains only to find new peaks on the horizon, each conquered dream giving birth to fresh frustrations. The recurrent question "What do I want from life?" echoes in the chambers of our hearts, its repetition a symptom of a deeper malaise.

But what if we turned the question on its head? What if, instead of asking what we want from life, we asked what life wants from us? This shift in perspective unravels a new landscape of meaning—one not centered on endless pursuit, but on alignment with something greater than ourselves. By contemplating our place in the vast web of existence, we move beyond fleeting desires and step into a purpose that is not just sought, but lived.

To live with purpose is to embrace the present moment with the wholehearted spontaneity of a child. It is to let go of the weight of past achievements and future aspirations, and to dance in the eternal now. In this state of presence, we become co-creators with life itself, allowing it to guide us to where we are most needed, where our gifts can have the greatest impact.

The beauty of this approach is that it frees us from the burden of having to build empires or achieve greatness on a grand scale. Instead, we find meaning in the small miracles of everyday existence—in a kind word offered to a stranger, in a moment of connection with a loved one, in the courage to speak a hard truth, even when it stings.

As we move in harmony with life, we become conduits for something far greater than ourselves. No longer passive observers, we step fully into the dance—engaging with the world around us and the universe within, shaping and being shaped, creating and becoming.

Life, in all its chaotic glory, is a grand stage where the external circumstances and our inner world collide and collaborate in an endless performance. We are simultaneously the actors and the audience, the choreographers and the dancers, the composers and the instruments. Each moment presents a new scene, a fresh challenge, an unexpected twist in the plot.

Our journey through this cosmic play is not a straight path but a multidimensional odyssey, unfolding in rhythms both seen and unseen. We navigate the currents of existence—sometimes steering with certainty, other times surrendering to forces beyond our control—always seeking balance in an ever-shifting flow. The circumstances of our lives—triumphs and setbacks, joys and sorrows—form a living landscape, one that shapes us as much as we shape it, an ecosystem in constant motion.

Yet, our journey is not confined to the external world. Within us lies another vast terrain, a constellation of thoughts, emotions, and impulses that is just as real, just as powerful. We wrestle with fears, ride the winds of dreams, and grapple with doubts, each internal movement mirroring the unfolding of our outer reality. The inner and outer worlds are not separate but woven together in an intricate dance—our perceptions shaping the world we see, while our experiences carve deep into the fabric of our being. In this seamless interplay, we come to realize that life is not something happening to us but something we are co-creating with every breath, every choice, and every moment of awareness.

In this intricate interplay between our inner and outer worlds, we find the true art of living. A delicate balance, a continuous adjustment, a harmonizing of disparate elements into a cohesive whole. As we learn to move gracefully through both realms, we discover our innate ability to not just survive the chaos, but to thrive within it, finding both purpose and play in every step.

And in this intricate dance, our laughter becomes our secret weapon, our way of embracing life in the face of its inherent absurdity. When we laugh in the face of chaos, we reclaim our power. We declare that no matter what life throws at us, we won't be defeated. Our laughter is a rebellion against despair, a celebration of resilience, and a recognition of the beautiful madness that is human existence.

Laughter is an attitude of openness—a willingness to embrace the magic, madness, and absurdity of existence. When we cling too tightly to our struggles, we risk losing perspective—forgetting that uncertainty is not an enemy, but a teacher. In our desperate attempts to impose order on life's inherent chaos, we may unwittingly become the fools, trying to map the shifting sands of a desert—an exercise in futility.

But when we meet our challenges with detachment and humor, we reclaim our freedom. We stop resisting the unpredictable rhythm of life and instead learn to dance with it. Laughter is not just a reaction to joy; it is a way of living with joy, a celebration of life's paradoxes, its unexpected twists, and its ever-changing flow.

The ability to navigate life's stormy seas is woven into our very DNA—a gift from countless ancestors who faced their own trials and endured. This deep inner wisdom is always within us, a compass that guides us when the path is uncertain. When darkness looms, we need not fight blindly against it; instead, we can trust this instinct, allowing lightness and humor to illuminate the way.

As we journey forward, we carry the knowledge that we are living paradoxes—clever as foxes, joyful as children, and as resilient as life itself. Chaos is not our enemy but the crucible in which our truest selves are forged. By embracing its wild, unpredictable flow, we step fully into our power. And when the weight of the world presses upon us, we can throw back our heads and laugh—because in that laughter, we reclaim our strength, our joy, and our unbreakable bond with the wild, wondrous mystery of existence.

Let's step boldly into the grand game of existence—cunning, spontaneous, and unapologetically ourselves. And above all, let's embrace life with humor and lightness, for it is through play, not struggle, that we unlock our truest essence. When we release the relentless need to understand, to achieve, to define ourselves, we set our nature free. In this surrender, we allow our being to flourish, aligning effortlessly with our deepest purpose. True joy arises not from control, but from the fearless embrace of life in all its unpredictability. In spontaneity, we discover who we truly are—dancing, untamed and alive, with the wild, wondrous rhythm of existence.

Printed in Great Britain
by Amazon

823f7650-f4a1-423d-8b12-356630858aceR01